I0050639

Managing Brand Crises

Managing Brand Crises

A Guide to Navigating the Storm

Eugene Y. Chan

BUSINESS EXPERT PRESS
Leader in applied, concise business books

Managing Brand Crises: A Guide to Navigating the Storm

Copyright © Business Expert Press, LLC, 2025

Cover design by Eugene Chan

Interior design by Exeter Premedia Services Private Ltd., Chennai, India

All rights reserved. No part of this publication may be reproduced, stored in a retrieval system, or transmitted in any form or by any means—electronic, mechanical, photocopy, recording, or any other—except for brief quotations, not exceeding 400 words, without the prior permission of the publisher.

First published in 2025 by
Business Expert Press, LLC
222 East 46th Street, New York, NY 10017
www.businessexpertpress.com

ISBN-13: 978-1-63742-823-8 (paperback)
ISBN-13: 978-1-63742-824-5 (e-book)

Business Expert Press Marketing Collection

First edition: 2025

10 9 8 7 6 5 4 3 2 1

EU SAFETY REPRESENTATIVE
Mare Nostrum Group B.V.
Mauritskade 21D
1091 GC Amsterdam
The Netherlands
gpsr@mare-nostrum.co.uk

Description

In today's fast-paced digital world, brand crises are no longer a question of "if" but "when." With the power of social media amplifying every misstep, a poorly timed campaign, a product recall, or a public relations blunder can quickly spiral out of control, jeopardizing a brand's reputation and financial future. *Managing Brand Crises: A Guide to Navigating the Storm* equips brand managers, PR professionals, and business leaders with the tools they need to weather the storm and emerge stronger.

This insightful guide explores the critical skills required to anticipate potential pitfalls, respond swiftly and transparently, and rebuild consumer trust. From mastering stakeholder engagement to crafting strategies for reputation recovery, this book provides actionable steps for transforming crises into opportunities for growth and innovation. Packed with real-world examples and expert advice, it demonstrates that with the right preparation and response, crises can become defining moments that strengthen a brand's identity.

Whether you're a seasoned professional or new to the field, *Managing Brand Crises* is an essential resource for navigating the challenges of today's high-stakes marketplace. Learn how to stay ahead of the curve, safeguard your brand, and turn moments of adversity into opportunities for success.

Contents

CHAPTER 1

Navigating the Unpredictable Waters of Brand Crises

In today's rapidly evolving marketplace, brand crises have become an all-too-frequent reality for companies across various sectors. The digital age, characterized by social media and instant communication, amplifies the impact of crises, making it easier for information—both positive and negative—to spread like wildfire. A single misstep, whether it be a poorly timed marketing campaign, a product recall, or a public relations blunder, can quickly escalate into a full-blown crisis, jeopardizing a brand's reputation and financial stability. As consumers become more vocal and vigilant, brands face heightened scrutiny, and even well-established organizations are not immune to the fallout from a crisis.

Given this precarious landscape, it is crucial for practitioners, brand managers, and public relations officials to be equipped with the skills and strategies necessary to effectively navigate these turbulent waters. Understanding the dynamics of a brand crisis is no longer optional; it is essential. The ability to anticipate potential pitfalls, respond swiftly and transparently, and rebuild trust can determine whether a brand emerges from a crisis unscathed or faces lasting damage. In an era where consumer loyalty can be easily swayed, the stakes have never been higher for those tasked with protecting and promoting their brands.

As crises continue to proliferate, the demand for knowledgeable practitioners who can skillfully manage brand crises is paramount. Effective crisis management requires a comprehensive understanding of the nuances involved in communication, stakeholder engagement, and reputation recovery. It is not enough to simply react; proactive preparation and strategic response are vital to safeguarding a brand's identity. With the right knowledge and tools, brand managers and Public Relation (PR) officials can transform potential crises into opportunities for growth and innovation, ensuring their brands not only survive the storm but thrive in its aftermath. In this landscape, learning to navigate the storm is essential for anyone invested in the long-term success of a brand.

The STORM Framework

This book, *Managing Brand Crises: A Guide to Navigating the Storm*, is designed for practitioners across various sectors, providing a comprehensive roadmap for managing crises. By adopting the **STORM Framework** —swift response, transparent communication, ownership of the problem, rebuilding trust, and monitoring and learning—brands can proactively prepare for potential crises, respond effectively when challenges arise, and foster a culture of resilience. Each chapter delves into critical aspects of crisis management, offering practical tools, real-world examples, and actionable strategies that can be implemented immediately.

In Chapter 1, we define what constitutes a brand crisis and explore the different types, common causes, and the crisis life cycle. Understanding this foundation is vital for recognizing the signs of an impending crisis and the urgency of being crisis-ready. By establishing a clear definition, practitioners can differentiate between minor setbacks and significant crises that require immediate attention. Chapter 2 examines the brand crisis life cycle, highlighting the stages from precrisis preparation to postrecovery. This chapter emphasizes the importance of proactive measures in enhancing stakeholder engagement and ensuring long-term success, enabling organizations to shift their focus from reactive to proactive crisis management.

Chapter 3 focuses on crisis communication dynamics, emphasizing the key principles of effective messaging. It explores the necessity of timeliness, transparency, consistency, and empathy in communicating with stakeholders, particularly in the era of social media. In an age where information spreads rapidly, the way a brand communicates during a crisis can make or break its reputation. Chapter 4 discusses the stakes involved in crisis management, showcasing examples of brands that faltered and those that emerged stronger. By analyzing both failures and successes, we underscore why every organization needs a crisis management plan tailored to its unique challenges and opportunities.

The subsequent chapters delve deeper into the **STORM Framework**. Chapters 5 through 9 dissect each component: the necessity of a swift response, the power of transparent communication, the importance of owning problems, the strategies for rebuilding trust, and the need for ongoing monitoring and learning postcrisis. Each chapter provides real-life case studies that illustrate the effectiveness of these principles and offer insights into best practices. For instance, we examine how brands that responded swiftly were able to mitigate damage and maintain consumer loyalty, while those that hesitated faced severe repercussions.

In Chapter 10, we emphasize preparation for future crises, revisiting the key elements of the **STORM Framework** and underscoring the need for continuous improvement and risk mitigation. Organizations must cultivate a culture that encourages proactive identification of potential threats and the development of contingency plans. The conclusion wraps up the discussion by reiterating the importance of resilience in today's brand landscape. It conveys that while brand crises are inevitable, they are also manageable with the right strategies in place. By fostering a mindset that views crises as opportunities for growth rather than mere threats, brands can emerge stronger and more connected to their stakeholders.

Ultimately, the **STORM Framework** serves as a vital resource for practitioners, offering a comprehensive guide to not just survive crises but to turn them into opportunities for growth and transformation. By fostering a culture of preparedness, organizations can face challenges head-on, enhancing their reputations and deepening their connections with stakeholders. This book is an essential tool for anyone seeking to navigate the complexities of brand crises and emerge stronger in the face of adversity.

How to Use This Book

The **STORM Framework** serves as a powerful tool for practitioners seeking to effectively manage brand crises. By focusing on the five essential components—swift response, transparent communication, ownership of the problem, rebuilding trust, and monitoring and learning—this framework provides a structured approach that equips brand managers and public relations officials with the strategies necessary for navigating the complexities of crisis situations. Each element of the **STORM Framework** offers actionable insights, enabling professionals to prepare for potential crises, respond decisively, and emerge stronger from adversity.

To leverage the **STORM Framework** effectively, practitioners can begin by embedding its principles into their organizational culture and crisis management plans. This involves conducting regular training sessions that emphasize the importance of swift responses and transparent communication. By fostering a culture of ownership, organizations can empower employees to take responsibility during crises, ensuring that everyone is aligned and prepared to act. The book will guide readers through the practical steps required to implement these strategies, drawing on real-world case studies that illustrate the successful application of each component.

Moreover, the information presented throughout the book can serve as a comprehensive resource for ongoing learning and adaptation. Practitioners are encouraged to engage in continuous monitoring of brand health and stakeholder sentiment postcrisis, utilizing the insights gained to refine their strategies and prevent future issues. The emphasis on learning from past experiences not only enhances a brand's resilience but also promotes a proactive approach to crisis management. By applying the lessons outlined in *Managing Brand Crises*, professionals can turn challenges into opportunities, fostering deeper connections with their stakeholders and building a robust brand identity that withstands the test of time.

The **STORM Framework** and the insights provided in this book empower practitioners to face brand crises with confidence and competence. In an era where the potential for crises is ever-present, understanding how to navigate these challenges is crucial for ensuring long-term brand success. By embracing the principles outlined in this guide, practitioners can not only manage crises effectively but also cultivate a culture of resilience that transforms challenges into pathways for growth and innovation.

CHAPTER 2

What Is a Brand Crisis?

Overview

- Defines a brand crisis and its potential impact on reputation, trust, and sales.
- Outlines the main types of brand crises, including public relations disasters, product failures, and ethical scandals.
- Explores common causes of crises, such as corporate missteps or external pressures.
- Discusses the role of social media in amplifying or mitigating crises.
- Highlights the importance of crisis preparedness to safeguard brand integrity.

In an era where brand reputation can be incredibly fragile and quickly diminished, understanding the intricate dynamics of a brand crisis is essential for any organization striving for long-term success and stability. With consumers more connected and informed than ever, a brand's reputation can be put at risk with just a single misstep, whether intentional or accidental. This potential vulnerability means that brands must remain vigilant, proactive, and well-prepared to address any challenges that may arise. A brand crisis can emerge from various factors, often catching brands off guard and leaving them scrambling to respond in a way that mitigates damage and restores public confidence.

The consequences of neglecting crisis management can be profound, affecting not only a brand's reputation but also its financial performance and stakeholder trust. In an age where information spreads rapidly through social media and online platforms, the ripple effects of a crisis can extend far beyond the initial incident. Negative perceptions can become entrenched, making recovery increasingly difficult. Therefore, it is crucial for brands to develop a thorough understanding of what constitutes a crisis, as well as the specific contexts in which they can occur.

As we explore the nuances of brand crises in this chapter, we will provide an essential overview that includes their definition, types, common causes, life cycle, and the paramount importance of being prepared for the unexpected. This foundational knowledge is key for organizations aiming to not only survive a crisis but also to emerge from it with their reputations intact and their consumer trust reaffirmed. A proactive approach to crisis management enables brands to better navigate potential pitfalls, minimizing the impact of adverse events and maintaining their credibility in the eyes of the public. Equipping organizations with the tools to recognize, respond to, and recover from brand crises is vital in fostering a resilient and adaptive brand that can thrive in an increasingly unpredictable marketplace.

Definition of a Brand Crisis

A brand crisis refers to any unexpected event or situation that negatively impacts the perception of a brand, leading to potential damage to its reputation and financial health. This encompasses a broad range of incidents, from PR disasters and product recalls to ethical scandals and executive misconduct. Each type of crisis has its own unique implications, and the way a brand responds can significantly influence the outcome. The repercussions of a crisis can manifest in various ways, such as a loss of consumer trust and loyalty, which can ultimately affect sales and market share. Additionally, a crisis can lead to significant financial repercussions, including legal fees, increased insurance premiums, and diminished stock prices. The stakes are high, as a well-managed crisis can sometimes lead to stronger consumer relationships, while a poorly handled one can result in irreparable damage.

In today's world, which is driven by instantaneous communication and an ever-accelerating news cycle, a brand crisis can escalate quickly, transforming a minor issue into a major scandal within a matter of hours. Social media platforms amplify consumer voices, allowing dissatisfaction to spread like wildfire and reaching millions in an instant. This underscores the necessity for organizations to understand what constitutes a crisis, as well as the strategies and tactics for managing it effectively. Being crisis-ready is not just a defensive strategy; it is an opportunity to demonstrate commitment to transparency and accountability, reinforcing a brand's core values and strengthening consumer relationships in the long run.

As we delve deeper into this chapter, we will also examine the various types of brand crises that can occur, categorizing them based on their origin and impact. By understanding these distinctions, organizations can better anticipate potential risks and tailor their crisis management plans accordingly. Furthermore, we will discuss common causes of brand crises, which often include lapses in product quality, failures in ethical standards, and unforeseen external factors such as market volatility or social unrest. Recognizing these underlying issues will empower brands to proactively address vulnerabilities and develop comprehensive strategies that not only protect their reputation but also enhance their resilience.

The life cycle of a brand crisis typically follows a defined trajectory, beginning with its onset and leading to escalation, resolution, and recovery. By analyzing this life cycle, organizations can identify critical moments when decisive action can either mitigate damage or exacerbate the situation. This chapter will highlight the importance of monitoring these stages and adapting responses as needed to ensure effective crisis management. Additionally, we will emphasize the critical role of preparation, illustrating how a proactive approach to crisis planning can make a significant difference when a crisis inevitably arises. Organizations that invest time and resources in developing crisis management strategies are better equipped to navigate the tumultuous waters of brand crises, ultimately emerging stronger and more resilient.

As we move forward in this discussion, it's essential to remember that understanding the dynamics of a brand crisis is not merely about identifying risks; it's about fostering a culture of preparedness and adaptability. Organizations must instill a mindset that views potential crises as opportunities for learning and growth. By embracing this perspective, brands can not only weather the storm when crises occur but also turn challenges into valuable lessons that enhance their overall effectiveness and strengthen their market position.

Ultimately, navigating the complexities of brand crises requires a multifaceted approach that encompasses understanding the nature of crises, recognizing their potential triggers, and implementing effective strategies for response and recovery. In doing so, organizations can safeguard their reputation, maintain consumer trust, and ensure their long-term viability in a highly competitive marketplace.

Types of Brand Crises

Brand crises can take many forms, each requiring different approaches to management and communication strategies tailored to the specific circumstances at hand. Understanding these varied types is crucial for organizations to navigate the complexities of crisis management effectively. The ability to recognize the distinct characteristics of each crisis type allows brands to respond appropriately and mitigate potential damage. Below are some of the most common types of brand crises, each with its unique challenges and implications for the brand's reputation.

In today's interconnected world, the repercussions of a brand crisis can ripple through various stakeholders, impacting not just consumer perception but also employee morale, investor confidence, and partner relationships. A well-defined understanding of the specific type of crisis enables organizations to deploy targeted strategies that address the underlying issues effectively. Each crisis type presents its own set of risks, necessitating a tailored approach to communication, resolution, and reputation management. By being well-versed in these various crisis types, organizations can enhance their preparedness and resilience, ensuring they are equipped to tackle any challenges that arise in a timely and effective manner.

Public Relations (PR) Disasters

PR disasters arise from miscommunication, poorly handled public statements, or insensitive actions that attract negative media attention and public scrutiny. These crises can escalate rapidly, especially in the age of social media, where public sentiment can shift quickly and unpredictably. In this environment, the potential for misinformation and rapid dissemination of negative narratives amplifies the impact of PR crises, making it crucial for brands to be prepared for swift action. For example, a controversial advertisement that fails to resonate with audiences can trigger widespread backlash, drawing criticism from consumers and stakeholders alike.

Similarly, an executive's ill-timed or thoughtless comment, especially in a sensitive social or political context, can ignite outrage and lead to calls for accountability. The repercussions of such statements can extend beyond immediate backlash, leading to long-term damage to the brand's image and customer relationships. Effective management of PR disasters requires immediate acknowledgment of the issue, transparent communication, and a well-thought-out response strategy to mitigate reputational damage. Additionally, brands must be proactive in monitoring public sentiment and media coverage to respond swiftly and appropriately, ensuring they maintain credibility and trust with their audience throughout the crisis.

> **Example:** A notable PR crisis for Starbucks occurred in 2018 when two Black men were arrested in a Philadelphia store while waiting for a friend. The men hadn't made a purchase, prompting a Starbucks employee to call the police, resulting in their arrest. Video footage of the incident quickly went viral, sparking public outrage and accusations of racial profiling. In response, Starbucks took swift action by publicly apologizing, meeting with the men involved, and closing over 8,000 U.S. stores for a day of racial bias training. The incident highlighted the importance of swift and transparent crisis management while underscoring the need for brands to address underlying cultural issues proactively.

Product Failures

Product failures can have severe consequences when a brand's product fails to meet quality standards or safety expectations. This often leads to significant public outcry, potential legal ramifications, and financial losses for the company. The impact of a product failure can extend beyond immediate financial losses; it can also damage the brand's reputation and market position. Common examples include product recalls, safety issues, and manufacturing defects that endanger consumers.

A notable instance is the Ford Pinto case, where design flaws led to serious safety concerns and a subsequent recall. The fallout from such crises can be detrimental, as they not only erode consumer trust but also invite regulatory scrutiny and legal challenges. In today's digital age, news of product failures can spread rapidly through social media and news outlets, exacerbating the crisis and further damaging the brand's reputation. Brands must be prepared to act swiftly to address product failures, provide clear information to consumers, and take responsibility for rectifying the situation.

This involves not only issuing recalls and apologies but also communicating transparently about the steps being taken to resolve the issues and prevent future occurrences. Proactive measures, such as quality control enhancements and consumer education, can also help restore confidence and demonstrate the brand's commitment to safety and quality. Ultimately, how a brand responds to a product failure can significantly influence consumer perceptions and loyalty in the long term.

Example: Samsung's Galaxy Note 7 was recalled in 2016 after reports emerged of the devices catching fire due to battery issues. Despite efforts to rectify the problem, replacement phones also ignited, leading to a second recall. Ultimately, Samsung discontinued the Galaxy Note 7, resulting in billions of dollars in losses and a significant blow to its reputation, as consumer trust was undermined.

The company subsequently implemented stricter quality control measures for future products to prevent similar failures.

Ethical Scandals

Ethical crises involve misconduct or unethical behavior by the brand or its representatives, fundamentally undermining the trust and credibility of the organization. This could encompass a wide range of issues, including fraud, discrimination, harassment, or violations of ethical norms and standards. When such unethical behavior comes to light, it can lead to significant backlash from consumers, regulators, and the media. Brands like Enron and Volkswagen have faced devastating crises due to ethical scandals that revealed deep-rooted issues within their organizational cultures.

The ramifications of ethical scandals can be particularly far-reaching, impacting employee morale, stakeholder relationships, and overall brand reputation. Employees may feel disillusioned and demotivated, leading to a decline in productivity and increased turnover. Stakeholders, including investors and partners, may re-evaluate their relationships with the brand, resulting in potential financial losses and diminished support.

To effectively manage ethical crises, organizations must not only address the immediate concerns but also undertake a thorough examination of their internal practices and culture to prevent recurrence. This includes implementing robust ethical training programs, establishing clear reporting mechanisms for unethical behavior, and fostering an organizational culture that prioritizes integrity and accountability. Transparency in addressing the scandal and taking decisive action to rectify the situation is essential for rebuilding trust with both internal and external audiences. By taking these steps, organizations can work toward restoring their reputations and ensuring a commitment to ethical standards moving forward.

> **Example:** In 2016, Wells Fargo found itself embroiled in an ethical scandal when it was revealed that employees had opened millions of unauthorized accounts to meet aggressive sales targets. This unethical practice led to substantial fines and numerous lawsuits. The scandal prompted the resignation of CEO John Stumpf and left a lasting stain on the bank's reputation, raising broader concerns about corporate ethics and the pressures placed on employees to achieve unrealistic goals.

Social Media Backlash

In today's digital landscape, a single mis-step can lead to swift and widespread backlash on social media platforms. The interconnectedness of online communities means that consumers are quick to voice their discontent, often amplifying issues that may have otherwise gone unnoticed. A single viral post, whether it be a customer complaint, a negative review, or a perceived injustice, can escalate a minor issue into a full-blown crisis, making effective social media management critical for brands.

Organizations must remain vigilant and develop proactive social media strategies that include monitoring various platforms for emerging issues, responding promptly to customer concerns, and engaging transparently with their audience. This vigilance is essential, as the fast-paced nature of social media can result in an issue gaining traction within minutes. Brands need to be aware of the sentiments circulating online and be prepared to counter misinformation or negative narratives as they arise.

Furthermore, the importance of building strong relationships with consumers cannot be overstated. Engaging with followers in a genuine and authentic manner helps establish trust, making it more likely that they will support the brand during challenging times. Additionally, training staff to handle social media interactions professionally can mitigate risks associated with backlash.

The fast-paced nature of social media means that brands must be agile and prepared to adjust their communication strategies to address any backlash swiftly and effectively. This may involve crafting thoughtful responses, issuing public statements, or even making changes to products or policies based on consumer feedback. By being proactive and responsive, organizations can navigate social media backlash and work toward maintaining their reputation even in the face of adversity.

> **Example:** Gillette faced social media backlash in January 2019 with the release of its advertisement titled "We Believe: The Best Men Can Be." The ad tackled issues of toxic masculinity and challenged traditional notions of manhood, eliciting mixed reactions. While many praised the brand for its stance, others criticized it for being politically correct and disconnected from its consumer base. The controversy impacted sales and brand perception, igniting discussions about the role of companies in addressing social issues.

Employee Misconduct

Employee misconduct can also lead to brand crises, particularly when the behavior of high-profile executives or other prominent employees comes to light. Whether it's sexual harassment, discrimination, or unethical behavior, employee misconduct reflects poorly on the company's leadership and culture. This type of crisis is often exacerbated by the public's growing expectation that companies should foster inclusive and respectful workplaces. Organizations must take a proactive stance in promoting a healthy corporate culture and ensuring that employees are held accountable for their actions.

Failure to address employee misconduct can lead to increased turnover, difficulties in attracting top talent, and a tarnished reputation that extends beyond the immediate crisis. Companies should prioritize training and development programs that emphasize ethical behavior, inclusivity, and respect in the workplace. Having clear policies and procedures for addressing misconduct is crucial in demonstrating a commitment to creating a safe and positive work environment.

Example: In 2017, Uber was rocked by revelations from former engineer Susan Fowler, who published a blog post detailing a toxic workplace culture that included incidents of sexual harassment and discrimination. The post prompted widespread backlash against the company, leading to an internal investigation, the resignation of CEO Travis Kalanick, and significant changes in the company's leadership and culture. Uber faced reputational damage and mounting pressure to reform its workplace policies.

Leadership Misconduct

Crises can also stem from the actions of key executives or employees, leading to significant reputational damage for the brand. Leadership misconduct can encompass a variety of behaviors, including harassment, discrimination, or financial impropriety. Such incidents not only tarnish the reputation of the individual involved but can also lead to a significant loss of credibility for the entire organization. The fallout from leadership-related crises often extends beyond the individual's actions, impacting the morale and trust of employees and stakeholders alike.

In response to such crises, organizations must take decisive action to demonstrate accountability, implement corrective measures, and restore confidence in their leadership. This means that the response should not be limited to addressing the misconduct of the individual but should also encompass broader efforts to rebuild the organization's integrity. Effective crisis management involves not only dealing with the immediate fallout but also engaging in a comprehensive evaluation of the organization's policies and practices to prevent similar incidents in the future.

Example: Nike encountered a crisis in 2021 when allegations of inappropriate behavior by senior executives came to light, highlighting issues of sexism and a toxic corporate culture. This scrutiny led to internal and external examination of the company's leadership practices, resulting in resignations and shifts in executive leadership. The crisis underscored the importance of gender equality and accountability in the workplace.

Cybersecurity Breaches

As companies become increasingly reliant on digital platforms and data-driven operations, cybersecurity breaches have emerged as a growing threat to brand reputations. A data breach can expose sensitive customer information, leading to identity theft, financial loss, and widespread distrust in the brand's ability to protect personal data. Organizations must prioritize cybersecurity measures and invest in robust systems to safeguard against potential threats. Regular security audits, employee training on data protection, and incident response plans are essential components of an effective cybersecurity strategy.

Additionally, transparency and communication play vital roles in how a company handles a data breach. Promptly informing affected customers about the breach and providing guidance on how to protect their information can help mitigate reputational damage. Companies should also be prepared to respond to inquiries and concerns from stakeholders in the wake of a breach to maintain trust and credibility.

Example: Target experienced a massive data breach in 2013 that compromised the credit and debit card information of over 40 million customers during the holiday shopping season. The breach was traced back to malware installed on point-of-sale systems. Target faced substantial reputational damage and financial losses, including costs for credit monitoring services for affected customers. This incident sparked discussions about cybersecurity practices in the retail sector and prompted Target to enhance its data security measures.

Common Causes of Brand Crises

Understanding the root causes of brand crises is vital for organizations seeking to anticipate and mitigate potential risks before they escalate into significant issues. By identifying these common causes, brands can implement proactive measures to protect their reputation and maintain consumer trust. Here are some of the most prevalent causes of brand crises.

Poor Communication

Inadequate or unclear communication during critical moments can significantly exacerbate crises. When brands fail to provide timely updates, accurate information, or clear messaging, it can breed distrust among their audience. For instance, during a crisis, stakeholders expect transparency and consistent communication; a lack of these elements can lead to confusion, speculation, and anger among consumers. Effective crisis communication strategies should prioritize clarity, timeliness, and accessibility of information to minimize the negative impact on the brand's reputation.

In addition, brands should ensure that their communication channels are well established and capable of reaching their audience effectively. Whether through social media, press releases, or direct customer communications, the chosen methods should reflect the urgency and importance of the message. By developing a comprehensive communication plan that includes potential scenarios and responses, brands can ensure they are prepared to respond swiftly and accurately during a crisis.

Quality Control Issues

Lapses in quality control can lead to product failures and serious safety concerns, which can trigger crises for brands. Maintaining rigorous quality control standards is essential to prevent issues that could escalate into significant crises. When consumers encounter defective products or experience safety-related problems, their trust in the brand diminishes, leading to potential boycotts and negative word-of-mouth.

Brands must implement comprehensive quality assurance processes, conduct regular audits, and respond promptly to any signs of quality issues to uphold their reputation and protect their customers. Furthermore, involving consumers in feedback loops and encouraging reviews can help brands identify potential quality issues before they escalate into crises. By prioritizing quality control and actively seeking customer input, brands can strengthen their reputation and ensure customer safety.

Cultural Insensitivity

As brands expand their reach globally, a lack of cultural awareness and sensitivity can lead to missteps that offend consumers and various communities. Insensitive marketing campaigns, public statements, or product launches that fail to consider cultural nuances can result in backlash and severe reputational damage. Brands must conduct thorough market research, engage with diverse consumer segments, and foster cultural competency within their organizations to avoid alienating audiences and creating crises.

By being aware of cultural differences and showing respect for diverse perspectives, brands can minimize the risk of cultural insensitivity-related crises. Additionally, brands should consider hiring culturally diverse teams and consultants to guide their messaging and marketing strategies, ensuring that they resonate positively with various audiences. Engaging with local communities and seeking feedback on campaigns can further enhance cultural sensitivity and prevent potential crises.

Negligence In Ethical Standards

Ethical lapses, whether intentional or accidental, can lead to severe consequences for brands and diminish consumer trust. Failure to adhere to ethical practices, such as transparency in sourcing, fair labor practices, and honesty in advertising, can result in public outrage and a significant loss of customer loyalty. For example, brands that engage in misleading advertising or fail to disclose critical information can face legal repercussions and damage their reputation.

Organizations must establish and enforce strong ethical guidelines, promote a culture of integrity, and regularly assess their practices to uphold their commitment to ethical standards. This includes training employees on ethical decision making, conducting regular audits of business practices, and creating channels for whistleblowers to report unethical behavior without fear of retaliation. By fostering a culture of accountability and ethical responsibility, brands can prevent crises related to ethical misconduct and maintain consumer trust.

External Factors

Some crises arise from factors beyond a brand's control, such as economic downturns, political unrest, natural disasters, or global pandemics. While brands cannot predict these events, they can prepare for how to respond effectively. Developing crisis management plans that address potential external threats, conducting risk assessments, and establishing communication protocols can enable brands to navigate challenging situations with greater resilience.

By being proactive and adaptable, organizations can minimize the impact of unforeseen external factors on their operations and reputation. Additionally, brands should consider building strong relationships with stakeholders, including government agencies and community organizations, to facilitate collaboration and support during crises. By remaining agile and ready to adapt their strategies, brands can effectively manage external crises and protect their reputation in the face of adversity.

The Role of Social Media In Brand Crises

Social media has fundamentally transformed the landscape of brand crises, reshaping not only how crises are communicated but also how they escalate and are perceived by the public. In the past, crisis management often involved a controlled process, managed through traditional PR channels such as press releases and controlled messaging. However, the advent of social media has introduced a chaotic and rapidly evolving environment, characterized by instantaneous communication and global reach. This shift has fundamentally altered the dynamics of crisis communication, presenting both significant challenges and unique opportunities for brands navigating turbulent waters.

The Acceleration of Crisis Development

Historically, the development of news regarding a crisis could take time, allowing companies a certain degree of leeway to respond and implement damage control before public sentiment shifted dramatically. However, in today's digital landscape, the speed at which information spreads on platforms like Twitter, Facebook, and Instagram means that brands often find themselves confronting a firestorm of public opinion and scrutiny before they have a chance to formulate a thoughtful response. The instantaneous nature of social media not only accelerates the development of a crisis but also amplifies its impact, leading to a whirlwind of commentary that can overshadow the brand's message.

For instance, during the United Airlines passenger removal incident in 2017, videos capturing the distressing event quickly went viral, generating widespread outrage and leading to a barrage of negative media coverage. The situation escalated rapidly, with social media users expressing their shock and anger, often through emotive posts and videos, making it abundantly clear that United Airlines was in the midst of a significant crisis long before the company had a chance to respond. This phenomenon illustrates the power of social media to turn isolated incidents into full-blown crises, highlighting the urgent need for brands to remain vigilant and proactive in their communication strategies.

Amplification of Consumer Voice

Social media has fundamentally empowered consumers in unprecedented ways, giving them an accessible platform to voice their opinions, share personal experiences, and mobilize others in a matter of moments.

This democratization of communication means that, during a crisis, it is not just the company that holds the microphone; customers, stakeholders, and even casual observers can easily share their views and experiences, often shaping the narrative surrounding the crisis in real time. Brands must now contend with a more vocal and engaged audience, where consumer sentiment can rapidly shift the tone of the conversation.

A notable example is the #DeleteUber campaign, which emerged in response to the company's perceived lack of a strong stance against the travel ban instituted by the Trump administration in 2017. Many consumers took to social media to express their dissatisfaction, posting messages that encouraged others to delete the app and seek alternatives. The wave of negativity surrounding Uber prompted significant media coverage and put intense pressure on the company to respond. This illustrates how social media can amplify the consumer voice, turning individual complaints into collective movements that can inflict considerable reputational damage. Brands must now actively monitor their online presence and respond to consumer concerns in real time to mitigate potential fallout and rebuild trust.

Transparency and Authenticity

In the age of social media, transparency and authenticity have become non-negotiable attributes for brands facing a crisis. Consumers expect brands to communicate honestly and forthrightly during difficult times, and any attempt to downplay the severity of a situation or obfuscate key details can lead to heightened backlash and further erosion of trust. Brands that fail to embrace transparency risk not only immediate reputational damage but also long-term consequences as consumers increasingly prioritize authenticity in their relationships with brands.

For example, in the aftermath of the BP Deepwater Horizon oil spill in 2010, the company's initial response was widely criticized for being overly scripted and lacking genuine remorse. BP's attempts to manage the crisis through controlled messaging and PR tactics further fueled public outrage, leading to significant and lasting damage to its reputation. In contrast, companies that adopt a transparent approach during crises often fare better in the long run, as they demonstrate a commitment to accountability and ethical behavior. This open communication fosters consumer trust, making it easier for brands to rebuild their reputations and maintain customer loyalty even in the face of adversity. Ultimately, the expectation for transparency in social media communication underscores the need for brands to engage authentically with their audiences, especially during challenging times.

Importance of Being Crisis-Ready

In today's fast-paced and interconnected environment, brands cannot afford to be complacent. The ability to navigate a crisis effectively is not just about implementing damage control measures; it's fundamentally about being prepared, proactive, and resilient in the face of challenges. Organizations that take a strategic approach to crisis management are better positioned to weather the storm and emerge with their reputations intact. Therefore, developing a comprehensive crisis management plan that encompasses clear communication strategies, stakeholder engagement protocols, and contingency measures is essential for any brand aiming to safeguard its integrity and trustworthiness.

Preparation as a Strategic Imperative

Being crisis-ready involves more than just having a plan on paper; it requires a thorough understanding of the potential crises that could affect the brand and the associated risks. This includes conducting a thorough risk assessment to identify vulnerabilities and evaluate possible scenarios that may arise. By anticipating potential crises, organizations can develop tailored strategies that address specific challenges and enable swift, effective responses when issues do occur.

Such foresight is not merely advantageous but essential for maintaining operational continuity and safeguarding the organization's reputation. This preparation should also include identifying key stakeholders and determining how they will be informed and engaged during a crisis.

Having a proactive stance on risk management can significantly reduce the likelihood of reputational damage when crises do arise.

Training and Simulation

Crucial to effective crisis readiness is training staff at all levels of the organization. Employees should be well-versed in the crisis management plan and familiar with their specific roles and responsibilities during a crisis. Regular training sessions, workshops, and seminars can help ensure that all staff members understand the protocols and are equipped to act decisively in high-pressure situations.

Conducting regular drills simulating various crisis scenarios is also invaluable; these exercises can reveal weaknesses in the plan and provide insights into areas needing improvement. Engaging employees in these drills fosters a sense of ownership and accountability, reinforcing the importance of each individual's role in crisis management. By investing in ongoing training, organizations can cultivate a workforce that is not only knowledgeable but also confident in their ability to respond effectively to crises.

Staying Informed

In addition to training, organizations must remain informed about potential risks and trends within their industry and the broader marketplace. This includes monitoring changes in consumer behavior, technological advancements, and emerging threats that could trigger a crisis. Utilizing tools such as social media monitoring, industry reports, and competitive analysis can provide vital insights that inform crisis preparedness.

Organizations should also foster relationships with key stakeholders, including suppliers, customers, and regulatory bodies, to ensure a coordinated response during crises. By staying informed and connected, brands can anticipate challenges and develop strategies that pre-emptively address potential crises before they escalate.

Fostering a Culture of Transparency and Accountability

Creating a crisis-ready organization necessitates fostering a culture of transparency and accountability. This culture should permeate every level of the organization, encouraging open communication and empowering employees to voice concerns or report potential issues before they escalate into full-blown crises.

Leadership must model these values by being open about challenges, admitting mistakes, and actively seeking feedback from employees. When employees feel supported and encouraged to communicate, they are more likely to contribute valuable insights that can aid in crisis prevention and management. A culture of transparency not only helps in crisis situations but also strengthens overall employee morale and trust in the organization.

Establishing Clear Communication Protocols

An integral aspect of being crisis-ready is establishing clear communication protocols that define how information will be disseminated during a crisis. These protocols should outline the chain of command for decision making, identify spokespersons, and specify how messages will be conveyed to various stakeholders, including employees, customers, media, and the public.

A well-structured communication strategy ensures that accurate information is delivered promptly, mitigating confusion and misinformation. It also reinforces the brand's commitment to transparency and accountability, essential elements in rebuilding trust postcrisis. Clear communication protocols also allow organizations to respond quickly and effectively, preserving the integrity of their messaging and reputation.

The Foundation for Effective Crisis Management

Ultimately, understanding what constitutes a brand crisis, its various types, common causes, and life cycle is the first step toward effective crisis management. With this foundational knowledge, organizations can better prepare themselves to navigate the storm when crises arise. Investing in crisis preparedness not only safeguards the brand's reputation but also enhances overall resilience, enabling organizations to adapt to unforeseen challenges and emerge stronger. By prioritizing crisis readiness, brands can maintain consumer trust and loyalty, ensuring long-term success in an unpredictable environment.

Conclusion

In an increasingly interconnected and fast-paced marketplace, understanding the nature of brand crises has never been more crucial. A brand crisis, defined as any significant disruption that threatens a brand's reputation and integrity, can arise from various sources—ranging from PR disasters and product failures to ethical scandals. These crises often stem from common causes, such as poor communication, lapses in quality control, or misalignment with consumer values.

Recognizing the distinct types of brand crises allows organizations to prepare and respond effectively, mitigating damage and safeguarding their reputation. The life cycle of a brand crisis—comprising the onset, escalation, and resolution phases—highlights the importance of timely and strategic communication in managing the narrative and restoring stakeholder trust.

Being crisis-ready is not merely a precaution; it is a strategic imperative that positions brands to navigate unforeseen challenges with resilience. By proactively developing comprehensive crisis management plans, investing in staff training, and fostering a culture of transparency, organizations can turn potential crises into opportunities for growth and reaffirmation of their commitment to their values and stakeholders. This foundational knowledge of what constitutes a brand crisis sets the stage for deeper exploration into strategies for effective crisis management in the chapters to come. As we move forward, we will delve into actionable insights and frameworks that will equip brands to not only survive crises but thrive in their aftermath.

Further Reading

Chandrasekar, K., and V. Rehman. 2023. "Synthesis of Forty Years of Brand Crisis Literature." *Marketing Intelligence and Planning* 41 (5): 525–43.

Coombs, W.T. 2007 "Crisis Management and Communications." *Institute for Public Relations.* https://instituteforpr.org/crisis-management-communications/.

Dutta, S., and C. Pullig. 2011. "Effectiveness of Corporate Responses to Brand Crises: The Role of Crisis Type and Response Strategies." *Journal of Business Research* 64 (12): 1281–87.

Greyser, S.A. 2007. "Corporate Brand Reputation and Brand Crisis Management." *Management Decision* 47 (4): 590–602.

Li, M., and H. Wei. 2016. "How to Save Brand After Crises? A Literature Review on Brand Crisis Management." *American Journal of Industrial and Business Management* 6 (2): 89–96.

Wang, L., E.Y. Chan., and A. Gohary. 2023. "Consumers' Attributions in Performance-and Values-Related Brand Crises." *European Journal of Marketing* 57 (12): 3162–81.

CHAPTER 3

The Brand Crisis Life cycle

Overview

- Breaks down the five stages of the life cycle: precrisis, crisis event, immediate response, recovery, and postcrisis.
- Explains how understanding this life cycle enhances proactive planning and response strategies.
- Stresses the importance of transitioning effectively between life cycle stages to minimize damage.
- Encourages long-term thinking for postcrisis recovery and reputation repair.

The brand crisis life cycle offers a detailed and structured framework that enables organizations to understand the full trajectory of a crisis, from its inception to its resolution. It highlights the various stages a brand experiences as a crisis unfolds, providing a step-by-step guide for managing each phase strategically. This model emphasizes the importance of not just reacting to the crisis as it happens but preparing in advance for potential threats, responding efficiently when they occur, and planning for a smooth recovery afterward. By following this framework, brands can minimize immediate damage to their reputation and operations, effectively manage stakeholder relations, and lay the groundwork for long-term recovery and success.

Understanding the stages of a crisis is crucial because each phase requires different strategies, tools, and communication methods. For instance, in the early stages of a crisis, rapid response and clear communication are essential to controlling the narrative and preventing misinformation. Later stages, such as the recovery phase, may focus more on restoring stakeholder trust, rebuilding the brand's image, and learning from the experience to improve future preparedness. Organizations that recognize these phases can tailor their approach at each point, ensuring that they meet the specific demands of the situation and maintain consistency in their overall strategy.

The brand crisis life cycle also stresses the importance of preparation, which is often overlooked until a crisis strikes. Brands that invest time and resources into preparing for potential crises—through training, simulation exercises, and developing crisis communication plans—are more likely to handle real crises effectively. Preparation allows brands to be more agile and responsive when a crisis occurs, reducing the time taken to implement solutions and minimizing reputational harm. Moreover, by anticipating different types of crises, whether operational, reputational, or external, brands can customize their response strategies and be ready for various scenarios.

By systematically managing their response at every stage of the life cycle, organizations not only address the immediate fallout of a crisis but also position themselves for a more resilient recovery. This approach helps brands to not merely survive crises but potentially emerge stronger and more trusted by their stakeholders. Brands that successfully navigate crises demonstrate their ability to handle adversity, which can enhance their reputation in the long run. Moreover, the lessons learned during a crisis can help refine business practices, improve customer relations, and ensure that the organization is better equipped to handle future challenges.

The brand crisis life cycle is not just a tool for navigating difficult times, but a comprehensive roadmap that helps brands emerge from crises stronger, more resilient, and better positioned for long-term success. By recognizing the distinct phases of a crisis—precrisis, crisis event, immediate response, recovery, and postcrisis reflection—organizations can develop tailored strategies for each stage, enabling them to mitigate harm, maintain stakeholder trust, and build a more robust foundation for the future.

Stages of the Brand Crisis Life cycle

The brand crisis life cycle consists of five distinct stages (Figure 3.1): precrisis, crisis event, immediate response, recovery, and postcrisis. Each stage presents unique challenges and opportunities for brands to manage effectively, with different demands in terms of communication, decision making, and strategy development. Understanding these stages in detail allows organizations to navigate the complexities of a crisis in

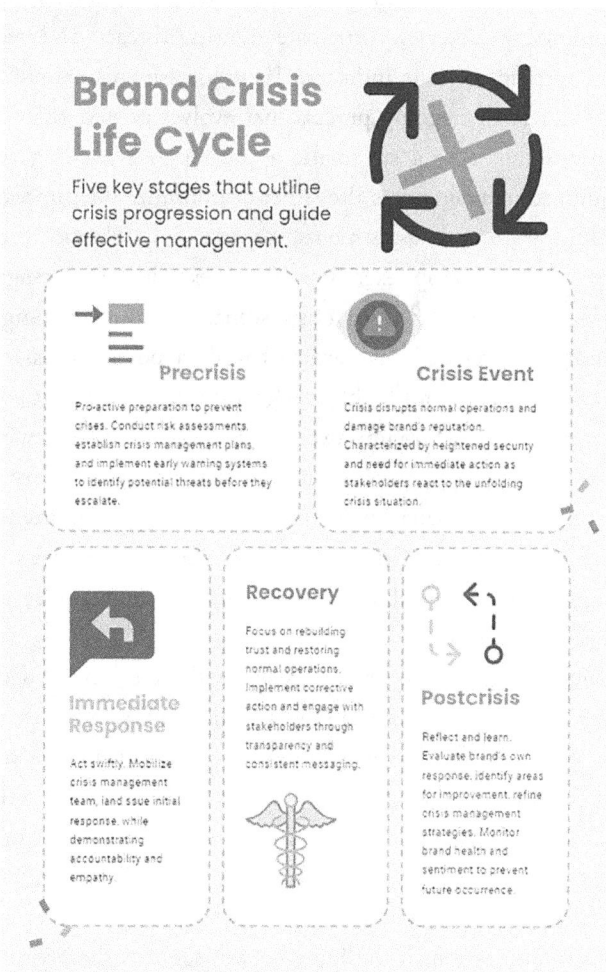

Figure 3.1 Brand crisis lifestyle

a structured and proactive way, mitigating the damage while positioning themselves for a quicker and more successful recovery.

Precrisis

The precrisis stage is fundamentally focused on proactive preparation and identifying potential risks that could lead to a crisis. This phase is crucial as it sets the foundation for how an organization will respond when a crisis arises. Organizations must cultivate a prevention-oriented mindset, continuously assessing both internal and external vulnerabilities. This involves conducting thorough risk assessments to identify operational weaknesses, anticipate external threats, and recognize challenges specific to their industry. These assessments should not be static, but rather an ongoing process that evolves as new risks emerge. Organizations that take a systematic approach to evaluating risks are better equipped to avoid crises altogether or minimize their impact.

In addition to risk assessments, organizations should run crisis simulations and tabletop exercises. These exercises can range from small-scale drills to full-fledged crisis scenario testing, helping teams understand how prepared they are to handle a potential crisis. These simulations are essential for highlighting weaknesses in current protocols and identifying areas where improvement is needed. By identifying gaps in crisis response early, organizations can implement necessary adjustments to their crisis management plans, enhancing their resilience in the face of future threats. Crisis simulations also prepare teams to react quickly and decisively, enabling them to remain calm under pressure when an actual crisis occurs.

A critical aspect of the precrisis stage is the creation of a detailed and robust crisis communication plan. This plan is not just a basic guide; it should be comprehensive enough to cover a wide range of potential crisis situations. The plan needs to include specific guidelines for developing messages tailored to different audiences, managing media relations, handling social media communications, and ensuring seamless internal communication. It should outline the key personnel involved in crisis communication, including who will serve as the organization's spokesperson, what kind of messaging will be delivered, and how quickly that communication will be disseminated. Having these clear communication protocols in place is essential for ensuring that responses are not delayed or disjointed when a crisis strikes.

Moreover, organizations should prepare key messages and templates in advance, customized for different types of crises. Whether the crisis is related to product recalls, legal issues, or reputation damage, predrafted statements can be adjusted and deployed swiftly to ensure that the organization's response is prompt and coherent. These prewritten messages save valuable time, allowing crisis teams to focus on managing the situation rather than scrambling to draft statements under pressure. The use of templates also ensures consistency in tone and messaging, which is vital for maintaining trust with stakeholders during the early stages of a crisis.

The precrisis stage also involves critical internal preparation. This includes providing crisis management training to staff and assigning specific roles to individuals within the crisis management team. Each team member should clearly understand their responsibilities and how they fit into the overall crisis response framework. Training sessions should be regular and updated to reflect changes in the organization's structure or the nature of potential threats. Well-trained staff can make the difference between a crisis spiraling out of control and one that is managed effectively. Designating specific roles—such as who will manage communications, who will liaise with legal teams, and who will handle internal coordination—ensures that no part of the response process is overlooked.

Building and maintaining strong relationships with stakeholders before a crisis occurs is an indispensable part of effective crisis preparedness. These stakeholders include customers, employees, investors, partners, suppliers, and the media. Proactively engaging with these key audiences to foster trust and goodwill creates a strong foundation for navigating crises. Trust built over time can serve as a buffer that softens the blow when a crisis hits, as stakeholders are more likely to give the organization the benefit of the doubt if it has a history of acting with integrity, transparency, and reliability.

Stakeholders are less likely to react negatively when an organization they trust encounters a crisis, making the recovery process smoother and more manageable. Effective stakeholder engagement also involves open lines of communication and regular updates on the organization's initiatives and values, which helps reinforce these relationships even in times of stability. In doing so, organizations can cultivate a level of goodwill that will sustain them during difficult times.

Additionally, organizations should invest in building a strong network of allies, such as industry influencers, media outlets, and community leaders, who can help amplify their voice during a crisis. These allies can be instrumental in shaping public perception and reinforcing the organization's messaging when it matters most. In the midst of a crisis, having a network of well-established relationships with media professionals and influencers allows the organization to communicate more effectively and control the narrative. These external voices can lend credibility to the organization's response and help ensure that accurate information reaches the public quickly.

By creating a strong crisis communication network and maintaining positive relationships with key external stakeholders, organizations can ensure that their messaging is not only heard but also trusted. Engaging with industry influencers, journalists, and media outlets before a crisis occurs helps solidify these partnerships, enabling a more cohesive and coordinated response when the organization needs it most. Media relations, in particular, can make or break the public's perception of how well an organization handles a crisis. A strong relationship with the press allows for more favorable coverage and ensures that the organization's side of the story is effectively communicated.

> **Example:** Imagine a popular fitness apparel brand, FitWear, detecting a potential issue during its routine quality checks. Engineers discover that a new line of running shoes has a minor defect in the sole, which could cause wear and tear faster than advertised. At this precrisis stage, the brand has not yet faced public backlash or complaints, but the defect poses a risk to customer satisfaction and the brand's

reputation. FitWear's proactive approach includes engaging its crisis management team, conducting a full assessment of the product line, and preparing a contingency plan for a potential recall. This vigilance allows the company to address the issue internally before it escalates into a public crisis, demonstrating the importance of identifying vulnerabilities early in the brand crisis life cycle.

Crisis Event

The crisis event phase is a pivotal moment when an incident occurs that poses a direct threat to the brand's reputation, disrupts operations, or negatively impacts stakeholders. The immediate task for organizations is recognizing that a crisis is unfolding, as the ability to identify it early can dramatically influence the outcome. Swift recognition can be the dividing line between a manageable situation and a full-blown disaster. Early detection allows organizations to take swift, decisive action before the crisis spirals out of control. To ensure timely recognition, organizations must have robust systems in place for real-time monitoring. This may involve social media tracking to capture shifts in public sentiment, customer feedback mechanisms to spot emerging complaints, or media monitoring tools to identify negative press. In today's fast-paced digital world, a small issue can escalate into a major crisis within hours, so continuous vigilance is key. Real-time monitoring helps organizations remain alert to subtle signs that a crisis is brewing, giving them more control over the narrative and more time to plan their response strategy.

Once a crisis is recognized, the next critical step is a thorough assessment of its severity. This assessment allows the organization to gauge the potential damage to the brand, employees, customers, and other stakeholders. The severity of the crisis is evaluated based on the scope, scale, and the potential for escalation. For example, is the crisis a localized issue, or is it spreading across regions or industries? What level of public attention is it garnering? The organization must also assess the risk to its reputation, financial standing, and long-term goals. In this phase, the crisis management team should anticipate how different stakeholders, including customers, employees, investors, and regulators, might react. Public opinion can play a crucial role in determining the depth of the crisis, and understanding these dynamics is key to shaping the appropriate response. This initial assessment also enables the crisis management team to prioritize which issues need immediate attention and which can be addressed later. By focusing on the most critical elements first, the organization can mitigate further damage and begin the process of regaining control over the situation.

The next crucial step after identifying and assessing the crisis is the immediate mobilization of the crisis management team. This team, which should already be established and well-prepared during the precrisis stage, must act quickly and efficiently. Speed is of the essence, as delays in response can exacerbate the crisis, allowing misinformation or speculation to fill the communication void. Each member of the crisis management team must have a clear understanding of their specific roles and responsibilities. For instance, there will be individuals responsible for internal communication with employees to ensure they are informed and reassured. Others will handle external communication, engaging with the media and stakeholders to provide updates and manage public perception. Legal experts may need to assess any potential liabilities or regulatory violations that could arise from the crisis. Additionally, operations management must ensure that the organization continues to function as smoothly as possible, minimizing disruption to day-to-day business activities.

Coordination within the crisis management team is critical for ensuring a timely and unified response. There should be seamless communication across all areas of responsibility, with regular updates and meetings to ensure everyone is aligned on the latest developments. The team's ability to work cohesively will determine how effectively the organization navigates the crisis. This is where the precrisis training and preparedness efforts come into play, as a well-rehearsed team can operate smoothly under pressure.

A vital component of this phase is appointing a trained spokesperson who will represent the organization publicly. This individual must be well-prepared and skilled in handling media inquiries, delivering press statements, and responding to stakeholder concerns in a calm and measured manner. The spokesperson's role is to ensure that the organization's messaging is clear, consistent, and empathetic. In the heat of a crisis, public perception is often shaped by the tone and transparency of communication, so the spokesperson must strike the right balance between providing necessary information and maintaining the organization's reputation. They should be well-versed in the organization's key messages and have the ability to adapt their communication style depending on the audience, whether it's customers, investors, or the media. By delivering timely updates and addressing concerns head-on, the spokesperson can help prevent the spread of misinformation and reduce public anxiety. This visibility and transparency are essential for maintaining trust and demonstrating that the organization is taking the crisis seriously and acting with integrity.

> **Example:** The crisis event stage begins when the issue with FitWear's defective running shoes becomes public. A viral post on social media from a dissatisfied customer shows images of the sole tearing apart after only a few uses, accompanied by a caption accusing FitWear of compromising quality. The post quickly gains traction, with other customers sharing similar experiences and expressing outrage. Media outlets pick up the story, and hashtags like #FitWearFail trend online, amplifying the negative attention. Retailers begin receiving returns en masse, and customers demand refunds, while questions about FitWear's quality assurance practices surface in public forums. At this stage, FitWear is fully immersed in the crisis, facing both reputational damage and operational challenges, as it scrambles to respond and contain the fallout. This is the turning point where swift, transparent, and well-coordinated action is critical to mitigate further harm.

Immediate Response

The immediate response stage is arguably the most crucial part of crisis management, as it sets the foundation for how the entire crisis will be handled and perceived by stakeholders. The timing of an organization's first communication during this stage can make or break the effectiveness of its crisis response. Acting quickly is of paramount importance, as the speed of communication can influence public perception and stakeholder trust. Any significant delay or hesitancy in acknowledging the issue can worsen the situation, as rumors and misinformation can spread unchecked, filling the information void and leading to even greater reputational damage. By moving swiftly and decisively, brands can seize control of the narrative before it spirals out of their hands. The initial communication should focus on providing clear, transparent, and accurate information. It is essential that the organization acknowledges the crisis, accepts responsibility where appropriate, and reassures stakeholders that immediate steps are being taken to resolve the issue. This transparency serves to demonstrate that the brand is operating in good faith and is committed to making things right.

Equally important in the immediate response phase is the tone of the communication. Brands should avoid vague or evasive statements, as this can be interpreted as an attempt to downplay or conceal the seriousness of the situation. Instead, the message should be grounded in facts and delivered in a way that conveys accountability, compassion, and urgency. By acknowledging the crisis openly and expressing empathy for those affected, organizations can begin to rebuild trust and reassure stakeholders that the issue is being taken seriously. Transparency during this stage is not just about sharing information—it is about fostering a sense of responsibility and integrity, which can help alleviate concerns and prevent stakeholders from feeling alienated or misled. Moreover, being open about the steps the organization is taking to resolve the crisis reinforces the idea that the brand is actively working to address the problem, which can help minimize damage to its reputation.

The immediate response stage should also emphasize proactive engagement with stakeholders, addressing their concerns and inquiries as quickly as possible. In a crisis, communication is not a one-way street—it is essential for organizations to listen carefully to the feedback, concerns, and questions coming from their various audiences, including customers, employees, investors, and partners. Engaging with stakeholders and making it clear that their voices are being heard fosters a sense of inclusion and respect. This not only builds trust but also helps the organization tailor its responses more effectively. Addressing stakeholder concerns directly can diffuse frustration or anger, as people tend to be more understanding and patient when they feel that their grievances are being taken seriously.

Tailored messaging is another key component of a successful immediate response. Not all stakeholders will have the same concerns or require the same level of detail, so it is important to customize communications for each audience. For example, customers may need reassurance that product quality and safety are being addressed, while investors will want to know about the potential financial impact of the crisis. Employees, on the other hand, may need information about their job security and the steps the organization is taking to manage the internal fallout of the situation. Crafting messages that are concise yet comprehensive, and that address the specific concerns of each audience, ensures that the response is well-received without overwhelming stakeholders with unnecessary or irrelevant details. Clarity in communication, combined with a sense of empathy and responsibility, helps maintain confidence among stakeholders and reinforces the message that the organization is in control of the situation.

Example: In the immediate response stage, FitWear's crisis management team is activated to address the fallout from the defective running shoes. Within hours of the viral post, FitWear issues an initial statement on social media, acknowledging the complaints and assuring customers that the issue is being investigated. The team designates a spokesperson who conducts a press briefing, explaining that FitWear is committed to resolving the matter swiftly and transparently. A product recall is announced, offering affected customers free replacements or full refunds, and a dedicated hotline is set up to handle inquiries. FitWear also uses its website to create a central hub for updates on the crisis, including FAQs about the recall process. Social media platforms are closely monitored for sentiment and feedback, and the brand actively engages with concerned customers by responding to comments and questions. By acting quickly and communicating openly, FitWear aims to take control of the narrative and demonstrate its commitment to accountability, while limiting further damage to its reputation.

Recovery

Once the initial shock of the crisis subsides, the recovery stage begins. At this point, organizations must evaluate the full impact of the crisis on their operations, brand reputation, and stakeholder relationships. Evaluating the effectiveness of the crisis response is critical for determining how well the organization managed the situation and whether the strategies used were successful. Key performance indicators (KPIs) can include metrics like media coverage, social media sentiment, and customer feedback. Analyzing these indicators will provide a comprehensive view of how the crisis affected the brand and its stakeholders, highlighting what worked well and what could be improved.

Following the evaluation, organizations should take concrete steps to implement changes based on the lessons learned. Whether these changes involve adjusting internal policies, improving communication protocols, or refining crisis management strategies, they are essential for enhancing future crisis preparedness. Organizations should also revise their crisis communication plan to reflect these improvements, ensuring that they are better equipped to handle future crises. Ongoing training and development for the crisis management team are also critical during this stage, reinforcing the need for continuous improvement in crisis response capabilities.

Example: In the recovery stage, FitWear focuses on restoring customer trust and rebuilding its brand reputation after the immediate crisis has been managed. The company sends personalized emails to customers who participated in the recall, thanking them for their understanding and offering a 20 percent discount on future purchases as a goodwill gesture. FitWear also rolls out a campaign highlighting its enhanced quality control measures, reassuring customers that the issues with the defective running shoes have been resolved. Additionally, FitWear engages in community outreach, partnering with fitness influencers and hosting free running events to reconnect with its customer base and rebuild its image. The company uses these opportunities to emphasize its commitment to quality and customer satisfaction. On its social media channels, FitWear shares testimonials from satisfied customers who received replacements and found the improved product to meet their expectations. These proactive measures help FitWear rebuild trust, regain loyalty, and re-establish its position as a reliable brand in the fitness apparel industry.

Postcrisis

Once the immediate shock of the crisis has been addressed, organizations enter the recovery stage, which is pivotal for regaining stability and rebuilding trust with stakeholders. During this phase, companies must conduct a thorough evaluation of the crisis's impact on various aspects of the business, such as operations, brand reputation, financial standing, and stakeholder relationships. It is crucial to not only assess the tangible effects but also to understand the deeper implications for the company's long-term objectives and public perception. A comprehensive postcrisis analysis is essential for determining whether the organization's crisis management strategies were effective and what areas require improvement. This evaluation involves gathering data on KPIs, including the volume and tone of media coverage, shifts in social media sentiment, customer feedback, employee morale, and financial repercussions. Analyzing these indicators will give the organization a holistic view of the crisis's consequences, providing insight into what strategies worked well and which ones fell short.

This stage of the crisis life cycle emphasizes learning from the experience. Once the data have been collected and the impact thoroughly evaluated, the organization must take concrete steps to apply the lessons learned. This might involve refining internal processes, adjusting communication strategies, or re-evaluating the decision-making hierarchy during a crisis. For example, if the organization discovered that its communication with the media or customers was insufficient or poorly timed, adjustments should be made to ensure a more effective and transparent flow of information in the future. Similarly, if certain operational weaknesses were exposed during the crisis, these should be addressed through updated policies and practices designed to prevent similar issues from recurring. The recovery stage is not just about returning to normal operations but about building a more resilient organization capable of handling future crises more effectively.

A significant part of this recovery phase involves revising and updating the organization's crisis communication plan. Based on the lessons learned during the crisis, companies should revisit their communication protocols to ensure they are better equipped to respond quickly and transparently in the future. This might include developing more detailed message templates, identifying additional spokespersons to handle different aspects of the crisis, or improving coordination between departments to streamline communication. By fine-tuning the crisis communication plan, organizations can reduce the chances of miscommunication or delayed responses in future crises. Additionally, integrating technology and digital tools, such as social media monitoring systems or crisis management software, can enhance the organization's ability to respond swiftly and strategically.

Employee training is another essential aspect of the recovery stage. Organizations should prioritize ongoing training and development for their crisis management team and other key staff members involved in crisis response. Regular simulations, workshops, and reviews of crisis scenarios will ensure that the team remains sharp, knowledgeable, and ready to take immediate action when needed. Continuous improvement in crisis response capabilities is vital, as no two crises are the same, and the organization must be adaptable to different types of challenges. Moreover, encouraging open dialogue within the organization about what went well and what could have been handled better helps foster a culture of transparency and learning, which is key to continuous growth and resilience.

Another critical factor during the recovery stage is rebuilding and strengthening stakeholder relationships that may have been strained during the crisis. Whether it's with customers, employees, investors, or the media, organizations should actively engage in relationship-rebuilding efforts. Apologizing where necessary, offering clear explanations, and showcasing tangible efforts to make amends can go a long way in restoring trust. Rebuilding these relationships is not just about addressing the immediate concerns raised during the crisis but also about demonstrating a long-term commitment to accountability, transparency, and improvement. For example, if customers were affected by the crisis, the organization could offer compensation or discounts as a gesture of goodwill. If internal employee trust was shaken, the company might implement new employee engagement initiatives or improve working conditions to show its dedication to its workforce.

Example: In the recovery stage, FitWear focuses on restoring customer trust and rebuilding its brand reputation after the immediate crisis has been managed. The company sends personalized emails to customers who participated in the recall, thanking them for their understanding and offering a 20 percent discount on future purchases as a goodwill gesture. FitWear also rolls out a campaign highlighting its enhanced quality control measures, reassuring customers that the issues with the defective running shoes have been resolved. Additionally, FitWear engages in community outreach, partnering with fitness influencers and hosting free running events to reconnect with its customer base and rebuild its image. The company uses these opportunities to emphasize its commitment to quality and customer satisfaction. On its social media channels, FitWear shares testimonials from satisfied customers who received replacements and found the improved product to meet their expectations. These proactive measures help FitWear rebuild trust, regain loyalty, and re-establish its position as a reliable brand in the fitness apparel industry.

The Importance of Understanding the Brand Crisis Life cycle

Understanding the complexities of the brand crisis life cycle is crucial for organizations striving to navigate crises with success, resilience, and long-term stability. In today's unpredictable business environment, no brand is immune to potential disruptions, whether they stem from external factors, such as economic downturns, technological failures, or social controversies, or internal issues, such as mismanagement, ethical lapses, or operational breakdowns. The key to weathering these challenges lies in an organization's ability to grasp the nuances of the brand crisis life cycle and to apply tailored strategies that align with the unique demands of each phase.

By recognizing the distinct stages of a crisis—from precrisis preparation to postcrisis recovery—organizations can implement targeted responses that minimize damage and maximize opportunities for growth (Table 3.1). This proactive approach ensures that brands are not merely reactive but are actively managing their reputation, stakeholder relationships, and operational resilience at every turn. The ability to anticipate potential risks, swiftly assess and address crises as they emerge, and then strategically recover allows companies to safeguard their brand's reputation and foster trust among stakeholders, which is essential for maintaining long-term loyalty and confidence.

Moreover, organizations that understand the full life cycle of a crisis are better positioned to adapt to the dynamic nature of crises as they evolve. Each phase of a crisis brings with it distinct challenges—whether it's managing initial communications, controlling the narrative in the media, or rebuilding stakeholder trust once the crisis subsides. By being well-versed in these stages, brands can avoid common pitfalls, such as delayed responses, poor messaging, or inadequate postcrisis evaluation, that could otherwise exacerbate the situation. Furthermore, this deep understanding enables companies to capitalize on the opportunities that crises often present—such as demonstrating leadership, innovation, and a commitment to values like transparency and accountability.

Ultimately, mastering the intricacies of the brand crisis life cycle not only enables organizations to survive crises but to emerge from

Table 3.1 This table outlines the five critical stages of the brand crisis life cycle: precrisis, crisis event, immediate response, recovery, and postcrisis. Each stage includes a description, key activities to undertake, and the objectives organizations should aim to achieve, providing a comprehensive framework for understanding and managing brand crises effectively

Stage	Description	Key activities	Objectives
Precrisis	The preparation phase where organizations identify potential risks and develop strategies to mitigate them.	• Conduct risk assessments • Develop crisis communication plans • Train crisis management teams	• Identify potential risks • Ensure readiness
Crisis event	The critical period when the crisis unfolds, requiring immediate action and communication.	• Activate crisis response team • Issue initial statements • Monitor social media and public sentiment	• Contain the crisis • Provide timely updates
Immediate response	The active management of the crisis, focusing on communication and containment.	• Issue initial statement • Communicate with stakeholders • Monitor social media and public sentiment	• Contain the crisis • Provide timely updates
Recovery	The phase where the organization begins to recover and restore operations, reputation, and stakeholder trust.	• Assess damage and impact • Implement recovery strategies • Rebuild stakeholder relationships	• Restore trust • Resume normal operations
Postcrisis	The final stage involves reflection and analysis to learn from the crisis and improve future preparedness.	• Conduct a postmortem analysis • Document findings and lessons learned • Revise crisis plans based on insights	• Improve future crisis management • Foster a culture of continuous improvement

them stronger, with a more resilient brand and a renewed sense of purpose. Those who can successfully navigate the challenges of a crisis will be better equipped to maintain their competitive edge, strengthen their market position, and foster deeper connections with their customers, employees, and partners. This comprehensive approach to crisis management transforms what could be a devastating event into an opportunity for growth, learning, and long-term success.

Proactive Crisis Management

One of the most significant advantages of understanding the brand crisis life cycle is the ability to adopt a proactive approach to crisis management. Organizations that fully embrace this life cycle are significantly better positioned to anticipate and recognize potential crises long before they escalate into full-blown emergencies. By identifying early warning signs—whether they arise from consumer dissatisfaction, social media missteps, operational vulnerabilities, or shifts in the competitive landscape—businesses can take timely, pre-emptive action. This proactive stance enables brands to develop and implement crisis prevention strategies that can effectively mitigate risks and significantly reduce the likelihood of crises occurring in the first place.

Moreover, proactive crisis management goes well beyond merely reacting to potential threats as they arise. It encompasses a comprehensive approach that involves the continuous monitoring of industry trends, consumer sentiment, regulatory changes, and global events that could impact the brand's reputation or operational capabilities. Organizations that prioritize proactive management are typically more likely to have established crisis communication plans and trained teams in place, ready to handle any situation that may arise. These brands enjoy a substantial advantage because they do not wait for a crisis to escalate before taking action—they are already prepared with the necessary tools and tactics to respond swiftly and effectively when the need arises.

By adopting a proactive stance, organizations can effectively demonstrate to their stakeholders that they are committed to safeguarding their interests and maintaining their well-being. This not only helps to prevent crises but also fosters a sense of security and trust among consumers, investors, employees, and other key audiences. Brands that successfully prevent or mitigate crises show their stakeholders that they are resilient, adaptable, and capable of navigating challenges without losing sight of their core values and mission. This proactive management approach not only preserves the brand's reputation but can also enhance its overall market position, reinforcing consumer loyalty and strengthening relationships with stakeholders.

Furthermore, organizations that engage in proactive crisis management can leverage their preparedness as a competitive advantage. They can position themselves as leaders in their industry, not just in terms of their products and services but also in their approach to risk management and stakeholder engagement. When a crisis is managed effectively, it can even lead to a strengthening of the brand's reputation, as stakeholders recognize the organization's commitment to transparency, accountability, and ethical conduct. As a result, a proactive crisis management strategy not only shields the organization from immediate threats but also lays the groundwork for long-term success, allowing brands to thrive even in challenging circumstances. This holistic approach to crisis management is essential for building a resilient organization that can withstand the uncertainties of today's rapidly changing environment.

Enhanced Stakeholder Engagement

Another critical aspect of understanding the brand crisis life cycle is its strong emphasis on the significance of stakeholder engagement throughout each stage of a crisis. Stakeholders—including customers, employees, suppliers, investors, partners, and the media—are integral to the survival and success of a brand during a crisis. How well a brand engages and communicates with its stakeholders can significantly influence the outcome of the crisis and the brand's ability to recover effectively. A well-informed and engaged stakeholder base can serve as a crucial buffer against negative perceptions, enabling the brand to navigate turbulent waters with greater ease.

In the precrisis stage, organizations should actively focus on building strong, trusting relationships with their stakeholders. This involves engaging in transparent communication about the brand's values, goals, and commitment to ethical practices and social responsibility. Establishing these robust connections before a crisis strikes creates a solid foundation of goodwill and trust that can prove invaluable during difficult times. When stakeholders feel valued and heard, they are more likely to offer their support and loyalty when a crisis occurs, standing by the brand during challenging moments instead of distancing themselves.

During the actual crisis event, timely, transparent, and empathetic communication becomes essential for maintaining stakeholder confidence. Brands that fully understand the life cycle appreciate the importance of addressing stakeholder concerns quickly and with sincerity, whether through social media updates, press releases, or direct communication methods. By keeping stakeholders informed and actively involved in the process, brands can reduce uncertainty and anxiety, which helps to prevent negative reactions that could exacerbate the situation. Ensuring stakeholders feel included in the narrative can also foster a sense of community and collective resilience during a crisis.

Postcrisis, the organization's relationship with stakeholders doesn't merely conclude; in fact, this stage provides a unique opportunity to further strengthen these connections by demonstrating accountability and a genuine commitment to improvement. Engaging stakeholders in the recovery process—whether through regular updates on corrective actions taken, participation in Corporate Social Responsibility (CSR) initiatives, or inviting them to provide feedback—can foster deeper loyalty and strengthen ties. The brand shows that it values its stakeholders not just when times are good, but also during challenging times, which significantly enhances its reputation and trustworthiness over the long term. This continuous engagement fosters a lasting relationship built on trust and mutual respect, ultimately leading to increased brand loyalty and a more resilient organizational identity.

By actively involving stakeholders throughout the brand crisis life cycle, organizations can create a supportive network that contributes to a more effective crisis response and recovery process. This holistic approach not only bolsters the brand's reputation but also cultivates a community of advocates who are willing to champion the brand during both prosperous and challenging times, thereby ensuring sustainable success and resilience in an unpredictable environment.

Long-Term Success

The ultimate goal of mastering the brand crisis life cycle is to ensure the long-term success and sustainability of the brand. Crises are inevitable in today's complex and fast-paced world, but how an organization responds to them determines whether it will merely survive or thrive in the aftermath. Brands that invest the time to understand the life cycle and manage it effectively position themselves for greater resilience and continued growth. They recognize that the ability to navigate crises is not just a reactive measure but a proactive strategy that shapes their future trajectory.

One of the key factors contributing to long-term success is learning from the crisis experience. Brands that conduct thorough postcrisis evaluations and take actionable steps to improve their processes, policies, and communication strategies are far more likely to emerge stronger. These organizations understand that each crisis provides valuable lessons—whether it's identifying weaknesses in operational procedures, recognizing gaps in stakeholder communication, or discovering new opportunities for innovation. By applying these lessons, organizations can enhance their crisis preparedness and prevent similar issues from arising in the future. This continuous cycle of learning and adaptation not only fortifies the brand's capabilities but also ingrains a culture of resilience and accountability.

Additionally, effectively managing the brand crisis life cycle helps organizations build a stronger brand reputation over time. When stakeholders observe that a brand is capable of handling crises with integrity, transparency, and accountability, they are more likely to trust and support that brand in the future. In fact, some brands manage to not only recover from crises but also enhance their reputation as a result of their adept handling. By demonstrating resilience, adaptability, and a genuine commitment to improvement, these organizations can transform a potentially damaging situation into an opportunity for growth and strengthened relationships with stakeholders. This ability to turn adversity into an advantage significantly boosts their standing in the market.

Furthermore, brands that excel in managing the life cycle gain a competitive advantage. In a world where consumer loyalty is often fragile and reputations can be quickly damaged, brands that have proven their ability to navigate crises effectively stand out in the marketplace. They become known as organizations that can be trusted in times of uncertainty, attracting customers, investors, and partners who value stability and reliability. This competitive edge contributes to the long-term sustainability and growth of the brand. A strong reputation built on crisis management not only enhances brand loyalty but also leads to increased market share and profitability.

In effect, understanding the brand crisis life cycle is not just about surviving a crisis—it's about thriving in the aftermath and using the experience as a catalyst for improvement. Proactive crisis management, enhanced stakeholder engagement, and a focus on long-term success all contribute to the brand's ability to emerge from crises stronger, more resilient, and better prepared for the future. Brands that master this life cycle not only protect their reputation during difficult times but also build a solid foundation for ongoing success and growth in the years to come. By continuously refining their strategies and fostering open lines of communication with stakeholders, these brands can ensure that they remain relevant, trusted, and capable of meeting challenges head-on. Ultimately, the mastery of the brand crisis life cycle becomes a cornerstone of organizational excellence, leading to sustained performance and a lasting legacy in the marketplace.

Conclusion

The brand crisis life cycle offers a crucial roadmap for organizations to navigate the complexities of a crisis with confidence and foresight. By understanding the various stages of a crisis—precrisis, crisis event, immediate response, recovery, and postcrisis—organizations can better prepare for challenges, respond effectively, and ensure long-term resilience. This structured approach enables brands to address the unique demands of each phase, helping to minimize reputational damage and maintain stakeholder trust.

Proactive preparation is key, allowing brands to identify potential risks before they escalate. Equally important is the way organizations engage with stakeholders during and after the crisis. Transparent communication, timely responses, and a commitment to addressing concerns can transform a difficult situation into an opportunity for deeper relationships and trust. Ultimately, embracing the brand crisis life cycle empowers organizations to turn crises into opportunities for growth. By learning from each experience, improving strategies, and fostering strong stakeholder connections, brands can emerge stronger, more adaptable, and better prepared for future challenges.

Further Reading

Boin, A., and P. 't Hart. 2007. "Public Leadership in Times of Crisis: Mission Impossible?" *Public Administration Review* 67 (5): 898–907.

Coombs, W.T. 2019. *Ongoing Crisis Communication: Planning, Managing, and Responding*, 5th ed. Thousand Oaks, CA: SAGE Publications.

Fink, S. 2013. *Crisis Management: Planning for the Inevitable*, 3rd ed. New York, NY: AMACOM.

Pearson, C.M., and J.A. Clair. 1998. "Reframing Crisis Management." *Academy of Management Review* 23 (1): 59–76.

Meer, V.D., P. Verhoeven., H.W.J. Beentjes., and R. Vliegenthart. 2017. "Communicating in Times of Crisis: The Stakeholder Relationship Under Pressure." *Public Relations Review* 43 (2): 426–40.

CHAPTER 4

The Dynamics of Brand Crisis Communication

Overview

- Introduces the principles of effective crisis communication: timeliness, transparency, consistency, and empathy.
- Guides readers on developing a robust crisis communication plan, including message development and stakeholder analysis.
- Examines the role of social media as both a tool and a challenge during crises.
- Highlights the need for postcrisis evaluation to refine communication strategies.

Crisis communication has become an essential element of modern brand management, particularly in a world characterized by instantaneous information exchange and heightened public scrutiny. The manner in which organizations communicate during crises can significantly influence their reputation, customer loyalty, and overall business continuity. With the proliferation of social media and digital communication channels, the stakes of effective crisis communication have never been higher. Brands often find themselves thrust into the spotlight, with social media users and news outlets rapidly amplifying crises to global audiences. Therefore, it is imperative that organizations develop proactive crisis communication strategies that not only address immediate concerns but also lay the groundwork for long-term recovery.

Understanding the principles of effective crisis communication is crucial for organizations striving to protect their reputations and maintain stakeholder trust. This chapter explores the fundamental elements of crisis communication, the types of crises that can occur, the importance of timely and transparent messaging, and the necessity of having a well-defined crisis communication plan. Additionally, the role of social media as both a tool for engagement and a potential minefield will be examined. Furthermore, this chapter will delve into postcrisis analysis and recovery, emphasizing the significance of learning from past experiences to enhance future crisis preparedness.

Ultimately, the ability to communicate effectively during a crisis is not just a skill but a vital component of a brand's resilience. Organizations that prioritize authenticity, transparency, and empathy in their crisis communication efforts are better positioned to weather the storm and emerge stronger in the face of adversity.

Understanding Crisis Communication

Crisis communication refers to the strategic approach that organizations adopt to convey information to stakeholders during and after a crisis. It encompasses not only the messaging delivered but also the strategies employed to mitigate damage to a brand's reputation and restore stakeholder trust. This aspect of communication is crucial because the effectiveness of a company's response to a crisis can significantly influence how it is perceived in the public eye. In an age of rapid information dissemination and heightened public scrutiny, organizations must navigate crises with care, ensuring that their messages resonate with various stakeholders, including consumers, employees, investors, and the media.

Effective crisis communication is vital for several compelling reasons. First, it helps organizations maintain trust among consumers, employees, and other stakeholders during challenging times. When a crisis strikes, stakeholders often look to the organization for guidance and information. A well-crafted communication strategy can help reassure them that the organization is taking the situation seriously and is committed to addressing their concerns. This trust is particularly important in times of uncertainty, as stakeholders are more likely to remain loyal to a brand that communicates openly and transparently.

Second, timely and transparent communication can mitigate the spread of misinformation, which can exacerbate a crisis. In the digital age, information spreads rapidly, and inaccuracies can quickly spiral out of control. If organizations fail to communicate effectively, rumors and false information can proliferate, leading to public confusion and further damage to the brand's reputation. Therefore, proactive communication that addresses potential misunderstandings is essential in containing the narrative surrounding a crisis.

Third, organizations that handle crises effectively are often viewed more favorably than those that respond poorly. Effective crisis communication can demonstrate an organization's commitment to accountability and ethical behavior. This favorable perception is critical for preserving brand equity and can even lead to increased customer loyalty in the long term. Consumers are more likely to support a brand that they perceive as being honest and transparent, particularly when a crisis occurs.

Moreover, successful crisis communication can have positive implications for an organization's financial performance. Research has shown that companies with strong reputations and effective crisis management strategies tend to recover more quickly from crises, often resulting in less financial loss and a faster return to normal operations. This underscores the importance of having a robust crisis communication framework in place.

The crisis communication process can be broken down into four key phases, each of which plays a critical role in ensuring that an organization is well-equipped to handle crises and mitigate their impact:

1. **Prevention:** Organizations must proactively identify potential crises before they occur. This involves conducting risk assessments, analyzing industry trends, and staying informed about emerging issues that could escalate into crises. By recognizing potential vulnerabilities, organizations can develop preventative measures and communication strategies that minimize the likelihood of crises occurring.

2. **Preparation:** Having a crisis communication plan in place is essential for ensuring that organizations can respond swiftly and effectively when a crisis arises. This plan should include detailed protocols for internal and external communication, designated spokespeople, and predefined messaging templates that can be adapted as needed. Training team members on their roles and responsibilities during a crisis is crucial for a coordinated response.

3. **Response:** This phase involves the actual communication during a crisis. Quick and transparent messaging is crucial to address stakeholder concerns. Organizations must provide timely updates, acknowledge the situation, and outline the steps being taken to resolve the issue. During this phase, organizations should be prepared to address questions and concerns from the media and the public, as well as monitor sentiment across communication channels to gauge the effectiveness of their messaging.

4. **Recovery:** After a crisis, organizations must evaluate their response and learn from the experience to improve future crisis management. This includes conducting a thorough review of the crisis communication plan, assessing the effectiveness of messaging, and identifying areas for improvement. Organizations should also communicate their commitment to transparency and accountability to stakeholders, reinforcing their dedication to rebuilding trust.

Each of these phases is interconnected and contributes to an organization's overall crisis management strategy. By recognizing the importance of each phase and taking proactive measures, organizations can enhance their ability to navigate crises effectively and emerge stronger on the other side.

Key Principles of Effective Crisis Communication

Crisis communication is a nuanced and challenging domain that requires organizations to adhere to several key principles to effectively manage their reputation and maintain stakeholder trust during turbulent times. These principles—timeliness, transparency, consistency, and empathy—are essential for navigating crises successfully. By understanding and implementing these principles, organizations can foster goodwill, mitigate damage, and ultimately emerge stronger from challenging situations (Figure 4.1).

Timeliness

Timeliness is perhaps the most critical factor in crisis communication. Organizations must respond quickly to crises to control the narrative

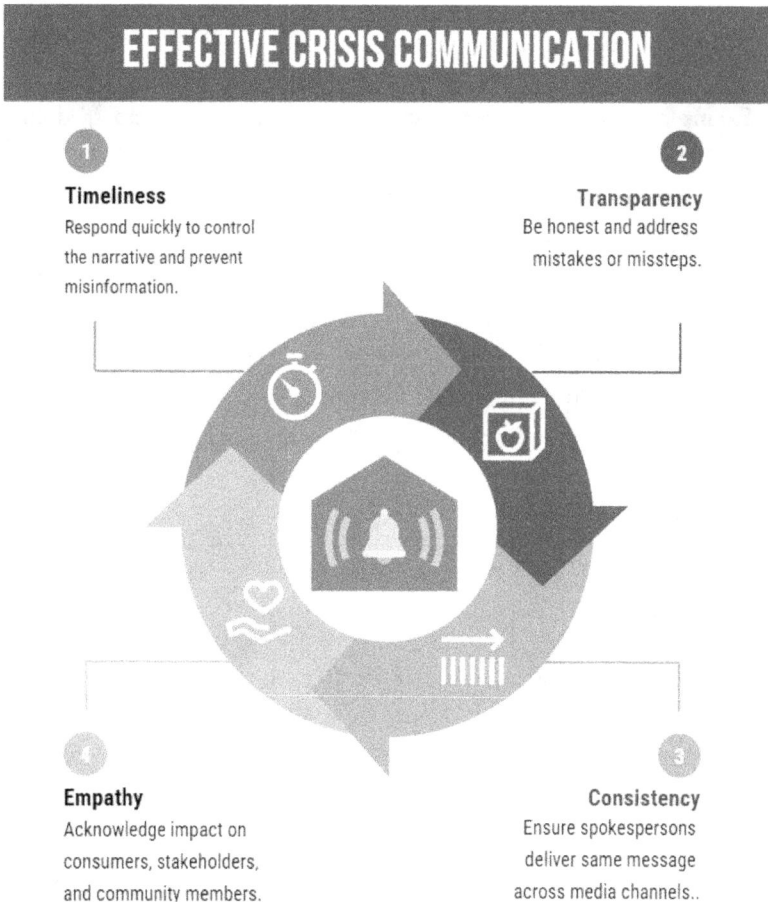

EFFECTIVE CRISIS COMMUNICATION

1 Timeliness
Respond quickly to control the narrative and prevent misinformation.

2 Transparency
Be honest and address mistakes or missteps.

4 Empathy
Acknowledge impact on consumers, stakeholders, and community members.

3 Consistency
Ensure spokespersons deliver same message across media channels..

Figure 4.1 Effective crisis communication

and prevent misinformation from spreading. In today's fast-paced digital environment, where news travels at lightning speed, even a slight delay in communication can lead to significant negative consequences. A failure to act promptly can result in a loss of trust and credibility among stakeholders, which may take years to rebuild.

Furthermore, timely communication allows organizations to clarify facts and provide necessary information to the public. This includes addressing concerns, outlining steps taken to remedy the situation, and offering reassurance. The more quickly an organization communicates, the more likely it is to control the narrative and prevent the escalation of the crisis. Additionally, a timely response can also mitigate the spread of misinformation, which can create further complications for the organization.

Example: When the Tylenol cyanide poisoning crisis emerged in 1982, Johnson & Johnson acted swiftly to protect consumers and address the issue. Upon learning that several people had died from tampered Tylenol capsules, the company immediately issued a nationwide recall of 31 million bottles, despite the significant financial cost. They communicated transparently with the public, implemented tamper-proof packaging, and launched a hotline for consumer concerns. This quick response not only mitigated further harm but also set a benchmark for crisis management, helping the company rebuild trust and maintain its reputation as a consumer-focused brand.

Transparency

Transparency is another essential element in crisis communication. Stakeholders appreciate honesty and are more likely to trust brands that openly address their mistakes or missteps. Transparent communication fosters goodwill and can help mitigate the negative effects of a crisis. For instance, when Johnson & Johnson faced the Tylenol poisoning crisis in the 1980s, the company quickly issued a recall and provided clear, honest information about the situation. Their decision to be forthright about the dangers posed by their product ultimately restored consumer trust in the brand.

Transparency involves more than just delivering information; it requires a commitment to openness and a willingness to share details about the crisis, including its causes and potential impacts. Organizations should communicate not only what happened but also the steps they are taking to address the issue and prevent future occurrences. By being transparent, organizations can demonstrate accountability and build credibility with their stakeholders, which is especially important in times of crisis when trust is fragile.

Moreover, transparent communication can help organizations create a narrative that counters misinformation. When stakeholders feel informed and included in the conversation, they are less likely to turn to external sources or speculate about the situation. This creates an environment where trust can be rebuilt, and relationships with consumers can be strengthened.

> **Example:** In 2015, the automaker Toyota faced a crisis when it had to recall millions of vehicles due to defective airbags supplied by Takata. Toyota responded transparently by promptly acknowledging the issue and providing clear details about the recall process. The company set up a dedicated website with real-time updates, FAQs, and a Vehicle Identification Number (VIN) lookup tool to help customers determine if their vehicles were affected. Toyota's transparency in openly addressing the issue and keeping stakeholders informed throughout the process helped the brand maintain consumer trust during a challenging time.

Consistency

Consistency in messaging is vital during a crisis. Organizations must ensure that all spokespersons deliver the same message across different platforms to avoid confusion and further damage to the brand's reputation. This requires effective internal communication and coordination among team members. Inconsistent messaging can lead to misunderstandings and may be perceived as a lack of accountability, causing stakeholders to question the organization's integrity and commitment to resolving the crisis.

To achieve consistency, organizations should develop a clear and unified message that outlines the situation, the organization's response, and any relevant actions taken. This message should be communicated through various channels, including press releases, social media, and internal communications. All team members involved in crisis management should be trained on the key messages to ensure they are communicated accurately and effectively.

Furthermore, organizations should regularly update stakeholders as new information becomes available, ensuring that everyone is on the same page. Consistent messaging not only helps to clarify the situation but also reinforces the organization's commitment to transparency and accountability. When stakeholders receive the same information from multiple sources, it reinforces the message and helps to build trust.

> **Example:** During the 2018 Facebook–Cambridge Analytica data scandal, Facebook faced intense scrutiny for its role in mishandling user data. While its initial response was criticized, the company eventually implemented a consistent strategy to rebuild trust. Facebook repeatedly communicated its commitment to improving user privacy through regular updates, public statements, and transparent reports on changes made to its data-handling policies. This consistency helped demonstrate the company's resolve to address the issue comprehensively, even if public skepticism persisted for some time.

Empathy

Empathy plays a crucial role in crisis communication. Brands that acknowledge the impact of the crisis on their stakeholders and express genuine concern are more likely to be viewed favorably. Empathetic responses can help to humanize a brand and build emotional connections with consumers. For instance, after the 2018 Starbucks racial bias incident, CEO Kevin Johnson issued a heartfelt apology and took immediate steps to address the issue, demonstrating empathy toward those affected and reinforcing the brand's commitment to inclusivity.

Empathy in crisis communication goes beyond simply expressing sympathy; it involves actively listening to stakeholders' concerns and feelings. Organizations should strive to understand how the crisis affects their stakeholders, and their messaging should reflect that understanding. By acknowledging the emotional toll of a crisis and validating stakeholders' feelings, organizations can foster goodwill and strengthen their relationships.

Moreover, empathetic communication can help to de-escalate tensions and reduce hostility. When stakeholders feel heard and understood, they are more likely to respond positively to the organization's efforts to address the situation. This can lead to a more constructive dialogue and pave the way for healing and reconciliation. Organizations that prioritize empathy in their crisis communication are better equipped to navigate the complexities of stakeholder emotions and expectations, ultimately leading to a more favorable resolution.

The key principles of effective crisis communication—timeliness, transparency, consistency, and empathy—are essential for organizations to navigate crises successfully. By adhering to these principles, organizations can mitigate the negative impacts of a crisis, maintain stakeholder trust, and preserve their reputation. As crises continue to evolve in complexity and scope, the importance of effective crisis communication will only grow, making it imperative for organizations to prioritize these principles in their crisis management strategies.

Example: Starbucks showed empathy in 2018 following an incident in Philadelphia where two Black men were arrested at one of its stores for sitting without making a purchase. Recognizing the racial biases inherent in the situation, the company issued a heartfelt apology and took immediate action. Starbucks closed over 8,000 stores for a day to conduct racial bias training for employees, signaling its commitment to addressing systemic issues and fostering inclusivity.

This empathetic response resonated with stakeholders and showcased Starbucks' willingness to take responsibility and drive positive change.

Developing a Crisis Communication Plan

A comprehensive crisis communication plan is an essential tool for organizations to effectively manage potential crises and protect their reputation. It serves as a blueprint for guiding actions, ensuring that responses are well-coordinated and timely. The development of such a plan involves several key components and processes that organizations must carefully consider to prepare for unforeseen events.

Key Components of a Crisis Communication Plan

A well-structured crisis communication plan includes several key components that work together to facilitate effective crisis management, ensuring organizations are prepared to respond promptly and efficiently when a crisis occurs. One foundational element is stakeholder identification, where organizations determine who will be most affected by potential crises and what specific information needs they have. Stakeholders may include customers, employees, investors, suppliers, regulators, the media, and the general public. Understanding the unique perspectives and concerns of each stakeholder group is critical for crafting effective messages. For instance, customers may prioritize safety and accountability, while investors might focus on financial implications and the long-term impact on the company's stability.

Another essential component is establishing clear communication protocols for both internal and external communication. These protocols should outline who is responsible for communication, what information will be shared, and how it will be disseminated. Creating a hierarchy of communication is vital, designating individuals who will speak on behalf of the organization, especially during media interactions. Moreover, protocols should include guidelines for timely reporting and information sharing to keep all relevant parties informed throughout the crisis.

Message development is equally important; organizations should prepare templates and key messages in advance to streamline the communication process during a crisis. Predeveloped messages save valuable time and ensure a consistent narrative when a crisis unfolds. These messages should be adaptable to various scenarios while addressing the core issues at hand, enabling organizations to maintain a clear and unified voice. Messages should focus on transparency, accountability, and a commitment to resolving the issue, fostering trust among stakeholders.

Lastly, conducting a thorough risk assessment is crucial for identifying potential vulnerabilities that could lead to crises. This involves analyzing past incidents, industry trends, and emerging threats that may impact the organization. By understanding these risks, organizations can develop specific strategies to mitigate them and create tailored communication plans for different scenarios. This proactive approach enhances the organization's ability to anticipate crises and respond effectively.

Designating a Crisis Management Team

A crisis management team is a critical component of an effective crisis communication plan, composed of individuals with defined roles and responsibilities who each contribute their expertise to navigate the complexities of a crisis. Typically, the team includes representatives from key departments such as public relations, legal, human resources, and operations. This diverse composition ensures that multiple perspectives are considered in the decision-making process, allowing for a well-rounded approach to crisis management. Each member should have a clear understanding of their role and the expectations placed upon them to ensure a coordinated response.

One of the primary responsibilities of the crisis management team is to monitor the crisis as it unfolds. This involves tracking media coverage, social media conversations, and stakeholder sentiments to gauge public reaction and adjust communication strategies as necessary. By staying informed, the team can respond to emerging concerns, counter misinformation, and ensure that accurate information is disseminated.

In addition to monitoring, the crisis management team is responsible for crafting responses that align with the organization's values and messaging. This includes drafting press releases, social media updates, and internal communications that specifically address the issues at hand. Collaboration among team members is crucial; they should review messages before dissemination to ensure consistency and accuracy.

Furthermore, designating trained spokespersons who are adept at handling media inquiries is essential for effectively representing the brand during a crisis. These individuals should possess strong communication skills, allowing them to convey the organization's message clearly and confidently. Regular training sessions should be conducted to prepare spokespersons for potential questions and scenarios they may encounter during media interactions. This preparation enables them to respond with poise and credibility, which is vital for maintaining stakeholder trust.

Message Development

Crafting effective crisis messages requires careful consideration of the audience and the specific context of the crisis, as effective messaging can significantly influence stakeholders' perceptions of the organization's response. A crucial aspect is audience-centric messaging, where messages should be clear, concise, and focused on addressing stakeholder concerns. Organizations must tailor their messages to different audiences, as illustrated in the stakeholder engagement map (Figure 4.2), ensuring that the tone and content resonate with each group. For example, messages directed at customers may emphasize safety and accountability, while those aimed at investors might focus on the financial implications of the crisis. This tailored approach not only enhances message effectiveness but also demonstrates an understanding of stakeholders' needs and priorities.

Additionally, clarity and simplicity are paramount in crisis messaging. Organizations should avoid jargon and technical language that may confuse stakeholders; instead, messages should be straightforward and easily understandable. Providing specific information about the crisis, the organization's response, and any actions being taken can help alleviate concerns and foster trust. Clear messaging also prevents misinterpretation and allows stakeholders to quickly grasp the situation. Regular updates are essential as a crisis evolves, and organizations should keep stakeholders informed of developments through ongoing communication, reinforcing their commitment to transparency and accountability. Stakeholders appreciate being kept in the loop, and consistent updates help build confidence in the organization's ability to manage the situation.

Finally, after the crisis has been managed, organizations should conduct a thorough evaluation of their messaging. This postcrisis reflection allows them to identify what worked well, what could be improved, and how to enhance future crisis communication strategies. By analyzing past responses, organizations can develop better messaging

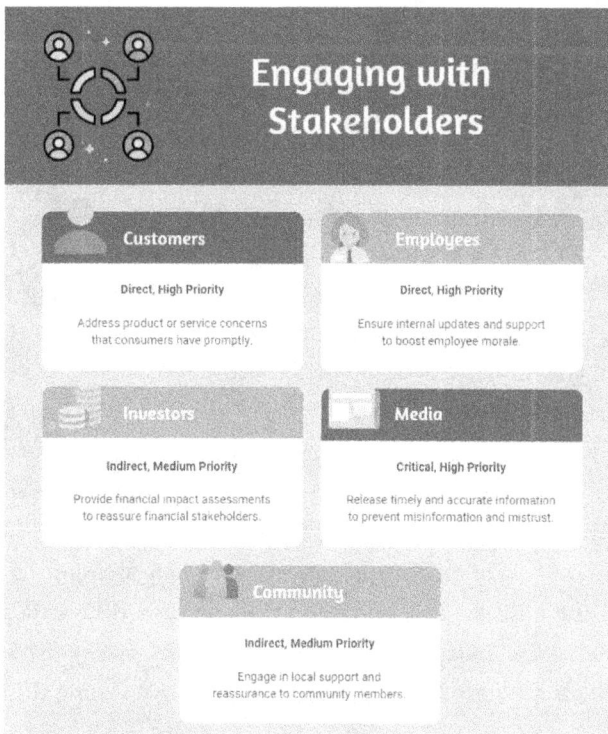

Figure 4.2 Engaging with stakeholders

frameworks that are tailored to their stakeholders' needs, ultimately strengthening their crisis communication efforts. Incorporating insights from the stakeholder engagement map throughout this process can further ensure that messaging aligns with stakeholder expectations and fosters a strong, trust-based relationship moving forward.

Utilizing Communication Channels

Utilizing various communication channels effectively is crucial for organizations during a crisis, as each channel offers unique advantages and challenges. Social media platforms, for example, provide real-time updates and facilitate engagement with consumers, allowing organizations to connect directly with their audience. During a crisis, social media can serve as an immediate channel for disseminating information, responding to inquiries, and addressing concerns. Organizations should actively monitor social media conversations and respond promptly to stakeholder questions and comments, demonstrating engagement and accountability.

While social media is essential for real-time updates, press releases are invaluable for conveying more detailed information to the media and stakeholders. These documents can outline the organization's response to the crisis, the steps being taken to resolve the issue, and any relevant background information. Well-crafted press releases can serve as a valuable resource for journalists, ensuring accurate reporting and reducing the likelihood of misinformation.

Email communication also proves effective for reaching stakeholders during a crisis. Organizations can send targeted messages to different groups, such as employees, customers, and investors, to keep them informed and address specific concerns. Timely, clear, and personalized email communication enhances its effectiveness.

Moreover, organizations should leverage their websites as a central hub for crisis-related information. Creating a dedicated page or section for crisis updates allows stakeholders easy access to the latest news, official statements, and resources. Regularly updating the website ensures that stakeholders have access to accurate information, minimizing confusion and uncertainty.

Lastly, while digital channels are increasingly dominant, traditional media still plays a vital role in crisis communication. Organizations should engage with journalists and news outlets to share their narrative and ensure accurate coverage. This engagement may involve participating in interviews, providing background information, or issuing statements to clarify any misconceptions presented in the media. By effectively utilizing these various communication channels, organizations can navigate crises more successfully and maintain stakeholder trust.

The Role of Social Media in Crisis Communication

Social media has fundamentally transformed the landscape of crisis communication, becoming an essential tool for organizations navigating challenging situations. However, it also presents unique challenges that can complicate the communication process. As a result, organizations must adopt strategic approaches to leverage social media effectively while mitigating its potential pitfalls.

Social Media as a Double-Edged Sword

Social media can serve as both a powerful tool for effective crisis communication and a potential minefield for brands. On one hand, platforms like Twitter, Facebook, Instagram, and TikTok enable brands to communicate directly with consumers, providing real-time updates and addressing concerns. This immediacy allows organizations to share their perspectives, clarify misinformation, and present their narratives directly to their audience. For instance, during a crisis, organizations can use social media to disseminate vital information quickly, ensuring that stakeholders are kept informed about developments and organizational responses.

On the other hand, social media can amplify negative sentiment and spread misinformation if not managed properly. The speed at which information can be shared means that false narratives can quickly gain traction, potentially damaging an organization's reputation before it has a chance to respond. Moreover, social media allows for public commentary and backlash, where individuals can express their dissatisfaction, often leading to viral outrage that can escalate quickly. As such, organizations must be vigilant in monitoring their social media presence and proactive in addressing any negative sentiment that arises.

Example: In 2017, Pepsi faced a backlash after releasing an ad featuring Kendall Jenner that was criticized for trivializing social justice movements. In response to the uproar on social media, Pepsi quickly pulled the ad and issued a statement via Twitter apologizing for "missing the mark." However, the brand's response was criticized as tone-deaf and insufficient, with many feeling that it failed to address the core issue of exploiting activism for commercial gain. Pepsi's attempt to use social media to quell the controversy only amplified the criticism, as users dissected both the ad and the apology, demonstrating how social media can exacerbate a crisis if not handled thoughtfully.

Monitoring Social Media Sentiment

Organizations must actively monitor social media sentiment during a crisis to gauge public perception and adjust their communication strategies accordingly. The ability to track real-time feedback from consumers can provide invaluable insights into how the crisis is being perceived and what specific concerns need to be addressed. Tools such as sentiment analysis software can help brands track mentions across various platforms and assess overall sentiment trends. These tools analyze data from social media conversations to determine whether public sentiment is predominantly positive, negative, or neutral, offering organizations a clearer picture of the prevailing attitudes toward the crisis.

By understanding how consumers feel about the crisis, organizations can tailor their responses to address specific concerns and restore trust. For example, if sentiment analysis reveals a high level of frustration among customers regarding a product recall, the organization can craft messages that specifically address those concerns, providing reassurance and outlining steps being taken to rectify the situation. Moreover, organizations can identify key influencers and advocates within their social media audience, leveraging their support to amplify positive messages and counteract negative narratives.

The Importance of Transparency and Timeliness

One of the key lessons from these case studies is the importance of transparency and timeliness in crisis communication on social media. When organizations are open about their challenges and proactive in providing updates, they are more likely to foster trust among stakeholders. Consumers appreciate authenticity and a willingness to engage in honest conversations, especially during difficult times. Organizations that prioritize transparent communication can better navigate the complexities of public sentiment, minimizing potential backlash and maintaining their reputations.

Building a Social Media Crisis Strategy

To effectively harness the power of social media during a crisis, organizations should develop a comprehensive social media crisis strategy that encompasses several key elements. First, preparedness is essential; organizations should establish protocols for social media monitoring and engagement before a crisis occurs. This proactive approach involves identifying potential risks and creating preapproved messaging templates that can be quickly adapted in response to various scenarios.

Second, training is crucial for all team members involved in crisis communication. They should receive instruction on effective social media practices, including how to respond to negative comments and engage constructively with stakeholders. This training ensures that the organization speaks with one voice and maintains a consistent message across all platforms.

During a crisis, engagement becomes vital. Organizations should actively interact with their audience on social media, addressing concerns, answering questions, and providing updates. By fostering two-way communication, organizations can demonstrate their commitment to transparency and accountability.

After managing a crisis, organizations should conduct a thorough postcrisis analysis of their social media responses. This analysis involves evaluating the effectiveness of their messaging, understanding how stakeholders reacted, and identifying areas for improvement in future crisis communication efforts. By learning from past experiences, organizations can refine their social media strategies and enhance their preparedness for future crises.

The role of social media in crisis communication is multifaceted, presenting both opportunities and challenges for organizations. By recognizing social media's dual nature as a tool for engagement and a potential source of risk, organizations can better navigate crises and protect their reputations. Through effective monitoring, tailored messaging, and proactive engagement, organizations can leverage social media to communicate effectively during a crisis, ensuring that they address stakeholder concerns and maintain public trust. Ultimately, a strategic approach to social media crisis communication is essential for organizations seeking to thrive in an increasingly interconnected digital landscape.

Postcrisis Analysis and Recovery

Evaluating Crisis Response Effectiveness

After the dust has settled on a crisis, it is imperative for organizations to conduct a thorough evaluation of their crisis communication efforts. This evaluation is a critical process that involves assessing multiple aspects of the response, including whether the messaging effectively reached the intended audiences, addressed stakeholder concerns, and ultimately helped to mitigate damage to the brand's reputation. The analysis should not only focus on the immediate outcomes but also consider the long-term implications of the communication strategies employed during the crisis.

To effectively evaluate the crisis response, organizations can utilize KPIs that provide valuable insights into the success of their efforts. These KPIs may include metrics such as media coverage volume, sentiment analysis from social media, and direct stakeholder feedback. Media coverage can be evaluated by measuring the tone and reach of articles and broadcasts, identifying whether the coverage was predominantly positive, negative, or neutral. Social media sentiment analysis allows organizations to gauge public opinion in real time, providing insights into how stakeholders are perceiving the organization postcrisis. Stakeholder feedback can be gathered through surveys or focus groups, allowing organizations to understand the concerns and sentiments of those most affected by the crisis.

Additionally, organizations should analyze their internal communication processes during the crisis. Were team members adequately informed? Did the internal messaging align with external communications? Understanding these dynamics can highlight areas for improvement and reinforce the importance of a cohesive communication strategy in future crises.

Learning From Crises

Conducting a postcrisis review is essential for identifying lessons learned and improving future crisis communication strategies. This review process should be systematic and comprehensive, involving all key stakeholders who played a role during the crisis response. By facilitating a collaborative environment where team members can openly discuss their experiences and perspectives, organizations can uncover valuable insights that may not have been evident during the heat of the moment.

Organizations should analyze what worked well and what did not during the crisis response. This could involve reviewing the effectiveness of the messaging, the channels used for communication, and the speed of the response. Identifying strengths in the communication strategy can help build a foundation for future crisis plans, while recognizing weaknesses allows for targeted improvements.

Furthermore, organizations should conduct scenario planning exercises as part of their postcrisis analysis. By simulating various crisis scenarios and discussing potential responses, organizations can enhance their preparedness and adaptability. These exercises foster a culture of continuous learning and resilience, ensuring that team members are equipped to handle future challenges more effectively.

The insights gained from a postcrisis review should inform the development of updated crisis communication plans and training for team members. This includes refining messaging templates, establishing clearer protocols for crisis responses, and incorporating feedback from stakeholders to better address their concerns. By continuously evolving their crisis communication strategies, organizations can build a more robust framework that enhances their readiness for future crises.

Rebuilding Brand Reputation

Rebuilding trust and repairing a brand's reputation after a crisis can take considerable time and effort. Organizations must be proactive in communicating their commitment to improvement and accountability. This involves acknowledging past mistakes and demonstrating genuine efforts to rectify them. Transparency in these communications is crucial, as stakeholders are more likely to respond positively when they perceive sincerity and a willingness to change.

Long-term strategies are essential for restoring brand equity. Engaging with the community, launching launching Corporate Social Responsibility (CSR) initiatives, and fostering open communication can significantly aid in rebuilding trust. For example, after the BP oil spill in 2010, the company recognized the need to take substantial corrective measures to regain public trust. In response, BP invested heavily in environmental restoration projects and committed to transparency regarding its safety practices and environmental impact. This long-term commitment aimed not only to repair its image but also to demonstrate a genuine dedication to sustainable practices and corporate responsibility.

Organizations can also engage in reputation management campaigns that highlight positive stories and community engagement initiatives postcrisis. These campaigns can help shift public perception from the crisis to the organization's efforts to make amends and contribute positively to society. Collaborating with local organizations, supporting community initiatives, and showcasing positive employee stories can humanize the brand and foster a sense of connection with stakeholders.

Furthermore, organizations should focus on building a culture of accountability and ethical behavior within their teams. By prioritizing ethical decision making and transparency at all organizational levels, brands can establish a strong foundation of trust that extends beyond crisis management. Training programs focused on ethical communication, CSR, and stakeholder engagement can further reinforce these values.

Conclusion

Effective crisis communication is not just a reactive measure for brands facing the complexities of modern crises; it is an essential strategic approach that can determine an organization's survival and long-term success. In today's interconnected and fast-paced world, the landscape of communication has evolved dramatically, with social media and digital platforms allowing information to spread rapidly. This environment necessitates that organizations are not only prepared to manage crises as they arise but also to understand the broader implications of their communication strategies on their brand reputation and stakeholder relationships.

By understanding the key principles of crisis communication, organizations can develop a comprehensive framework that guides their actions during difficult times. These principles include timely and transparent communication, empathy toward stakeholders, and a commitment to addressing concerns proactively. Having a well-defined crisis communication plan that outlines roles, responsibilities, and protocols is crucial for ensuring that everyone involved is aligned and knows how to respond effectively. This preparation allows organizations to act swiftly and decisively, which is vital for minimizing damage during a crisis.

Leveraging social media effectively also plays a critical role in modern crisis communication. Social media platforms serve as both a channel for real-time communication and a tool for engaging with stakeholders directly. Brands can use social media to provide updates, clarify misinformation, and connect with their audience on a personal level. However, organizations must also be aware of the risks associated with social media, including the potential for misinformation to spread rapidly and the challenge of managing public sentiment. By actively monitoring social media and responding promptly to stakeholder inquiries, organizations can maintain control over their narrative and mitigate the negative impacts of a crisis.

Moreover, conducting thorough postcrisis evaluations is essential for learning from past experiences and improving future crisis communication strategies. These evaluations should include a comprehensive analysis of what worked well and what did not during the crisis response. By identifying strengths and weaknesses, organizations can refine their crisis communication plans and enhance their training programs for team members. This ongoing learning process ensures that organizations remain adaptable and resilient, equipped to handle future challenges with greater effectiveness.

Rebuilding brand reputation after a crisis is another critical aspect that requires time and effort. Organizations must be proactive in communicating their commitment to improvement and accountability to their stakeholders. Long-term strategies, such as engaging with the community, investing in CSR initiatives, and maintaining transparency in operations, can significantly contribute to restoring brand equity. For instance, after the BP oil spill in 2010, the company took steps to invest in environmental restoration and committed to transparency regarding safety practices, which were pivotal in its efforts to rebuild trust with stakeholders.

A well-executed crisis communication strategy is not merely about managing crises as they arise; it is fundamentally about building a robust foundation of trust and credibility that endures long after the storm has passed. Organizations that prioritize effective crisis communication will not only navigate crises more successfully but will also cultivate stronger relationships with their stakeholders, enhancing their reputation and resilience in the long run. This proactive approach to crisis communication will ultimately position brands to emerge from crises with renewed strength and a deeper commitment to their values, ensuring that they are better prepared for the inevitable challenges that lie ahead.

Further Reading

Argenti, P.A. 2022. "Crisis Communication: Lessons From 9/11." *Harvard Business Review.*

Breakenridge, D.K. 2012. *Social Media and Public Relations: Eight New Practices for the PR Professional.* Upper Saddle River, New Jersey, NJ: FT Press.

Fearn-Banks, K. 2016. *Crisis Communications: A Casebook Approach,* 5th ed. New York, NY: Routledge.

Gao, Y, and F. Liu. 2023. "Brand Crisis Management in the Era of New Media: A Social Media Analysis of Crisis Communication." *Research in Media and Communication* 1 (1): 30–40.

Greyser, S.A. 2009. "Corporate Brand Reputation and Brand Crisis Management." *Management Decision* 47 (4): 590–602.

Romenti, S., E. Murtarelli, and C. Valentini. 2014. "Organizations' Conversations in Social Media: Applying Dialogue Strategies in Times of Crisis." *Corporate Communications: An International Journal* 19 (1): 66–82.

Seeger, M.W., and R.R. Ulmer. 2003. "Explaining Enron: Communication and Responsible Leadership." *Management Communication Quarterly* 17(1): 58–84.

Wang, Y. 2016. "Brand Crisis Communication Through Social Media: A Dialogue Between Brand Competitors on Sina Weibo." *Corporate Communications* 21 (1): 56–72.

CHAPTER 5

The Stakes of Crisis Management

Overview

- Explores the consequences of brand crises on reputation, sales, and stakeholder trust.
- Discusses the critical elements of an effective crisis management strategy.
- Provides examples of brands that succeeded or failed based on their crisis management approaches.
- Introduces the STORM Framework as a comprehensive solution for managing crises.

In today's hyper-connected world, the stakes of crisis management in branding have never been higher. A single misstep, whether it's a product defect, public relations mishap, or ethical breach, can quickly spiral out of control, thanks to the rapid spread of information across social media and global news outlets. What might begin as a small issue can rapidly escalate into a full-blown crisis with severe consequences for a brand's reputation, customer loyalty, and bottom line. The ripple effects of such incidents can be profound, impacting not only short-term sales but also long-term consumer trust and investor confidence.

For brands, the damage inflicted by a poorly handled crisis can take years to repair, with consumers increasingly holding companies accountable for their actions. In this environment, the margin for error is slim, and the ability to respond quickly, transparently, and strategically can mean the difference between recovery and ruin. Effective crisis management is no longer just about damage control—it's about safeguarding a brand's identity and core values in the face of adversity.

Understanding these high stakes is essential for brand managers, marketers, and leaders who seek to navigate the complexities of modern crisis management. It requires not only a deep knowledge of potential risks but also the foresight to anticipate crises before they escalate and the preparedness to respond decisively when they do. Being equipped to manage a crisis in this interconnected landscape involves strategic planning, robust communication skills, and an unwavering commitment to transparency and accountability.

The Impact of Brand Crises on Reputation, Sales, and Trust

A brand crisis can have devastating effects on multiple fronts, significantly undermining its reputation, sales, and consumer trust. The most immediate impact of a crisis is often on the brand's reputation. When a brand faces negative publicity, whether from a public relations disaster, ethical scandal, or product failure, it can tarnish the carefully cultivated image that the brand has built over time. A damaged reputation can result in a loss of credibility, making consumers question the brand's integrity and reliability. As the public perception shifts, the brand may find itself labeled as untrustworthy or irresponsible, which can take years to rebuild.

The financial repercussions of a brand crisis can be equally severe. Consumer boycotts, negative reviews, and diminished interests can lead to a sharp decline in sales. When customers lose confidence in a brand, they are likely to turn to competitors, resulting in lost revenue and market share. The impact on sales can extend beyond immediate financial losses; it can also influence stock prices, investor confidence, and overall business sustainability. In some cases, the fallout from a crisis can lead to significant long-term damage, requiring substantial investments in marketing and public relations to regain consumer interest.

Perhaps the most critical casualty of a brand crisis is consumer trust. Trust is a foundational element of any successful brand–consumer relationship, and once it is eroded, it can be incredibly challenging to restore. Consumers expect transparency and accountability from brands, and failure to meet these expectations during a crisis can lead to a deep-seated skepticism. Rebuilding trust requires consistent, honest communication, as well as a demonstrated commitment to corrective action and improvement. Brands that fail to effectively manage crises risk losing loyal customers and struggling to attract new ones.

Reputation

A brand's reputation is its most valuable asset, serving as the cornerstone of consumer trust and loyalty. When a crisis occurs, public perception can shift dramatically and often instantaneously. Negative headlines can overshadow a brand's previous achievements and tarnish its carefully crafted image, leading to an immediate loss of credibility. This shift in perception can be exacerbated by the speed of information dissemination in today's digital age, where news travels rapidly across social media platforms, amplifying the impact of any adverse event.

Research indicates that consumers are less likely to engage with a brand that has faced a significant crisis, and the repercussions can extend far beyond immediate sales declines. The long-term effects can include decreased customer loyalty, lower brand equity, and challenges in attracting new customers. Moreover, the damage to a brand's image can persist over time, as negative associations linger in the minds of consumers, making it difficult for brands to reclaim their former status.

In essence, the fallout from a crisis can lead to a protracted struggle for recovery, requiring brands to invest considerable resources in rebuilding their reputation and restoring consumer trust. A tarnished image may necessitate extensive public relations efforts, rebranding strategies, and a commitment to transparency and accountability to demonstrate to consumers that the brand has learned from its mistakes and is dedicated to improvement. Thus, safeguarding a brand's reputation is paramount, as it is not only a reflection of the brand's identity but also a critical driver of its long-term success in the marketplace.

Example: Example: In 2017, Pepsi faced a backlash after releasing an ad featuring Kendall Jenner that was criticized for trivializing social justice movements. In response to the uproar on social media, Pepsi quickly pulled the ad and issued a statement via Twitter apologizing for "missing the mark." However, the brand's response was criticized as tone-deaf and insufficient, with many feeling that it failed to address the core issue of exploiting activism for commercial gain. Pepsi's attempt to use social media to quell the controversy only amplified the criticism, as users dissected both the ad and the apology, demonstrating how social media can exacerbate a crisis if not handled thoughtfully.

Sales

The impact of a crisis on sales can be immediate and substantial, creating a ripple effect that can threaten the financial stability of a brand. When consumers perceive a brand as associated with controversy or negative events, they may choose to distance themselves from it, resulting in a significant decline in sales. This reaction is often driven by a desire to align with brands that reflect their values and ethics, prompting consumers to seek alternatives when they feel disillusioned or disappointed by a brand's actions.

A study conducted by the American Marketing Association found that brands embroiled in crises experienced an average sales drop of 20 percent, with some brands facing even more severe losses. These figures highlight the critical importance of swift and effective crisis management, as the financial ramifications can extend beyond immediate sales declines. For instance, a prolonged loss of consumer trust can lead to lasting damage that hinders a brand's ability to recover fully, impacting future sales and overall market positioning.

Moreover, the impact on sales can vary depending on the nature and visibility of the crisis. High-profile scandals or safety issues may trigger a more pronounced consumer backlash, while more subtle crises could lead to gradual erosion of sales over time. In today's interconnected world, where information spreads rapidly, brands must recognize the urgency of addressing crises head-on to mitigate potential losses. Engaging in proactive communication, demonstrating accountability, and implementing corrective measures can help brands regain consumer confidence and ultimately protect their bottom line in the face of adversity.

> **Example:** Volkswagen suffered a major sales impact after the 2015 emissions scandal, in which the company was found to have installed software to cheat emissions tests on diesel vehicles. In the aftermath, sales of diesel models plummeted in key markets like the United States and Europe. Volkswagen had to recall millions of vehicles and pay hefty fines, which significantly strained the company's finances. The scandal not only affected sales of diesel cars but also tarnished the appeal of other models, as consumers grew skeptical of the brand.

Trust

Trust is fundamental to consumer relationships, serving as the bedrock upon which brand loyalty is built. When a crisis arises, it fundamentally challenges this foundation of trust, often leading consumers to question a brand's integrity and commitment to its values. The erosion of trust can be swift and significant, as consumers may feel betrayed or misled, prompting them to reconsider their loyalty and association with the brand.

Rebuilding trust after a crisis can be a lengthy and complex process, requiring sustained efforts in transparency, effective communication, and demonstrated accountability. Brands must engage in open dialogues with their consumers, acknowledging the issues at hand and outlining clear plans for rectification. According to the Edelman Trust Barometer, trust in brands can diminish rapidly in the wake of a crisis, with many consumers reporting a loss of confidence that can persist long after the initial incident. This highlights the urgency for organizations to address issues head-on rather than adopting a defensive posture.

To effectively restore consumer trust, organizations need to go beyond mere statements of regret. They must take meaningful actions that reflect a genuine commitment to change. This might include implementing new policies, investing in quality control measures, or enhancing ethical practices. Brands that demonstrate a willingness to learn from their mistakes and prioritize the needs and concerns of their consumers are more likely to regain trust over time. Ultimately, the path to rebuilding trust is not merely about recovering from a crisis; it is about transforming the relationship with consumers to foster deeper connections based on transparency and accountability, ensuring that the brand emerges stronger and more resilient in the long run.

Example: The Facebook–Cambridge Analytica data scandal in 2018 shattered trust in the social media giant. Revelations that the personal data of millions of users had been harvested without consent and used for political advertising led to widespread criticism of Facebook's data privacy practices. Despite apologies and promises of reform from CEO Mark Zuckerberg, many users and stakeholders remained unconvinced. The incident sparked a global conversation about data security and privacy, leading to increased regulatory scrutiny and a significant trust deficit that continues to challenge Facebook's reputation.

Key Elements of an Effective Crisis Management Strategy

To mitigate the negative impact of brand crises, organizations must develop effective crisis management strategies that incorporate several key elements. Proactive handling involves anticipating potential crises before they occur, allowing brands to prepare response plans and minimize risks effectively. This proactive stance can involve regular risk assessments and establishing protocols for various scenarios. Timely communications are crucial during a crisis; organizations must provide prompt and accurate information to stakeholders to prevent misinformation and confusion. Maintaining transparency is essential for building trust with the public.

Furthermore, demonstrating empathy and accountability can significantly impact how consumers perceive a brand during a crisis. Acknowledging mistakes and expressing genuine concern for those affected can help in rebuilding trust and fostering goodwill. Finally, organizations should prioritize monitoring and adaptation, continuously tracking public sentiment and media coverage throughout the crisis. This allows for adjustments to communication strategies and responses as the situation evolves, ensuring that the brand remains aligned with stakeholder expectations and can recover more effectively. By integrating these elements into their crisis management plans, organizations can better navigate turbulent times and emerge with their reputations intact.

Proactive Planning

A well-prepared organization can respond quickly and effectively to potential crises, significantly reducing the impact on its reputation and operations. This preparedness begins with a thorough identification of potential risks that could threaten the organization, ranging from operational issues to public relations disasters. By understanding the specific vulnerabilities within their environment, organizations can proactively address them before they escalate into full-blown crises.

Conducting regular crisis simulations is another critical component of effective crisis readiness. These drills allow team members to practice their responses in a controlled environment, helping to identify weaknesses in the crisis management plan and improve team coordination. Through realistic scenarios, employees can become familiar with their roles and responsibilities during a crisis, ensuring that everyone knows what is expected of them when the time comes to act.

Additionally, creating a comprehensive crisis management plan is essential for any organization aiming to navigate crises successfully. This plan should outline clear roles and responsibilities for each team member, detailing who will handle communications, manage the crisis response, and liaise with stakeholders. Having defined responsibilities ensures that everyone knows their specific tasks, reducing confusion and enabling a swift response.

Together, these elements form a robust foundation for crisis management, allowing organizations to act decisively and efficiently when faced with unexpected challenges. In a world where the landscape can change rapidly, being well-prepared is not just advantageous; it is a strategic imperative for safeguarding the brand's integrity and trustworthiness.

Timely Communication

During a crisis, timely and transparent communication is paramount to effectively managing the situation and preserving a brand's reputation. Brands must prioritize providing accurate and up-to-date information to stakeholders, ensuring that concerns are addressed and questions are answered promptly. This proactive approach helps to establish trust, as stakeholders appreciate clear communication in times of uncertainty.

An open dialogue is essential, allowing stakeholders to express their concerns and receive reassurance from the brand. By fostering a two-way communication channel, organizations can gain valuable insights into public sentiment and adjust their strategies accordingly. Rapid response is also crucial in mitigating misinformation, which can spread quickly during a crisis, exacerbating the situation. By being the first to communicate accurate information, brands can shape the narrative, prevent speculation, and reduce the likelihood of escalation.

Moreover, maintaining transparency throughout the crisis helps to reinforce the brand's commitment to accountability. Stakeholders are more likely to forgive mistakes if they perceive the brand as honest and forthcoming about the situation. In this way, effective communication not only serves as a tool for immediate crisis management but also lays the groundwork for rebuilding trust and loyalty in the long term. Ultimately, by prioritizing timely and transparent communication, brands can navigate crises more effectively and emerge stronger on the other side.

Empathy and Accountability

Demonstrating empathy toward affected stakeholders is crucial during a brand crisis, as it can significantly influence the brand's recovery trajectory. Brands must not only recognize the immediate impact of the crisis on their customers, employees, and the broader community but also actively engage in efforts to address these concerns. Acknowledging the emotional and practical repercussions of the crisis is essential in fostering a sense of connection and understanding with stakeholders. This involves being transparent about the situation and expressing genuine remorse for any harm caused.

Taking accountability for their actions is equally important; brands should be willing to accept responsibility for their role in the crisis. This requires open acknowledgment of mistakes, whether they stem from negligence, oversight, or poor judgment. When a brand openly admits to its shortcomings, it demonstrates integrity and a commitment to improvement. Consumers appreciate honesty, and this level of transparency can help to mend relationships that may have been strained during the crisis.

Furthermore, brands should not only apologize but also outline a clear plan of action to make amends and prevent similar incidents in the future. This may involve implementing new safety protocols, enhancing customer service practices, or offering compensation to affected parties. When a brand shows that it is taking proactive steps to rectify the situation and ensure accountability, it can foster goodwill among stakeholders. Such actions signal to consumers that the brand values their trust and is committed to learning from its mistakes.

Ultimately, the combination of empathy and accountability creates a pathway for rebuilding trust. Consumers are more likely to forgive brands that demonstrate genuine concern for their well-being and a willingness to take corrective measures. By prioritizing empathy and accountability during a crisis, brands can reinforce their commitment to their stakeholders and pave the way for recovery and renewal, ultimately strengthening their reputation in the long run.

Monitoring and Adaptation

Continuous monitoring of public sentiment and media coverage during a crisis is essential for brands aiming to navigate the turbulent waters of a brand crisis effectively. This ongoing vigilance allows organizations to stay attuned to how their stakeholders are reacting and what narratives are gaining traction in the media. By leveraging tools such as social media listening platforms and analytics, brands can gain real-time insights into public perceptions, enabling them to identify emerging concerns or shifts in sentiment promptly.

Being aware of these dynamics empowers brands to adapt their strategies based on the evolving situation and feedback from stakeholders. If public reactions indicate a need for more transparency or specific information, brands can adjust their communications to address these gaps. This agility in response can significantly mitigate the risk of further escalation and demonstrate to stakeholders that the brand is committed to open dialogue and responsiveness.

Moreover, monitoring allows brands to evaluate the effectiveness of their crisis management efforts continuously. By analyzing the outcomes of their communications and interventions, brands can determine what strategies are resonating with their audience and which may require re-evaluation. This adaptability not only helps in managing the current crisis but also contributes to long-term improvements in crisis preparedness, ensuring that organizations are better equipped for future challenges. In an age where information spreads rapidly, being proactive and responsive through continuous monitoring is critical for safeguarding brand reputation and maintaining stakeholder trust.

Why Every Brand Needs a Crisis Management Plan

The unpredictable nature of crises underscores the necessity for every brand to have a comprehensive crisis management plan in place. A well-defined plan serves as a vital roadmap for navigating challenging situations, enabling organizations to act swiftly and effectively in times of uncertainty. Without a strategic plan, brands risk becoming paralyzed during a crisis, leading to poor decision making, miscommunication, and ultimately exacerbating the situation. In such high-stress scenarios, a lack of preparation can transform a manageable issue into a full-blown disaster.

Moreover, a crisis management plan is not merely a reactive measure; it actively protects a brand's reputation while enhancing its resilience against future challenges. By investing in crisis preparedness, organizations can build stronger relationships with stakeholders, instilling confidence that the brand can handle adverse situations with professionalism and care. This proactive approach fosters a culture of transparency and accountability, encouraging open communication and collaboration among all employees. When staff at all levels understand their roles and responsibilities within the plan, they are better equipped to respond effectively, turning potential crises into opportunities for demonstrating the brand's commitment to its values and customers.

Ultimately, a robust crisis management plan empowers organizations to not only survive crises but also emerge from them with enhanced credibility and trust. Brands that prioritize crisis preparedness position themselves to navigate turbulent waters, reinforcing their reputation as responsible and reliable entities in the eyes of their stakeholders. By recognizing the importance of a crisis management plan, organizations can transform uncertainty into resilience, ensuring long-term success in an ever-changing landscape.

Overview of the STORM Framework as a Guiding Principle

To aid practitioners in managing brand crises, the **STORM Framework** (Figure 5.1) serves as a guiding principle, encapsulating the critical components of effective crisis management. The **S** in **STORM** stands for swift response, emphasizing the need for brands to understand the context of the crisis, monitor developments closely, and quickly respond to the situation at hand. **T** represents transparent communication, highlighting the importance of open and honest communication with stakeholders, as it fosters trust and demonstrates accountability. The **O** stands for ownership of the problem, which signifies the necessity for brands to take responsibility for their actions and show a willingness to

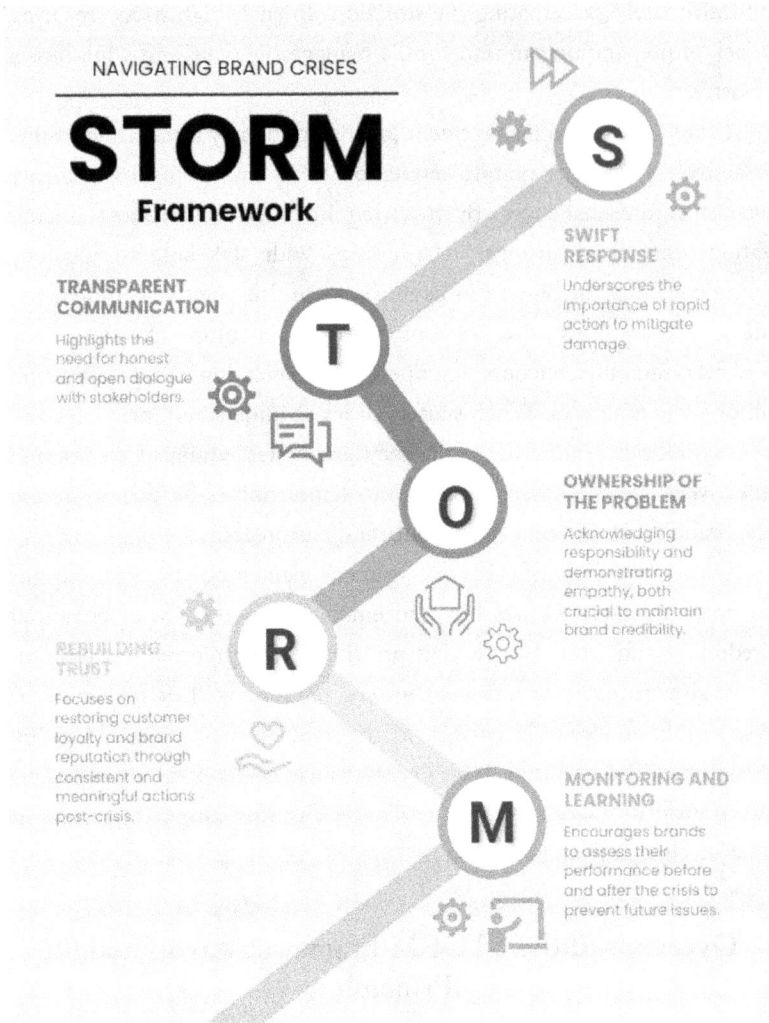

NAVIGATING BRAND CRISES

STORM
Framework

TRANSPARENT COMMUNICATION

Highlights the need for honest and open dialogue with stakeholders.

SWIFT RESPONSE

Underscores the importance of rapid action to mitigate damage.

OWNERSHIP OF THE PROBLEM

Acknowledging responsibility and demonstrating empathy, both crucial to maintain brand credibility.

REBUILDING TRUST

Focuses on restoring customer loyalty and brand reputation through consistent and meaningful actions post-crisis.

MONITORING AND LEARNING

Encourages brands to assess their performance before and after the crisis to prevent future issues.

Figure 5.1 STORM Framework

implement corrective measures. **R** denotes the rebuilding trust, which involves creating a structured plan of action to address the crisis, including approaches to rebuild the trust of customers and stakeholders. Lastly, the **M** stands for monitoring and learning, stressing the need for continuous monitoring of public sentiment and media coverage to allow brands to adapt their strategies effectively in response to the evolving situation.

By integrating these elements into their crisis management practices, organizations can enhance their resilience and safeguard their reputations in the face of challenges. In the chapters that follow, we will explore each component of the **STORM Framework** in detail, equipping practitioners with the knowledge and tools necessary to effectively manage brand crises.

S: *Swift Response*

Swift response is a cornerstone of the **STORM Framework**, emphasizing the need for brands to act quickly and decisively in the face of a crisis. In today's fast-paced digital environment, news spreads rapidly, and delays in response can exacerbate a situation. A swift response is not only about speed but also about demonstrating accountability and commitment to stakeholders. When brands react promptly, they convey a sense of responsibility, which can foster trust among consumers and other stakeholders. This immediate acknowledgment of the crisis helps to mitigate misinformation and allows the brand to shape the narrative surrounding the event.

Acting swiftly also enables brands to minimize potential damage. The longer a crisis remains unaddressed, the more likely it is to spiral out of control, leading to negative public sentiment, financial loss, and long-term reputational harm. By responding quickly, organizations can contain the fallout, address stakeholder concerns, and limit the impact on their reputation and bottom line. Furthermore, a timely response helps reassure stakeholders that the brand is in control and actively working to resolve the issue, which can strengthen customer loyalty even in difficult circumstances.

Incorporating swift response into crisis management plans involves several key actions. Brands should develop clear communication strategies that allow for rapid dissemination of information and ensure that designated spokespeople are prepared to address the media and the public. Additionally, organizations must regularly train their crisis management teams and conduct simulations to ensure everyone knows their roles and responsibilities when a crisis occurs. Ultimately, by prioritizing swift responses, brands can enhance their resilience and protect their reputation during challenging times.

T: Transparent Communication

Transparent communication is a fundamental pillar of effective crisis management, emphasizing the importance of engaging in open and honest dialogue with stakeholders. During a crisis, misinformation and speculation can quickly spread, leading to confusion and eroding trust. By proactively communicating accurate information, organizations can mitigate these risks and establish themselves as credible sources amidst the chaos. Transparency involves not only sharing what is known but also acknowledging uncertainties and limitations regarding the situation. This approach fosters an environment where stakeholders feel informed and valued, enhancing their connection to the brand.

Moreover, transparent communication allows organizations to demonstrate empathy and accountability, reinforcing their commitment to addressing stakeholder concerns. Regular updates throughout the crisis are essential, as they keep stakeholders informed of developments and the organization's response efforts. Additionally, brands should actively encourage feedback and questions from stakeholders, further promoting an inclusive dialogue that builds trust and understanding. By prioritizing transparency in their communication strategies, organizations can navigate crises more effectively, reduce potential fallout, and ultimately strengthen their relationships with stakeholders long after the crisis has passed.

O: Ownership of the Problem

Ownership of the problem is a critical component of the **STORM Framework** in crisis management, emphasizing the importance of brands taking responsibility for the issues they face. When a crisis occurs, stakeholders expect the brand to acknowledge its role in the situation rather than deflecting blame or minimizing the issue. This accountability is essential for rebuilding trust and credibility with customers, employees, and other stakeholders.

Taking ownership means publicly admitting the problem, outlining the brand's involvement, and accepting the consequences. For instance, in the case of the 2010 BP Deepwater Horizon oil spill, BP faced severe criticism for its attempts to downplay the severity of the crisis and shift blame onto contractors. This lack of ownership exacerbated public outrage, leading to lasting damage to the brand's reputation and significant financial penalties. In contrast, brands that take proactive steps to own their mistakes can mitigate damage more effectively.

A clear example of ownership can be seen in Johnson & Johnson's response to the 1982 Tylenol crisis. The company quickly acknowledged the severity of the situation, taking full responsibility for the product tampering that resulted in several fatalities. By voluntarily recalling over 31 million bottles of Tylenol and cooperating fully with authorities, Johnson & Johnson demonstrated a commitment to consumer safety and transparency. This decisive ownership of the problem not only helped to restore consumer confidence but also set a precedent for crisis management best practices. Ultimately, brands that embrace ownership of the problem can effectively navigate crises and rebuild their reputations in the long term.

R: Rebuilding Trust

Rebuilding trust is a critical component of effective crisis management, especially after a brand has faced significant challenges. Trust is often the foundation of a strong brand–consumer relationship, and when crises occur, that foundation can be severely shaken. This chapter discusses the importance of rebuilding trust, the strategies brands can employ to restore confidence among stakeholders, and highlights examples of brands that have successfully regained trust after crises.

To rebuild trust, brands must first acknowledge the impact of the crisis on their stakeholders. This acknowledgment shows that the brand values its audience and is committed to addressing their concerns. Following this recognition, it is crucial to demonstrate genuine empathy. Engaging with affected stakeholders and understanding their feelings can significantly aid in mending relationships. Brands should craft messages that resonate with their audience, clearly addressing the specific concerns of various groups and making them feel heard and valued. This empathetic approach lays the groundwork for trust to be rebuilt.

In addition to empathetic communication, brands need to take concrete actions that reflect their commitment to improvement. This involves implementing changes to prevent similar issues from arising in the future. By demonstrating accountability through specific measures, such as policy changes or enhanced safety protocols, brands can reassure stakeholders that they are taking the necessary steps to rectify the situation. Transparency about these changes is essential; sharing progress updates can further reinforce stakeholders' confidence in the brand.

Ultimately, rebuilding trust is a gradual process that requires ongoing effort and dedication. Brands must remain consistent in their messaging and actions, continuously engaging with stakeholders and showing a genuine commitment to improvement. Successful examples of trust rebuilding can serve as valuable lessons for brands navigating their own crises, illustrating that while regaining trust may be challenging, it is not impossible with the right approach.

M: Monitoring and Learning

Monitoring and learning form a crucial aspect of the **STORM Framework**, emphasizing the need for continuous evaluation of the crisis response to enhance future strategies. This component highlights the importance of assessing both the effectiveness of the actions taken during the crisis and the overall impact on stakeholders. By closely tracking public sentiment, media coverage, and stakeholder feedback, organizations can gain valuable insights into how their responses were perceived and what adjustments might be necessary.

Effective monitoring involves utilizing various tools and channels, including social media analytics, surveys, and traditional media analysis, to gauge public reaction and sentiment. This real-time feedback allows brands to identify areas for improvement and to make necessary adjustments swiftly. Learning from each crisis is essential for refining crisis management strategies, as it equips organizations with the knowledge needed to anticipate and respond to potential future challenges more effectively.

Incorporating lessons learned into crisis management plans not only fosters a culture of continuous improvement but also demonstrates to stakeholders that the organization values feedback and is committed to evolving its practices. Ultimately, monitoring and learning create a proactive approach to crisis management, ensuring that brands are better prepared to handle future incidents and can maintain their integrity and trustworthiness in the eyes of their consumers.

Conclusion

Brand crises are unavoidable in today's interconnected world, but their outcomes are largely determined by how organizations respond. As explored in this chapter, crises can significantly impact a brand's reputation, financial performance, and customer trust. However, these challenges also offer brands an opportunity to demonstrate resilience, accountability, and a commitment to stakeholders. The stakes of crisis management are high, but so are the rewards for organizations that navigate these moments effectively.

Understanding the potential consequences of a crisis underscores the importance of being prepared. The examples discussed highlight the stark contrast between brands that managed crises effectively and those that faltered. Effective crisis management hinges on swift, decisive action, clear communication, and a genuine effort to rebuild relationships with stakeholders. These elements not only mitigate damage but can also position the brand for a stronger recovery.

To provide a structured approach to crisis management, the STORM Framework offers a comprehensive strategy that practitioners can rely on during turbulent times. The five components—swift response, transparent communication, ownership of the problem, rebuilding trust, and monitoring and learning—serve as actionable pillars that address both immediate and long-term needs in a crisis. This framework ensures that organizations are not just reactive but also proactive in safeguarding their brand's reputation and stakeholder relationships.

As the chapter transitions to the STORM Framework, we invite readers to delve deeper into each of these components in subsequent chapters. By embracing the principles of the STORM Framework, practitioners can turn crises into opportunities for growth and resilience, ensuring their organizations emerge stronger and more trusted than before.

Further Reading

Adamska, M. 2017. "How These Three Brands Have Survived a Reputation Crisis." *BrandStruck: Brand Strategy / Positioning Case Studies.*

Byrd, S. 2012. "Hi Fans! Tell Us Your Story! Incorporating a Stewardship-Based Social Media Strategy to Maintain Brand Reputation During a Crisis." *Corporate Communications* 17 (3): 241–54.

Claeys, An-Sofie., and V. Cauberghe. 2015. "Crisis Response and Crisis Timing Strategies, Two Sides of the Same Coin." *Journal of Business Communication* 52 (4): 415–31.

Dawar, N., and M. Pillutla. 2000. "Impact of Product-Harm Crises on Brand Equity: The Moderating Role of Consumer Expectations." *Journal of Marketing Research* 37 (2): 215–26.

Deloitte. 2019. "Stepping in: The Board's Role in Crisis Management." www2.deloitte.com/content/dam/Deloitte/uk/Documents/risk/deloitte-uk-risk-global-on-the-boards-agenda-crisis-management.pdf.

Dutta, S., and C. Pullig. 2011 "Effectiveness of Corporate Responses to Brand Crises: The Role of Crisis Type and Response Strategies." *Journal of Business Research* 64 (12): 1281–7.

Fombrun, C.J., B. Cees and M.V. Riel. 2004. *Fame & Fortune: How Successful Companies Build Winning Reputations.* Prentice Hall.

Jin, Y., A. Pang, and G.T. Cameron. 2010. "Integrated Crisis Mapping: Toward a Publics-Based, Emotion-Driven Conceptualization in Crisis Communication." *Sphera Publica* 1 (1): 81–96.

CHAPTER 6

S = Swift Response

Overview

- Highlights why immediate action is crucial during a crisis to control damage.
- Offers practical steps for preparing response plans and mobilizing crisis management teams.
- Outlines actions to take within the first 24 hours to set the tone for an effective response.
- Includes case studies of brands that exemplify or fail to demonstrate timely responses.

In the realm of crisis management, speed is not just important; it is often the defining factor that can determine the severity of a brand crisis and the extent of its repercussions. The ability to respond quickly is crucial because it allows a brand to take control of the narrative before misinformation spreads, public sentiment turns hostile, or the crisis escalates beyond repair. A swift response demonstrates to stakeholders, including customers, employees, and the public, that the organization is aware of the issue and is taking immediate steps to address it. This proactive approach not only helps in minimizing the immediate damage but also plays a critical role in preserving the brand's long-term reputation and trustworthiness.

Failing to act quickly, on the other hand, can lead to a range of negative consequences. Delayed responses often allow the crisis to spiral out of control, as the lack of timely communication may create a vacuum that is quickly filled with rumors, speculations, and negative press. In the digital age, where news spreads rapidly across social media and other platforms, even a few hours of inaction can result in a significant backlash, eroding years of carefully built brand equity. Speed, therefore, is not just about limiting the damage—it is about demonstrating responsibility and transparency, two key factors that can influence public perception and stakeholder confidence during a crisis.

This chapter explores the vital role that speed plays in crisis management, examining why a fast response can make the difference between a minor issue and a full-scale crisis that threatens the very survival of a brand. It also delves into how organizations can prepare for such rapid responses, from having clear communication protocols in place to training teams for quick decision making under pressure. By looking at real-world examples of both successful and failed responses, this chapter illustrates the tangible impact that timeliness can have on a crisis's outcome, providing valuable lessons for brands looking to strengthen their crisis readiness.

Why Speed Matters in a Brand Crisis

The immediacy of a brand's response during a crisis is critical, as it can significantly shape stakeholder perceptions and influence the overall trajectory of the situation. A rapid response signals not only that the brand is aware of the issue but also that it prioritizes accountability and transparency, demonstrating care for those affected. When brands act swiftly, they are able to accomplish several key objectives.

Control the Narrative

In the fast-moving digital world, news, whether true or false, can spread like wildfire, often gaining momentum with little regard for factual accuracy. When a brand delays its response during a crisis, it leaves a void that is quickly filled by rumors, misinformations, and harmful speculations. As social media and online platforms amplify these inaccuracies, the crisis can rapidly spiral out of control, making it increasingly difficult for the brand to regain control over the situation. The longer the delay, the more entrenched these false narratives become, causing even more confusion and distrust among the public.

By responding promptly, a brand can take the reins of the situation and assert control over how the crisis is perceived. Providing accurate information early on helps to counteract the spread of false or misleading claims, reducing the risk of the narrative slipping out of the brand's control. Not only does this timely intervention help clarify the facts, but it also demonstrates that the brand is taking the issue seriously, which can foster a sense of responsibility and transparency. The earlier a brand steps in to provide clarity, the more effectively it can mitigate the confusion and prevent further escalation of the crisis. A swift and decisive response is therefore essential to containing the crisis and protecting the brand's reputation.

Build Trust

In moments of crisis, trust becomes especially fragile, and how a brand responds can either erode or strengthen that trust. Consumers naturally gravitate toward brands that show they are responsive and proactive in addressing issues, as this demonstrates a sense of responsibility and commitment. A swift and decisive reaction sends a clear message that the brand is not shying away from the problem but rather tackling it head-on. This level of responsiveness reassures stakeholders—customers, partners, and investors alike—that the brand is actively engaged in resolving the crisis.

A rapid response also signals accountability. It shows that the brand is willing to own up to any missteps and is taking immediate steps to rectify the situation. In doing so, the brand demonstrates transparency and responsibility, which are crucial factors in maintaining and rebuilding trust. Such actions can prevent the loss of consumer loyalty and, in some cases, may even deepen it, as customers appreciate a brand that stands by its values even in difficult times. By turning a crisis into an opportunity to showcase accountability and dedication, brands can restore confidence and potentially emerge stronger, with their core values reaffirmed in the eyes of their audience.

Minimize Damage

The longer a crisis remains unaddressed, the greater the potential for long-term damage to a brand's reputation and financial performance. As uncertainty lingers, consumers, investors, and stakeholders may lose confidence in the brand's ability to manage the situation, leading to heightened criticism, declining customer engagement, and loss of business. Unresolved crises often fuel negative sentiment, which can spread quickly through social media and other channels, amplifying the damage and making recovery even more challenging.

On the financial side, a delay in addressing the crisis can lead to significant revenue losses, as consumers distance themselves from the brand. Competitors may seize the opportunity to capture market share, further undermining the brand's position. Moreover, operational disruptions can arise as internal resources are stretched thin, and external partners may reconsider their associations with a brand seen as mishandling a crisis.

Conversely, when brands act quickly, they can mitigate these risks by containing the fallout and minimizing further harm. Proactive and decisive action can help limit reputational damage, prevent the crisis from escalating, and reassure customers that the brand is taking responsibility. Swift responses also help preserve financial stability by addressing the root cause of the crisis before it leads to more profound operational and revenue losses.

How to Prepare a Response Plan in Advance

Preparation is crucial for ensuring a swift and effective response when a crisis strikes. By developing a robust crisis response plan, brands position themselves to act decisively, which helps to minimize potential damage and maintain control over the narrative. A well-prepared brand can quickly address issues before they escalate, reducing the risk of confusion and preventing misinformation from spreading. Moreover, having a detailed plan in place allows brands to focus on delivering clear, consistent communication, reinforcing trust with stakeholders, and demonstrating a proactive approach to problem-solving during challenging times.

Crisis Scenarios

Identifying potential crisis scenarios is a critical first step in effective crisis management. Brands should proactively consider various situations that could negatively affect their reputation or operations. These scenarios may include product recalls, where faulty or unsafe products necessitate widespread withdrawals from the market, potentially undermining customer trust and generating negative publicity. Such recalls can create a ripple effect, leading to increased scrutiny from regulators and consumers alike, which can further damage a brand's standing in the market. Public relations disasters can also arise from missteps in communication or controversial statements made by brand representatives, which can quickly escalate into larger crises. A poorly worded social media post or an insensitive comment during a public appearance can provoke backlash, resulting in a loss of credibility and support from stakeholders.

Additionally, ethical scandals, such as corporate misconduct, employee misbehavior, or unethical business practices, can severely damage a brand's image. High-profile incidents of fraud, harassment, or discrimination can not only lead to legal repercussions but also erode the trust that consumers and employees place in the organization. Moreover, the impact of such scandals can linger long after the initial event, affecting long-term brand loyalty and customer relationships. By anticipating these various events, brands can develop tailored response strategies that prepare them to address specific challenges effectively, ensuring they can respond swiftly and decisively when a crisis strikes. This proactive approach not only mitigates the potential damage during a crisis but also reinforces the organization's commitment to accountability and integrity, ultimately strengthening its reputation in the eyes of stakeholders.

Predefined Roles and Responsibilities

Clearly outlining roles and responsibilities during a crisis is essential for effective crisis management. Brands should establish a dedicated crisis management team responsible for coordinating the response. This team typically includes key individuals from various departments, such as public relations, legal, operations, and senior management, ensuring a comprehensive approach to the situation. Each member of the team brings their unique expertise to the table, allowing for a well-rounded strategy that addresses all facets of the crisis. Designating a spokesperson is equally critical; this individual will serve as the primary point of contact for all communications, ensuring consistent messaging across all channels. This consistency is vital in maintaining public trust and preventing mixed messages that could further complicate the crisis.

By having clearly defined roles, organizations can streamline decision-making processes and enhance the overall efficiency of the response. When every team member understands their specific responsibilities, it reduces the likelihood of miscommunication and overlapping efforts, allowing for a more cohesive and effective response. This clarity helps prevent confusion and ensures that all team members are aligned with the organization's objectives during a crisis. Additionally, with clear roles established, the crisis management team can react more swiftly and effectively, minimizing potential damage to the brand's reputation and facilitating a quicker recovery. Ultimately, this structured approach not only helps in addressing the immediate challenges posed by the crisis but also strengthens the organization's resilience for future incidents.

Response Templates

Creating response templates for various crisis scenarios is a vital part of crisis preparedness that can significantly expedite communication during challenging times. These preprepared statements allow brands to react swiftly and consistently when a crisis arises, reducing the time spent crafting messages under pressure. Templates should cover a range of potential situations, including product recalls, public relations disasters, and ethical scandals, each tailored to address the specific nuances of the scenario.

For instance, a product recall template could include a clear acknowledgment of the issue, a commitment to customer safety, and instructions on how customers can return products. This template ensures that the brand communicates essential information while demonstrating a proactive approach to customer concerns. In contrast, a template for a public relations crisis might focus on expressing regret for any harm caused, outlining steps the company is taking to rectify the situation, and emphasizing the brand's commitment to transparency. Such messaging is crucial in managing public perception and mitigating potential backlash.

By having these templates ready, organizations can ensure that critical messages are communicated effectively, maintaining clarity and focus amidst the chaos of a crisis. This preparedness not only helps to preserve stakeholder trust but also enhances the brand's reputation for responsiveness and accountability. Furthermore, response templates can serve as a foundational tool for training crisis management teams, equipping them with the necessary language and structure to address crises confidently and competently. Ultimately, having these templates in place enables organizations to navigate crises more smoothly and emerge with their reputation intact.

Regular Training and Drills

Conducting regular crisis management drills is essential for keeping the crisis response team sharp and ensuring that each member understands their specific roles during a crisis. These drills simulate real-world scenarios, allowing team members to practice their responses in a controlled environment. By immersing themselves in these simulated situations, team members can gain hands-on experience and familiarize themselves with the intricacies of the crisis response plan. This practice not only prepares them for potential challenges but also helps to build confidence in their abilities to respond effectively.

Through this training, organizations can identify gaps or weaknesses in their response plan, providing valuable insights that can be addressed before an actual crisis occurs. By analyzing the outcomes of these drills, organizations can refine their strategies, ensuring that every detail of the response plan is effective and comprehensive. Additionally, these exercises foster teamwork and improve communication among team members, which is crucial when time is of the essence during a crisis. Improved collaboration ensures that all individuals are on the same page, enabling a more fluid and efficient response to unexpected events.

By repeatedly engaging in these drills, team members become more confident and adept at executing the plan under pressure, leading to a more coordinated and effective response when faced with real challenges. Regular training sessions not only enhance individual capabilities but also solidify the collective strength of the team, promoting a culture of preparedness. Ultimately, this proactive approach enhances the overall resilience of the organization, ensuring that it can navigate crises with agility and efficiency while maintaining stakeholder trust and confidence. The ability to respond decisively during a crisis is not merely about having a plan; it is about the preparedness and poise of the individuals executing that plan.

Mobilizing Your Crisis Management Team Immediately

When a crisis strikes, the first step is to mobilize the crisis management team. This team should be composed of individuals with diverse skills and expertise, including public relations, legal counsel, and senior management. Each member should bring a unique perspective that contributes to a comprehensive response strategy. Public relations professionals are essential for managing communication and maintaining the brand's image, while legal counsel ensures that all actions comply with regulations and minimize legal risks. Senior management provides leadership and direction, facilitating quick decision making and resource allocation. The diverse backgrounds and expertise of team members allow for a well-rounded approach to crisis management, enabling the organization to address various aspects of the situation effectively. By quickly assembling a capable crisis management team, brands can respond more effectively, minimizing damage and restoring stakeholder trust.

Immediate Notification

As soon as a crisis is detected, it is essential to notify all members of the crisis management team immediately. Timely communication is critical to ensure that everyone involved is fully informed about the situation at hand. Utilizing multiple communication channels can significantly enhance the effectiveness of this notification process. Consider employing a combination of email, instant messaging, phone calls, and, if necessary, video conferencing to reach all team members efficiently. Each of these channels serves a distinct purpose and can cater to different circumstances; for instance, instant messaging allows for quick, real-time updates, while emails provide detailed information that team members can refer back to as needed.

By employing a multichannel approach, the organization can ensure that every team member receives the critical information they need to respond effectively to the crisis. Moreover, this redundancy helps minimize the risk of any team member being left out of the loop, which could lead to confusion or miscommunication during a high-pressure situation. Prompt and clear communication is vital for coordinating an effective response, and by prioritizing this aspect, the crisis management team can work collaboratively to mitigate the impact of the crisis.

Gathering Information

The crisis management team must swiftly collect all relevant information regarding the crisis to effectively assess the situation. This involves gathering details about what has transpired, the parties involved, and any immediate impacts on the brand. Understanding the context is essential, as it allows the team to grasp the nuances of the crisis and identify potential risks and challenges that may arise during the response process.

In addition to factual information, the team should also seek insights into public sentiment and media coverage surrounding the crisis. This can help the team gauge how the situation is being perceived by stakeholders and the general public. Analyzing social media conversations, news articles, and customer feedbacks can provide valuable perspectives that inform the response strategy.

Once all pertinent information is collected, the crisis management team can engage in thorough discussions to develop a well-informed and tailored response. This understanding not only aids in crafting effective messaging but also allows the team to anticipate potential questions or concerns from stakeholders. By taking the time to fully understand the specifics of the crisis, the team can enhance their decision making and ultimately work toward a resolution that mitigates the impact on the brand.

Setting up a Command Center

Establishing a central location for the crisis management team to convene is essential for effective crisis response. This dedicated space serves as a hub where team members can gather to monitor developments, share information, and coordinate their actions in real time. Having a designated area fosters collaboration and ensures that everyone involved in the crisis response is on the same page.

In this central location, the team can set up necessary tools and technologies, such as screens displaying live news feeds, social media monitoring tools, and communication platforms, allowing for quick access to the latest information. This setup helps streamline communication, as team members can discuss updates, strategize responses, and make decisions collaboratively, all in one place.

Moreover, having a centralized command center helps reduce confusion during a crisis. Team members know where to go for information and support, which is crucial in high-pressure situations. By facilitating clear and efficient communication, the team can act more decisively and swiftly, ultimately enhancing the organization's ability to manage the crisis effectively and minimize its impact on the brand.

The First 24 Hours: What Needs to Happen

The first 24 hours following the onset of a crisis are critical for effective management and can significantly influence the overall outcome.

During this period, several key actions must be taken to ensure a coordinated and strategic response. First, conducting a thorough assessment of the situation is essential. This involves gathering all relevant information to understand the nature and scope of the crisis, identifying key stakeholders, and evaluating potential impacts on the brand. With this knowledge in hand, the crisis management team can formulate an appropriate initial response. This response should be timely, empathetic, and transparent, addressing the concerns of stakeholders while conveying the organization's commitment to resolving the issue.

Monitoring public sentiment is another crucial action during the initial hours of a crisis. Keeping a close eye on social media channels, news coverage, and public reactions helps the team gauge how the situation is being perceived and allows for adjustments to the communication strategy as needed. Establishing effective communication channels is also vital. This means not only disseminating information to the public but also ensuring that there are internal lines of communication among team members to facilitate collaboration. Finally, providing regular updates throughout the first 24 hours is essential. Frequent communication keeps stakeholders informed, reduces uncertainty, and demonstrates that the organization is actively engaged in addressing the crisis. By implementing these key actions, brands can lay the groundwork for effective crisis management and mitigate potential damage to their reputation and operations. Table 6.1 presents the ideal timeline for actions to take place in the first 24 hours of a crisis, including responsibilities and communication points.

Assessment

Evaluating the scope and impact of a crisis is essential for effective management and response. This assessment involves determining the number of stakeholders affected, including customers, employees, suppliers, and the broader community. Understanding the breadth of the impact helps organizations gauge the seriousness of the situation and prioritize their response efforts. For example, a crisis that affects

Table 6.1 This table outlines the key actions, responsibilities, and communication points for organizations to follow during the critical first 24 hours of a crisis, ensuring a swift and effective response to mitigate impact and maintain stakeholder trust

Timeframe (in hours)	Action	Responsibilities	Communication points
0–1	Crisis identification	Crisis response team leader	Initial assessment of the crisis
	Gather key information	Team members	Ensure all relevant data is collected
	Alert crisis response team	Team leader	Inform team members to convene
1–3	Draft initial response	Communication team	Prepare key messages for stakeholders
	Establish monitoring systems	Social media monitoring team	Set up alerts for mentions and sentiment
	Engage with key stakeholders	Team leader	Inform key stakeholders about the situation
3–6	Launch initial public statement	Communication team	Share initial response on website/social media
	Monitor reactions	Social media monitoring team	Track feedback and sentiment
6–12	Conduct internal briefing	Team leader	Update employees on the crisis status
	Refine messaging based on feedback	Communication team	Adjust messaging as needed
12–24	Release detailed updates	Communication team	Provide further details and action plan
	Engage with media	Public relations team	Conduct press briefings or interviews
	Evaluate stakeholder sentiment	Monitoring team	Assess how stakeholders are responding

a large segment of the customer base may require immediate and comprehensive action, while a more localized issue might allow for a more measured response.

In addition to identifying affected stakeholders, it is crucial to analyze the potential consequences for the brand. This includes examining financial implications, reputational damages, and legal ramifications. Brands need to consider how the crisis might impact sales, investor confidence, and overall market position. For instance, a major product recall not only incurs direct financial costs but can also lead to a significant loss of customer trust, which may take years to rebuild. By comprehensively assessing these factors, brands can develop targeted strategies to address the crisis, allocate resources effectively, and implement communication plans that resonate with the stakeholders involved.

This thorough evaluation not only guides immediate action but also aids in long-term recovery and reputation rebuilding efforts. Understanding the full impact of a crisis allows organizations to create a more focused response strategy that aligns with the needs of their stakeholders. It enables brands to communicate transparently and empathetically, addressing concerns while demonstrating their commitment to rectifying the situation. Ultimately, effective evaluation equips organizations with the insights needed to navigate the crisis landscape, mitigating damage and laying the groundwork for a stronger future.

Initial Response

Releasing an initial statement acknowledging the situation is a vital step in crisis management. This statement should be concise yet informative, clearly conveying that the brand is aware of the crisis and is actively investigating the matter. Effective communication at this stage is crucial; it not only demonstrates that the organization takes the situation seriously but also reassures stakeholders of its commitment to addressing the issue.

For example, the statement could read:

We are aware of the recent events impacting our brand and want
to assure our stakeholders that we are investigating the situation
thoroughly. Our priority is to understand the circumstances and
address any concerns as quickly as possible. We appreciate your
patience and support as we work to resolve this matter.

This message is straightforward, expressing concern while emphasizing the brand's dedication to finding a resolution.

By issuing this initial statement, brands can demonstrate transparency, establish accountability, and begin to manage the narrative
surrounding the crisis. Proactive communication in the early stages of a
crisis helps reassure stakeholders that the brand is engaged and working
diligently to rectify the situation. It sets the tone for future communications and can significantly influence public perception, as stakeholders
are more likely to respond positively to brands that are upfront about
their challenges. Moreover, a well-crafted initial statement can prevent
misinformation from spreading, allowing the organization to maintain
control over the situation as it develops.

In April 2019, Sephora addressed an incident involving SZA,
who experienced racial profiling in a California store. Following her
report on Twitter, Sephora took immediate action by issuing a public
apology on the same platform (Figure 6.1) and scheduling a nationwide
closure of all U.S. stores for inclusivity training. This swift and public
response on social media served as a proactive measure to acknowledge customer concerns and demonstrate Sephora's commitment to
inclusivity and accountability. By reacting quickly and visibly on social
media, Sephora contained the crisis, preventing it from escalating
and potentially damaging the brand further. The swift initial response
and subsequent store closure underscored Sephora's commitment to
fostering an inclusive shopping environment and reassured stakeholders,
helping to reinforce trust and stabilize the brand's reputation amidst the
situation.

Utilizing social media and news monitoring tools is essential
for gauging public reaction during a crisis. In today's digital age,
where information spreads rapidly, these tools empower brands to

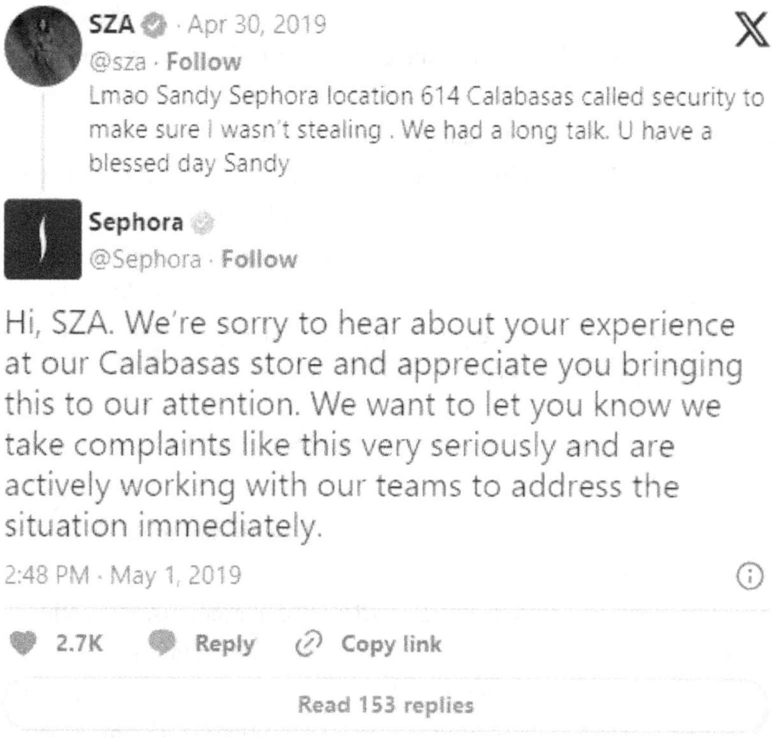

Figure 6.1 SZA/Sephora

track conversations, sentiments, and emerging narratives in real time, providing valuable insights into how stakeholders perceive the situation. By analyzing comments, shares, and news coverage, organizations can better understand the concerns and emotions of their audience, allowing them to navigate the crisis more effectively.

This understanding can significantly inform further communications. For instance, if monitoring reveals that stakeholders are expressing confusion or anger about a specific aspect of the crisis, the brand can tailor its messaging to address those concerns directly. By identifying the key issues that resonate with the public, brands can proactively provide clarity and context. Additionally, monitoring tools can highlight frequently asked questions or misinformation circulating online, enabling the organization to ensure that its response is both timely and relevant.

By actively engaging with public sentiment through these tools, brands can adapt their crisis management strategies, making informed decisions that align with stakeholder expectations. This responsive approach not only aids in managing the current situation but also plays a crucial role in rebuilding trust and credibility with the audience in the long run. Effective use of social media and monitoring tools allows organizations to demonstrate their commitment to transparency and accountability, fostering a sense of connection with stakeholders during challenging times. Ultimately, this can lead to stronger relationships and a more resilient brand reputation moving forward.

Establish Communication Channels

Establishing clear communication channels with stakeholders is vital during a crisis. Brands should create dedicated platforms, such as a crisis management web pages, social media accounts, or hotlines, where stakeholders can access accurate and up-to-date information. This transparency not only helps to inform but also reassures stakeholders that the organization is actively managing the situation and prioritizing their concerns.

For customers, providing regular updates through email newsletters, social media posts, and the brand's website can keep them informed of the latest developments and any steps being taken to address the crisis. This consistent communication fosters a sense of security and keeps the customer base engaged, ensuring they feel valued and informed throughout the ordeal. Employees should also have a reliable internal communication channel, such as an intranet or dedicated email list, to receive real-time updates and guidance on how to respond to inquiries. This empowers employees to act as informed representatives of the brand, maintaining a unified front during challenging times.

In terms of media relations, appointing a designated spokesperson is crucial to ensure consistent messaging and provide a single point of contact for journalists. This helps prevent the spread of misinformation and ensures that all communications are clear, accurate, and aligned with the brand's crisis response strategy. By prioritizing these communication channels, brands can effectively manage the narrative, mitigate misinformation, and foster trust among all stakeholders during a crisis. A proactive and organized communication strategy not only helps in navigating the immediate challenges but also strengthens the brand's reputation and relationships for the future.

Regular Updates

Committing to providing regular updates as new information emerges is essential for effective crisis management. By keeping stakeholders informed, brands demonstrate their commitment to transparency and accountability, which can help mitigate negative sentiments and rebuild trust. Regular communication can take various forms, including press releases, social media updates, email newsletters, and dedicated crisis management web pages, allowing stakeholders to access information through their preferred channels.

Establishing a consistent schedule for updates—whether hourly, daily, or as needed—ensures that stakeholders know when to expect new information. This predictability helps manage their expectations and reinforces the brand's proactive approach to handling the crisis. Additionally, responding to inquiries and feedback during this period can further enhance stakeholder trust and confidence. When stakeholders feel their voices are heard, they are more likely to remain supportive and engaged.

It's important to ensure that these updates are clear, accurate, and focused on addressing the key concerns of stakeholders. Acknowledging any uncertainties or ongoing investigations can also be beneficial, as it fosters a sense of honesty and authenticity. Transparency about what is known, what is being investigated, and what steps are being taken to resolve the issue can help stakeholders feel more secure. By prioritizing communication and providing regular updates, brands can navigate the complexities of a crisis more effectively while maintaining strong relationships with their stakeholders. This strategic approach not only mitigates immediate backlash but also lays the groundwork for long-term reputation recovery and resilience.

Case Studies

In the realm of crisis management, the speed of a brand's response can determine the trajectory of its reputation and consumer trust. Johnson & Johnson's handling of the 1982 Tylenol crisis is often heralded as a model of effective crisis management, characterized by a swift and decisive response that prioritized consumer safety. In stark contrast, both BP's reaction to the Deepwater Horizon oil spill and Volkswagen's response to the emissions scandal were marked by significant delays. Another example of slow response in the nonprofit sector came from Hockey Canada and the scandal surrounding sexual allegations involving junior hockey players. These slow reactions not only allowed misinformation to proliferate but also led to severe financial repercussions and long-lasting damage to their brand reputations. Analyzing these differing responses provides valuable insights into the critical importance of acting swiftly during a crisis.

Johnson & Johnson and the Tylenol Crisis

Johnson & Johnson's response to the 1982 Tylenol crisis exemplifies the effectiveness of swift action in crisis management. When seven people died after consuming cyanide-laced Tylenol capsules, the company acted almost immediately by recalling 31 million bottles of the product from store shelves nationwide. This pre-emptive measure was taken despite the fact that the contamination was not directly linked to the company itself. Johnson & Johnson also launched a comprehensive communication campaign, keeping the public informed about the steps being taken to ensure safety and prevent further incidents.

The swift response had several positive effects for Johnson & Johnson. First, the company's commitment to consumer safety and transparency helped to maintain public trust. By prioritizing the well-being of its customers over profits, Johnson & Johnson reinforced its reputation as a responsible and ethical brand. This approach not only prevented a more significant decline in consumer confidence but also showcased the company's commitment to doing what was right, ultimately winning the loyalty of its customers in the long run.

Moreover, Johnson & Johnson's effective crisis management set a precedent for the entire industry. The introduction of tamper-proof packaging in response to the crisis established new safety standards for over-the-counter medications. This proactive measure not only reassured consumers but also positioned Johnson & Johnson as a leader in safety innovation. Ultimately, the company's quick and effective handling of the crisis allowed it to recover market share relatively quickly, and it was able to return Tylenol to the shelves with renewed consumer trust. In many ways, the Tylenol crisis transformed Johnson & Johnson's approach to crisis management and set a benchmark for other companies, proving that a swift and responsible response can turn a potentially disastrous situation into an opportunity for strengthening brand loyalty.

BP and the Deepwater Horizon Oil Spill

BP's response to the Deepwater Horizon oil spill in April 2010 (Figure 6.2) is often cited as a textbook example of how a delayed reaction can exacerbate a crisis. Initially, BP did not fully grasp the magnitude of the disaster, which allowed the spill to continue for several months before adequate measures were implemented. Despite the immediacy of the situation, BP's leadership downplayed the severity of the spill, resulting in a slow and insufficient initial response. This hesitation led to the uncontrolled release of millions of barrels of oil into the Gulf of Mexico, causing extensive environmental damage and impacting local communities, wildlife, and businesses.

The lack of a swift response had dire consequences for BP. As public awareness of the spill grew, so did criticism of the company's handling of the crisis. BP's CEO, Tony Hayward, faced immense scrutiny for his comments that seemed to minimize the disaster, such as expressing concern over the impact on the company's image rather than the environmental and human toll. This further damaged the company's reputation and trust with stakeholders, leading to widespread outrage among consumers and environmental activists.

The financial repercussions of BP's sluggish response were substantial. The company faced billions of dollars in fines and legal settlements as a result of the spill, including penalties from the federal government

Figure 6.2 Deep waters horizontal oil spill

and compensation claims from affected businesses and individuals. In total, BP estimated that the total cost of the spill, including fines, clean-up efforts, and compensation, could exceed $65 billion. Additionally, the delay in addressing the crisis allowed negative sentiment to fester, leading to a significant decline in BP's stock value and long-term damage to its brand reputation. Overall, BP's lack of a swift response in the face of a major crisis serves as a cautionary tale for corporations about the critical importance of timely action and communication in crisis management.

Volkswagen and the Emissions Scandal

Volkswagen's handling of the emissions scandal that erupted in September 2015 is often cited as a cautionary tale in crisis management, particularly regarding the importance of a swift response. When it was revealed that Volkswagen had installed software to cheat emissions tests on millions of diesel vehicles, the company's initial reaction was marked by significant delays in acknowledgment and accountability. Instead of promptly addressing the allegations, Volkswagen's leadership opted for a defensive stance, which only fueled public outrage and skepticism. This slow response allowed misinformation to flourish and left stakeholders, including customers and regulatory bodies, feeling uninformed and frustrated.

The consequences of Volkswagen's sluggish response were severe. As the scandal unfolded, the company faced an avalanche of legal challenges, resulting in billions of dollars in fines and settlements. In total, Volkswagen has paid over $30 billion in various penalties, including civil and criminal fines, settlements with consumers, and costs associated with vehicle buybacks and fixes. The slow admission of wrongdoing not only led to massive financial liabilities but also significantly tarnished Volkswagen's reputation. Consumer trust plummeted, and sales of affected diesel models fell dramatically, with many potential customers choosing to turn to competitors instead.

Moreover, the delay in addressing the scandal created a protracted crisis period, during which public sentiment continued to deteriorate. By not responding swiftly, Volkswagen lost the opportunity to control the narrative and reassure stakeholders, further entrenching negative perceptions of the brand. The fallout from this crisis is still being felt today, as Volkswagen works to rebuild its image and regain consumer trust. The emissions scandal underscores the critical need for a swift response in crisis management; failing to act quickly can lead to devastating financial and reputational repercussions, as demonstrated by Volkswagen's experience.

Hockey Canada and Sexual Assault Allegations

Hockey Canada, the governing body for amateur hockey in Canada, found itself at the center of a significant scandal involving allegations of sexual assault by members of its national junior team. The crisis erupted in 2022 when it was reported that an unnamed player had been accused of sexual assault following a 2018 event. The allegations came to light amid scrutiny over Hockey Canada's handling of the situation, raising questions about the organization's culture and accountability.

One of the most glaring failures in Hockey Canada's response was its lack of swiftness in addressing the allegations. Initially, the organization chose to settle the claim discreetly, opting for a legal resolution rather than openly confronting the allegations. This decision was perceived as an attempt to shield the organization from public scrutiny, which only intensified backlash from stakeholders and the media. As public outrage grew, Hockey Canada was criticized for prioritizing its reputation over transparency and accountability.

The repercussions for Hockey Canada were severe and far-reaching. Sponsors, including major corporations, began to withdraw their support, significantly impacting the organization's financial stability. The federal government also took notice, launching investigations into Hockey Canada's practices and calling for reforms. In response to the mounting pressure, Hockey Canada eventually underwent leadership changes and implemented new policies aimed at addressing misconduct and promoting a safer environment within the sport. However, these efforts came after significant damage had already been done to its reputation, illustrating how a lack of a swift response can exacerbate the fallout from a brand crisis and undermine trust among stakeholders.

Overall, the Hockey Canada scandal serves as a stark reminder of the critical importance of a prompt and transparent response in crisis management. The organization's initial missteps and failure to act quickly ultimately resulted in a loss of credibility, stakeholder support, and a long road to rebuilding trust.

Conclusion

A swift response is the cornerstone of effective crisis management. As demonstrated throughout this chapter, the ability to act quickly and decisively can significantly reduce the impact of a crisis, safeguarding a brand's reputation and maintaining stakeholder trust. The case studies illustrate that while speed is critical, it must be paired with precision and preparation to deliver meaningful results.

Developing a well-structured response plan, assembling a dedicated crisis management team, and conducting regular drills are proactive steps brands can take to ensure readiness when crises arise. The first 24 hours are often the most critical period, and organizations that have clear protocols and predefined roles are better equipped to navigate this high-stakes window with confidence. Swift action not only helps control the narrative but also prevents misinformation from escalating and reassures stakeholders that the brand is committed to addressing the issue.

However, speed without strategy can backfire. This chapter emphasizes that a rapid response must also be thoughtful and informed by a clear understanding of the situation. Balancing urgency with careful decision making ensures that responses are not only timely but also effective in mitigating damage.

As we move forward in this book, the next chapters will delve into how a swift response aligns with other elements of the **STORM Framework**, such as transparent communication and ownership of the problem. Together, these components create a holistic approach to managing crises effectively and turning challenges into opportunities for growth and resilience.

Further Reading

Dutta, S., and C. Pullig. 2011. "Effectiveness of Corporate Responses to Brand Crises: The Role of Crisis Type and Response Strategies." *Journal of Business Research* 64 (12): 1281–7.

Garcia-Collart, T. 2024. "Speak up! Brands' Responsiveness Matters: Consumer Reactions to Brand Communications in the Early Stages of a Crisis." *Journal of Product & Brand Management* 33 (4): 449–59.

Iveson, A., M. Hultman, V. Davvetas, and P. Oghazi. 2023. "Less Speed More Haste: The Effect of Crisis Response Speed and Information Strategy on the Consumer-Brand Relationship." *Psychology & Marketing* 40 (2): 391–407.

Li, M., and H. Wei. 2016. "How to Save Brand After Crises? A Literature Review on Brand Crisis Management." *American Journal of Industrial and Business Management* 6 (2): 89–96.

Schultz, F, S. Utz, and A. Göritz. 2011. "Is the Medium the Message? Perceptions of and Reactions to Crisis Communication via Twitter, Blogs, and Traditional Media." *Public Relations Review* 37 (1): 20–7.

Ulmer, R.R., T.L. Sellnow, and M.W. Seeger. 2013. *Effective Crisis Communication: Moving from Crisis to Opportunity.* Sage Publications.

CHAPTER 7

T = Transparent Communication

Overview

- Explains how honesty and transparency strengthen stakeholder trust during crises.
- Provides strategies for tailoring messages to different stakeholder groups, including customers and employees.
- Emphasizes the importance of clarity and consistency in crisis messaging.
- Examines the role of social media in fostering transparency or exacerbating challenges.

In times of crisis, transparent communication is not merely a strategy; it is an absolute necessity. When a brand communicates honestly and openly, it builds trust with its stakeholders, fosters goodwill, and can significantly, influences how consumers perceive the brand during challenging times. Transparent communication allows for the dissemination of accurate information, which helps to dispel rumors and mitigate misunderstandings that can arise in high-pressure situations. This chapter delves into the critical importance of transparent communication in crisis management, exploring how brands can effectively engage with various stakeholders to maintain their credibility and integrity. Additionally, it examines examples of brands that have successfully navigated crises through honesty and openness, illustrating the positive effects of transparency on reputation and stakeholder relationships.

The role of transparent communication becomes even more pronounced in a crisis. Stakeholders, including customers, employees, and the media, are looking for clarity and reassurance. Brands that prioritize transparency are better positioned to address concerns and provide timely updates, thereby reducing uncertainty. This chapter will explore not only the importance of transparency but also practical strategies for engaging stakeholders effectively. By fostering an environment of open dialogue, brands can cultivate a sense of partnership and collaboration, reinforcing their commitment to accountability and ethical practices.

Furthermore, the chapter will highlight real-world examples of companies that embraced transparent communication during crises, demonstrating how honesty can lead to positive outcomes. These case studies will showcase how brands turned potential disasters into opportunities for rebuilding trust and reinforcing their values. In a landscape where consumers increasingly value authenticity and transparency, the ability to communicate openly during a crisis can be a significant differentiator for brands looking to maintain their reputations and ensure long-term success.

The Power of Honesty During a Crisis

Honesty is an indispensable tool in crisis management. When a crisis unfolds, stakeholders—including customers, employees, and the media—are actively seeking clear and truthful information. The importance of honesty in these situations cannot be overstated, as it plays a crucial role in shaping perceptions and guiding responses. One key reason why honesty matters is that it builds trust; stakeholders are more likely to feel confident in a brand that communicates openly, demonstrating accountability and integrity.

Additionally, honest communication helps reduce speculation and misinformation. In the absence of clear information, rumors and unfounded assumptions can quickly take root, leading to further complications and damage to a brand's reputation. By providing accurate updates and transparent messaging, brands can effectively quell speculation and maintain control over the narrative surrounding the crisis. This proactive approach not only mitigates potential harm but also enhances the brand's reputation, as stakeholders appreciate the transparency and forthrightness exhibited during challenging times.

Moreover, honesty can foster stronger relationships with stakeholders, as it creates a sense of partnership during difficult periods. When brands demonstrate a commitment to open communication, it reinforces their dedication to ethical practices and respect for their audience. Overall, embracing honesty as a cornerstone of crisis management can significantly influence the outcome, allowing brands to navigate crises more effectively and emerge with their reputations intact.

Building Trust

Being upfront about the situation, including acknowledging mistakes, is crucial for rebuilding trust with stakeholders during a crisis. When brands openly communicate the details of the crisis, it fosters an environment of transparency that stakeholders value. A sincere admission of errors not only highlights a brand's accountability but also signals a commitment to improvement and rectification. This authenticity can resonate deeply with stakeholders, who appreciate when brands own up to their missteps rather than deflecting blame or downplaying the severity of the situation.

Acknowledging mistakes also humanizes the brand, allowing stakeholders to see it as more than just a corporate entity but as an organization willing to learn and grow from its experiences. This approach can mitigate the negative impacts of the crisis and foster loyalty among consumers who recognize the brand's dedication to ethical practices. By being transparent and accountable, brands can begin to mend relationships, laying a foundation for recovery and positive engagement in the future.

Ultimately, the willingness to admit errors and communicate openly can transform a potentially damaging situation into an opportunity for growth and improvement. Stakeholders are more likely to support a brand that demonstrates humility and a proactive approach to crisis management, which can lead to a stronger reputation and renewed trust in the long run.

Reducing Speculation

Transparent communication plays a vital role in minimizing speculation and misinformation during a crisis. When brands proactively provide clear and accurate information, they effectively reduce the potential for rumors to spread, which can exacerbate the situation. In the absence of reliable communication, stakeholders often fill the information void with their assumptions, leading to misunderstandings and heightened anxiety.

By offering timely updates and clarifying the facts, brands can guide the narrative and ensure that stakeholders have the correct context regarding the crisis. This not only helps to maintain trust but also prevents the escalation of the crisis. When stakeholders feel informed, they are less likely to engage in harmful speculation, which can further damage the brand's reputation.

Moreover, transparent communication fosters an atmosphere of openness that encourages dialogue between the brand and its stakeholders. This two-way communication can provide valuable insights into stakeholder concerns and perceptions, allowing the brand to address specific issues directly. In this way, transparent communication serves as a critical tool in crisis management, protecting the brand's reputation and facilitating a smoother path toward recovery.

Enhancing Reputation

Brands that are perceived as honest and transparent during a crisis are significantly more likely to retain customer loyalty and support. When stakeholders witness a brand openly addressing issues, acknowledging mistakes, and providing clear information, they are more inclined to trust the brand. This trust is crucial for maintaining strong relationships with customers, who appreciate transparency as a sign of integrity and accountability.

Moreover, transparency during a crisis can enhance a brand's reputation in the long run. Brands that handle crises with openness often emerge stronger, as their willingness to confront challenges head-on can differentiate them from competitors. Stakeholders may view these brands as more relatable and responsible, fostering a deeper emotional connection. This positive perception can translate into increased customer loyalty, as consumers are more likely to support brands they believe are honest and committed to their values.

Ultimately, the long-term benefits of transparency extend beyond immediate crisis management. By building a reputation for honesty, brands can cultivate lasting goodwill among stakeholders, leading to enhanced brand equity and a competitive advantage in the marketplace. This underscores the importance of incorporating transparent communication as a core principle in crisis management strategies.

Communicating With Stakeholders: Customers, Employees, Media

Effective crisis communication involves crafting tailored messages for different stakeholder groups, as each group has unique concerns and needs. For customers, the primary focus is often on understanding the impact of the crisis on the products or services they rely on, as well as assurance regarding their safety and satisfaction. Clear and concise messaging can help alleviate fears and maintain trust, allowing customers to feel informed and valued.

Employees also require specific communication during a crisis. They may be concerned about job security, the organization's stability, and their roles in navigating the crisis. Providing transparent information and addressing their concerns can foster a sense of unity and commitment among employees, ensuring they remain engaged and motivated to support the organization through challenging times.

The media plays a crucial role in shaping public perception during a crisis. Effective communication with the media involves providing timely updates, clarifying misinformation, and maintaining an open line for inquiries. By proactively engaging with the media, brands can help ensure that accurate information is disseminated, ultimately influencing how the crisis is perceived by the wider public.

Overall, tailoring messages to meet the specific needs of each stakeholder group not only enhances the effectiveness of crisis communication but also helps mitigate potential reputational damage, fostering goodwill and trust among all parties involved. A matrix that outlines different stakeholder groups with tailored messaging strategies and channels for each group is shown in Table 7.1.

Customers

Communicating directly with customers through various channels is essential during a crisis. Utilizing emails, social media platforms, and press releases allows brands to reach their audience where they are most active and engaged. In this communication, it's crucial to address customer concerns head-on, acknowledging any impact the crisis may have on their experience or relationship with the brand.

For example, sending targeted emails can provide personalized messages that detail how the crisis affects specific customer segments, ensuring that the information is relevant and relatable. Social media, on the other hand, offers a real-time platform for updates and engagement, enabling brands to respond quickly to questions and comments, which can help alleviate customer anxiety.

Press releases serve as formal statements that provide essential information to the media and the public, ensuring that a consistent narrative is communicated. These releases should clarify the brand's position, outline steps being taken to resolve the issue, and reaffirm the brand's commitment to customer safety and satisfaction.

By proactively engaging with customers through these various channels, brands can foster a sense of transparency and trust. This direct communication not only keeps customers informed but also demonstrates that the brand is attentive to their needs and concerns during difficult times, ultimately helping to maintain loyalty and support.

Employees

Keeping employees informed during a crisis is critical for maintaining morale and trust within the organization. Clear internal communications help ensure that employees feel valued and included in the company's efforts to navigate the situation. When employees understand

Table 7.1 This table outlines tailored messaging strategies and communication channels for key stakeholder groups during a brand crisis, ensuring effective and clear communication to address their concerns and maintain trust.

Stakeholder group	Messaging strategies	Communication channels
Customers	Emphasize safety and accountability	Email newsletters
	Provide clear updates on the situation	Social media platforms
	Offer support options (e.g., refunds, FAQs)	Company website
Employees	Ensure transparency about the crisis	Internal emails
	Provide resources for support and assistance	Team meetings
	Encourage open dialogue and feedback	Intranet portal
Media	Issue factual statements to clarify the situation	Press releases
	Offer interviews or briefings with spokespeople	Media advisories
	Monitor coverage and correct misinformation	Social media engagement

how the crisis impacts the company and their roles, they are better equipped to manage their responsibilities and contribute positively.

It is essential to communicate openly about the nature of the crisis, the potential implications for the organization, and the specific steps being taken to address the issues at hand. This transparency not only helps alleviate uncertainty but also fosters a sense of solidarity among team members. Regular updates through emails, team meetings, and internal newsletters can keep everyone aligned and informed about developments, demonstrating the company's commitment to transparency and engagement.

Additionally, addressing employee concerns directly is vital. Providing forums for employees to ask questions and voice their worries allows for a two-way communication flow, reinforcing the message that their opinions matter. By fostering an environment of openness and trust, organizations can bolster employee confidence, ensuring that the workforce remains focused and motivated during challenging times. This proactive approach not only aids in crisis management but also strengthens the overall organizational culture in the long run.

Media

The media plays a crucial role in shaping public perception during a crisis. Establishing strong relationships with journalists and media outlets can significantly influence how a brand is portrayed in the news. By proactively engaging with the media, brands can ensure that their narratives are communicated effectively and that accurate information reaches the public.

Providing journalists with timely and accurate updates is essential in maintaining control over the narrative. When brands are transparent and responsive, they can help prevent the spread of misinformation and speculation that often accompanies a crisis. Being available for interviews and media inquiries demonstrates a commitment to transparency and accountability, reinforcing the brand's credibility during challenging times.

Furthermore, offering media briefings or press releases can help guide the coverage of the crisis. This proactive approach not only informs the media about the brand's perspective but also helps frame the conversation around the crisis in a way that aligns with the brand's values and message. By fostering positive relationships with the media and ensuring open lines of communication, brands can navigate crises more effectively and shape public perception in a way that mitigates reputational harm.

Crafting Transparent, Reassuring Messaging

When crafting messages during a crisis, clarity and reassurance are paramount. Effective communication can significantly influence how stakeholders perceive the brand and its response. One of the key principles is to be clear and concise. Messages should avoid jargon and complex language, ensuring that all stakeholders can easily understand the information being conveyed. This simplicity helps to prevent confusion and ensures that the core message is received loud and clear.

Acknowledging the situation is another essential principle. It's important to recognize the crisis openly and honestly, as this demonstrates accountability and transparency. Stakeholders appreciate brands that do not shy away from addressing the reality of the situation, which can foster trust during uncertain times.

Providing actionable information is crucial for helping stakeholders understand the steps being taken to address the crisis. This includes outlining what the brand is doing to resolve the issue and what stakeholders should do in response. Clear guidelines can empower customers and employees, enabling them to navigate the situation more effectively.

Lastly, expressing empathy is vital in crisis communication. Acknowledging the feelings and concerns of stakeholders shows that the brand cares about its audience. Empathetic messaging can help reassure stakeholders that the brand is aware of the impact the crisis may have on them and is committed to addressing their needs. By adhering to these principles, brands can craft effective messages that promote understanding and maintain confidence during challenging times.

Be Clear and Concise

When crafting messages during a crisis, clarity and reassurance are essential. Effective communication can greatly affect how people see the brand and its response. One key principle is to use straightforward language. Messages should avoid jargon and complicated terms, ensuring that everyone can easily understand the information being shared. This simplicity helps to prevent confusion and ensures that the main point is communicated clearly.

It's also important to acknowledge the situation openly. Recognizing the crisis shows accountability and transparency. Stakeholders appreciate brands that face the reality of the situation, which can help build trust during uncertain times.

Providing clear and actionable information is crucial. This means explaining what the brand is doing to fix the problem and what stakeholders should do next. Clear instructions can help customers and employees manage the situation more effectively.

Lastly, showing empathy is vital in crisis communication. Recognizing the feelings and concerns of stakeholders demonstrates that the brand cares about its audience. Empathetic messaging can help reassure people that the brand understands the impact of the crisis on them and is committed to addressing their needs. By following these principles, brands can create effective messages that promote understanding and maintain confidence during difficult times.

Acknowledge the Situation

Acknowledging the crisis and its implications is the first step in effective crisis communication. By being upfront about the issue, brands can establish credibility and show stakeholders that they are taking the situation seriously. This transparency is crucial in building trust, as it demonstrates that the brand is not trying to downplay or hide the problem.

When a brand openly addresses the crisis, it signals to customers, employees, and the media that it values honesty and accountability. This initial acknowledgment sets the tone for subsequent communications and reinforces the brand's commitment to resolving the issue. Moreover, recognizing the implications of the crisis allows the brand to convey its understanding of the potential impact on various stakeholders, thereby fostering a sense of empathy.

Following this acknowledgment, it is essential to provide clear, concise information about the steps being taken to address the situation. This includes outlining the measures implemented to rectify the problem and prevent future occurrences. By doing so, the brand can reassure stakeholders that it is actively engaged in finding solutions and maintaining a commitment to improvement. Overall, an upfront acknowledgment of the crisis lays the foundation for effective communication and helps manage stakeholder expectations during challenging times.

Provide Actionable Information

Clearly outlining the steps the brand is taking to address the crisis is essential in effective crisis communication. By detailing the actions being implemented, the brand not only reassures stakeholders but also demonstrates its proactive approach to resolving the issue.

First, the brand should communicate immediate actions taken to contain the crisis. This could include halting production, issuing recalls, or implementing safety measures. By highlighting these urgent steps, the brand conveys a sense of responsibility and urgency, reassuring stakeholders that their safety and interests are prioritized.

Next, the brand should outline longer-term strategies for addressing the root causes of the crisis. This could involve conducting thorough investigations, collaborating with relevant authorities, or engaging external experts to ensure comprehensive solutions. By sharing these plans, the brand emphasizes its commitment to accountability and improvement, fostering trust among stakeholders.

Additionally, providing updates on the progress of these actions is crucial. Regularly communicating the status of the crisis resolution efforts not only keeps stakeholders informed but also reinforces the brand's transparency. This ongoing communication builds confidence that the brand is actively engaged in addressing the situation and learning from the experience.

Ultimately, by clearly articulating the steps being taken, the brand can effectively manage stakeholder concerns and perceptions, demonstrating that it is not only responsive but also committed to maintaining the trust and loyalty of its audience.

Express Empathy

Showing understanding and concern for those affected by the crisis is vital in effective crisis communication. Empathetic messaging fosters a genuine connection with stakeholders and humanizes the brand, transforming a potentially damaging situation into an opportunity to demonstrate compassion and care.

When crafting messages during a crisis, it's essential to acknowledge the feelings and experiences of those impacted. By expressing empathy, brands can validate the emotions of stakeholders—be it customers, employees, or the community—showing that they are not just focused on mitigating reputational damage but are also genuinely concerned about the well-being of individuals affected by the situation.

In addition to acknowledging the crisis, brands should communicate a sincere commitment to support those impacted. This could include offering assistance, resources, or compensation for those who have been adversely affected. By taking tangible actions to help, the brand reinforces its dedication to its stakeholders, fostering trust and goodwill.

Furthermore, empathetic messaging should be reflected in the tone and language used. Employing straightforward and compassionate language can make a significant difference in how the message is received. Avoiding corporate jargon and focusing on clear, heartfelt communication helps to convey the brand's sincerity and reinforces the human aspect of the situation.

Ultimately, by prioritizing empathy in their messaging, brands can effectively navigate the complexities of a crisis while strengthening their relationships with stakeholders. This approach not only aids in crisis management but can also lead to long-term loyalty and support, as stakeholders are more likely to remember how a brand made them feel during challenging times.

The Role of Social Media in Transparent Crisis Communication

Social media platforms have become essential tools for crisis communication, offering brands the ability to communicate quickly and effectively with a broad audience. In the fast-paced environment of a crisis, the immediacy of social media allows brands to provide real-time updates, ensuring that stakeholders receive timely information about the situation as it unfolds. This immediacy can help mitigate confusion and speculation, demonstrating the brand's commitment to transparency.

Engagement on social media is also crucial during a crisis. Brands should actively monitor their platforms to respond to inquiries, concerns, and comments from stakeholders. This engagement fosters a sense of community and reassures audiences that their voices are being heard. By responding promptly and thoughtfully, brands can address misinformation and alleviate concerns, reinforcing trust during challenging times.

Additionally, monitoring sentiment on social media can provide valuable insights into how stakeholders are reacting to the crisis. Understanding public sentiment allows brands to adapt their communication strategies accordingly, addressing specific concerns and tailoring messages to meet the needs of their audience. By analyzing sentiment trends, brands can identify potential areas for improvement in their response efforts and adjust their messaging to resonate more effectively with stakeholders.

Overall, leveraging social media for crisis communication is vital for brands looking to navigate crises successfully. The combination of real-time updates, active engagement, and sentiment monitoring creates an opportunity for brands to build trust, manage public perception, and ultimately emerge stronger from challenging situations.

Real-Time Updates

Using social media to provide real-time updates during a crisis is crucial for brands aiming to control the narrative and keep stakeholders informed. In today's fast-paced digital landscape, information spreads rapidly, and social media platforms serve as immediate channels for communication. By delivering timely updates, brands can ensure that accurate information reaches their audience before misinformation or rumors take hold.

Real-time updates also demonstrate a brand's commitment to transparency, which is essential for maintaining trust during challenging times. When stakeholders see that a brand is proactively sharing information, they are more likely to feel reassured and engaged. This level of transparency not only helps manage expectations but also fosters goodwill among customers, employees, and the media.

Additionally, social media enables brands to interact with their audience directly. By responding to questions and addressing concerns in real time, brands can build a rapport with stakeholders and demonstrate that they value their input. This engagement not only helps mitigate the potential negative impact of the crisis but also reinforces the brand's commitment to open communication and accountability.

Utilizing social media for real-time updates is an effective strategy that empowers brands to control the narrative during a crisis, keep stakeholders informed, and maintain trust and credibility in the face of adversity.

Engagement

Encouraging dialogue with stakeholders through social media is a vital aspect of effective crisis communication. By actively responding to comments and questions, brands can demonstrate that they value their audience's input and are committed to maintaining transparency. This two-way communication fosters a sense of community and trust, allowing stakeholders to feel heard and understood during challenging times.

When a crisis arises, stakeholders often seek reassurance and clarity. Engaging in conversations on social media allows brands to address concerns directly, providing accurate information and alleviating fears. This interaction not only helps to mitigate the spread of misinformation but also reinforces the brand's reputation as approachable and accountable.

Moreover, responding to stakeholders shows that the brand is not just focused on delivering messages but is genuinely interested in understanding the sentiments and needs of its audience. This empathetic approach can significantly enhance customer loyalty, as stakeholders appreciate brands that take the time to engage and listen to their concerns.

Fostering dialogue through social media is essential for brands navigating a crisis. By encouraging interaction and responding thoughtfully to comments and questions, brands can reinforce their commitment to transparency, build trust, and ultimately strengthen their relationship with stakeholders.

Monitoring Sentiment

Monitoring sentiment on social media is crucial for brands during a crisis, as it provides real-time insights into public perception. By tracking conversations, comments, and mentions, brands can gauge how stakeholders are reacting to their responses and the overall situation. This continuous feedback loop allows companies to understand the mood of their audience—whether they feel reassured, frustrated, or confused.

By closely monitoring sentiment, brands can identify potential issues early on, allowing them to adjust their communication strategies accordingly. For instance, if a significant number of stakeholders express dissatisfaction with the brand's response, the company can pivot its messaging or take additional steps to address the concerns raised. This adaptability not only demonstrates responsiveness but also shows stakeholders that their opinions matter, fostering a deeper sense of trust and loyalty.

Moreover, understanding public sentiment can help brands avoid missteps in their communication. If the sentiment analysis reveals that certain messages are resonating well or generating backlash, brands can refine their messaging to better align with stakeholder expectations. This proactive approach to sentiment monitoring ensures that communication remains effective and relevant, ultimately helping to manage the crisis more successfully.

Monitoring sentiment on social media is an essential component of crisis management. By leveraging insights from public conversations, brands can adjust their communication strategies, enhance stakeholder trust, and navigate crises more effectively.

Case Studies

Several brands have effectively utilized transparent communication during crises, leading to successful damage mitigation. Johnson & Johnson responded swiftly during the 1982 Tylenol crisis by recalling millions of bottles and maintaining open communication about consumer safety, which helped restore its reputation. Starbucks addressed a racial bias incident in 2018 by publicly apologizing and implementing companywide training, reinforcing its commitment to inclusivity. The United Way also served as an example of taking ownership of the problem, coming from a nonprofit organization. However, Airbnb faced backlash during a 2015 incident involving a racial bias claim, and while it struggled with transparency initially, it eventually took steps to address the concerns and improve its policies. Chipotle, after a series of *E. coli* outbreaks, failed to engage in transparent communication by updating customers on safety measures and collaborating with health authorities, thereby harming customer trust. Lastly, Samsung also issued unclear communications after reports of its Galaxy Note 7 batteries catching fire.

Johnson & Johnson and the Tylenol Crisis

Johnson & Johnson's response to the 1982 Tylenol crisis is a prominent example of effective crisis management through transparent communication. When several individuals in Chicago died after consuming cyanide-laced Tylenol capsules, Johnson & Johnson swiftly took action. The company immediately recalled 31 million bottles of Tylenol from shelves, even before fully understanding the cause of the incidents. This proactive measure demonstrated the company's commitment to consumer safety, prioritizing public well-being over financial considerations.

Throughout the crisis, Johnson & Johnson maintained open and transparent communication with stakeholders. The company issued timely public statements, urging consumers to stop using Tylenol products and providing information on the ongoing investigation. They also established a dedicated hotline for consumers to address concerns and offer support. By holding press conferences and regularly updating the media, Johnson & Johnson ensured that accurate information was disseminated, helping to prevent the spread of misinformation and speculation.

The transparent approach taken by Johnson & Johnson during the Tylenol crisis significantly mitigated potential long-term reputational harm. While the immediate fallout resulted in a decline in sales and consumer confidence, the company's commitment to accountability and consumer safety ultimately fostered trust among stakeholders. Within a year, Tylenol regained a substantial share of the market, and the brand emerged from the crisis with a stronger reputation. The introduction of tamper-proof packaging, which became an industry standard, further reinforced Johnson & Johnson's commitment to consumer protection. This case serves as a powerful reminder of the importance of transparent communication in crisis management, illustrating how honesty and accountability can lead to successful brand recovery.

Starbucks and the Racial Bias Incident

In April 2018, Starbucks found itself at the center of a significant controversy when two Black men were arrested at a store in Philadelphia for allegedly trespassing. The incident unfolded when the men entered the cafe to meet a business associate but did not make a purchase while waiting. A store manager called the police, leading to the men's arrest. The situation sparked widespread outrage and accusations of racial profiling, leading to calls for boycotts and protests against the brand. The video of the incident, which circulated on social media, ignited discussions about race and bias in public spaces, putting immense pressure on Starbucks to respond swiftly and effectively.

Recognizing the gravity of the situation, Starbucks' CEO Kevin Johnson took immediate action. He publicly apologized for the incident and emphasized that the company would not tolerate any form of discrimination. Johnson described the arrest as "reprehensible" and stated that it was not reflective of the company's values. To address the situation head-on, he also met with the two men involved to listen to their experiences and understand their perspective. This move underscored Starbucks' commitment to accountability and reinforced the message that the brand was taking the matter seriously.

In addition to addressing the specific incident, Starbucks implemented companywide changes to prevent similar occurrences in the future. The company announced plans to close all its U.S. stores for a half-day to conduct racial bias training for employees, which impacted more than 8,000 locations. This training aimed to educate staff on implicit bias and create a more inclusive environment for all customers. By taking these steps, Starbucks not only sought to rebuild trust with its customers but also aimed to position itself as a leader in social responsibility. Ultimately, Starbucks' transparent communication and proactive measures helped the brand navigate the crisis effectively, preserving its reputation and reinforcing its commitment to diversity and inclusion.

United Way and Unethical CEO Practices

In the early 2000s, United Way faced a significant crisis when it was revealed that its then-CEO, Brian Gallagher, had engaged in unethical financial practices. The misconduct included misappropriation of funds and misleading financial statements, which not only put the organization's financial integrity at risk but also jeopardized its reputation as a leading nonprofit committed to serving communities. The scandal raised serious concerns among stakeholders, including donors, employees, and the public, who relied on United Way's transparency and accountability.

Upon learning of the misconduct, United Way's board of directors acted decisively. They recognized the severity of the situation and the importance of taking ownership of the problem. In a public statement, they expressed deep regret over the mismanagement and the breach of trust with their stakeholders. This acknowledgment was crucial, as it demonstrated a commitment to transparency and responsibility. The board initiated an independent investigation to assess the extent of Gallagher's actions, ensuring that the findings would be made public to restore credibility with donors and the community.

In the aftermath of the scandal, United Way implemented a series of reforms aimed at strengthening its governance and financial oversight. These changes included enhancing internal controls, increasing transparency in financial reporting, and establishing stricter accountability measures for leadership. The organization also launched a public relations campaign to rebuild its image and reassure stakeholders that it was committed to ethical practices. By proactively addressing the scandal and taking responsibility for the shortcomings, United Way was able to mitigate the backlash and gradually restore public trust. The crisis ultimately served as a pivotal moment for the organization, leading to increased accountability and a renewed focus on its mission to support communities effectively.

Airbnb and the San Francisco Incident

In 2015, Airbnb faced a significant crisis following a tragic incident in San Francisco, where a guest was murdered at an Airbnb property. The event raised serious concerns about safety and trust on the platform, prompting stakeholders—including users, hosts, and the media—to demand clarity and accountability from the company. Initially, Airbnb's response was criticized for lacking transparency. The company issued a brief statement expressing condolences to the victim's family but did not provide detailed information about the incident or its implications for user safety.

The lack of transparency during this crisis had notable repercussions for Airbnb's brand reputation. Stakeholders were left with many unanswered questions regarding the safety measures in place for guests and hosts, which led to a surge of negative sentiment online. Many users voiced their concerns on social media, and media coverage highlighted the perceived inadequacies in Airbnb's safety protocols. This atmosphere of uncertainty and mistrust threatened to erode the strong community that Airbnb had cultivated over the years.

As the situation unfolded, Airbnb eventually shifted its approach and began to implement more transparent communication practices. The company launched a series of initiatives aimed at improving safety and rebuilding trust, such as enhanced background checks for hosts, 24/7 customer support, and a commitment to increasing transparency about safety measures. By openly acknowledging the incident and detailing the steps being taken to address the concerns raised, Airbnb began to mend its relationship with stakeholders. This pivot toward transparency helped mitigate some of the reputational damage incurred during the initial response, demonstrating that proactive communication is essential for maintaining trust, especially in times of crisis.

Ultimately, the San Francisco incident served as a critical lesson for Airbnb and other brands regarding the importance of transparent communication during a crisis. While the company's initial response may have been lacking, its eventual commitment to clarity and accountability played a vital role in rebuilding trust and restoring its brand image.

Chipotle and the E. Coli Outbreak

In 2015, Chipotle Mexican Grill faced a major crisis due to multiple *E. coli* outbreaks linked to its restaurants. The situation unfolded in a way that put significant pressure on the brand's reputation and customer trust. Initially, the company struggled to communicate effectively about the outbreaks, leading to widespread concern and negative media coverage. Critics argued that Chipotle's responses lacked transparency, as the company was slow to provide detailed information about the source of the contamination and the specific locations affected.

The delayed and ambiguous communication contributed to a climate of fear and uncertainty among customers. Many consumers chose to avoid Chipotle due to health concerns, which resulted in a significant decline in sales. Social media played a crucial role during this crisis, with customers expressing their worries and frustration, which further amplified the negative sentiment toward the brand. The lack of timely and transparent communication made it difficult for Chipotle to control the narrative and ultimately harmed its reputation as a provider of fresh and safe food.

In response to the escalating crisis, Chipotle eventually shifted its strategy to prioritize transparency. The company publicly acknowledged the seriousness of the outbreaks and communicated its commitment to improving food safety protocols. It also provided regular updates on its efforts to investigate the source of the contamination and ensure that all food served met the highest safety standards. These efforts included implementing new food safety procedures, conducting thorough audits of its supply chain, and enhancing employee training on hygiene practices.

Chipotle's eventual transparency helped to restore some trust among customers, but the damage had already been significant. The crisis not only resulted in a substantial loss of revenue but also prompted an investigation by the Centers for Disease Control and Prevention and other health agencies. Additionally, Chipotle faced numerous lawsuits from affected customers, resulting in billions in legal costs and fines.

The *E. coli* outbreaks highlighted the critical importance of transparent communication during a crisis. Brands like Chipotle that fail to provide timely and clear information risk damaging their reputation and losing customer loyalty. The experience taught Chipotle that proactive and honest communication is vital for rebuilding trust and ensuring the long-term health of the brand.

Samsung and the Galaxy Note 7 Battery Crisis

The Samsung Galaxy Note 7 crisis serves as a notable example of how a lack of transparency in communication can exacerbate a brand crisis. In August 2016, Samsung launched the Galaxy Note 7 to considerable acclaim. However, reports soon emerged of devices catching fire due to battery defects. Instead of swiftly addressing the issue with clear and transparent communication, Samsung's initial response was marked by ambiguity and hesitation. The company announced a recall in early September but was criticized for not providing adequate information about the root cause of the problem or the extent of the risks associated with using the device.

As the crisis unfolded, Samsung faced mounting pressure as more incidents of overheating and fires were reported, even after the recall. The company's failure to clearly communicate the dangers posed by the device led to widespread public concern and distrust. While Samsung eventually decided to halt production of the Galaxy Note 7 entirely and issued a second recall, these measures came only after significant backlash and scrutiny from consumers, regulators, and the media. The delayed and unclear communication undermined consumer confidence and caused frustration among users, many of whom were unsure about the safety of their devices.

Samsung's initial lack of transparent communication not only fueled public outrage but also tarnished its brand reputation. The crisis led to billions in financial losses and forced the company to invest heavily in damage control efforts. Ultimately, while Samsung did work to rectify its approach as the situation developed, the early missteps in communication highlighted the critical importance of transparency during a crisis. The lesson learned from the Galaxy Note 7 incident emphasizes that brands must prioritize honest and timely communication to effectively manage crises and maintain stakeholder trust.

Conclusion

Transparent communication is a vital pillar of effective crisis management. As highlighted throughout this chapter, honesty and openness are not just ethical imperatives—they are strategic necessities for maintaining trust and credibility during a crisis. Stakeholders value brands that prioritize clarity, empathy, and accountability in their communications, especially when faced with challenges that test their integrity.

The case studies in this chapter demonstrate how transparent communication can mitigate backlash, address stakeholder concerns, and even strengthen brand loyalty in the aftermath of a crisis. Conversely, a lack of transparency often exacerbates the situation, leading to prolonged reputational damage and diminished trust.

Key takeaways from this chapter emphasize the importance of preparing communication templates, training spokespersons, and tailoring messages to meet the needs of diverse stakeholder groups. Leveraging social media as both a listening and messaging tool also underscores the power of real-time engagement in shaping public perception.

As we progress to the next elements of the **STORM Framework**, we will explore how transparent communication intersects with ownership of the problem and rebuilding trust. Together, these components provide a cohesive strategy for managing crises effectively while fostering lasting relationships with stakeholders. Transparency, at its core, is about more than managing a moment of difficulty—it is about laying the foundation for future trust and resilience.

Further Reading

Coombs, W.T. 2007. "Protecting Organization Reputations During a Crisis: The Development and Application of Situational Crisis Communication Theory." *Corporate Reputation Review* 10 (3): 163–76.

Fombrun, C.J., and M.D. Shanley. 1990. "What's in a Name? Reputation Building and Corporate Strategy." Academy of Management Journal 33 (2): 233–58.

Gillespie, N., G. Dietz, and V. Chao. 2010 "Trust Repair After an Organization-Level Failure." *Academy of Management Review* 35 (1): 127–45.

Soo-Yeon, K., and L. Jeong-Hyeon. 2022. "How to Maximize the Effectiveness of Stealing Thunder in Crisis Communication: The Significance of Follow-Up Actions and Transparent Communication." *Corporate Communications* 27 (3): 425–40.

Kim, Y. 2015. "Toward an Ethical Model of Effective Crisis Communication." *Business and Society Review* 120 (1): 57–81.

Rawlins, B.L. 2009. "Give the Emperor a Mirror: Toward Developing a Stakeholder Measurement of Organizational Transparency." *Journal of Public Relations Research* 21 (1): 71–99.

CHAPTER 8

O = Ownership of the Problem

Overview

- Stresses the necessity of acknowledging responsibility to build credibility.
- Discusses how to balance owning the problem with managing blame and liability.
- Highlights the importance of empathy and crafting sincere apologies.
- Features case studies of brands that successfully or unsuccessfully owned their crises.

In the midst of a brand crisis, ownership of the problem is not just a choice; it's an imperative. Taking responsibility for a crisis can significantly impact how stakeholders perceive the brand, the recovery process, and ultimately, the brand's reputation. By acknowledging their role in the situation, brands can foster trust and credibility among consumers, employees, and the media. This chapter discusses the importance of ownership, emphasizing that it is essential for effective crisis management. It will explore strategies for managing blame while demonstrating accountability, showcasing how proactive communication can help mitigate damage. Additionally, this chapter highlights examples of brands that turned crises into opportunities by embracing responsibility, illustrating that ownership can be a powerful tool in restoring and even enhancing a brand's standing in the market.

When a crisis strikes, brands face the critical decision of whether to take ownership of the problem. This choice can profoundly influence stakeholder perceptions and the trajectory of recovery efforts. Owner-ship signifies accountability, allowing brands to reshape the narrative surrounding the crisis and reinforce their commitment to integrity and transparency. In this chapter, we delve into the dynamics of ownership, offering insights on effectively managing blame while maintaining a focus on constructive solutions. Through various case studies, we will examine how brands that embraced responsibility not only navigated their crises more effectively but also emerged stronger, ultimately reinforcing their reputations in the eyes of consumers.

By illustrating how ownership plays a vital role in crisis manage-ment, this chapter aims to equip brands with the tools necessary for handling difficult situations. We will analyze the potential repercussions of evading responsibility, highlighting the risks of losing stakeholder trust and loyalty. In contrast, brands that own their challenges and communicate transparently often find opportunities for growth and improvement. The discussion will feature notable examples of brands that successfully turned crises into positive outcomes by embracing ownership, demonstrating the power of accountability in shaping long-term success and resilience in the marketplace.

Why Taking Responsibility is Non-Negotiable

Taking ownership of a crisis is critical for several reasons. First and foremost, it establishes credibility and trust with stakeholders. When a brand openly acknowledges its role in a crisis, it demonstrates transpar-ency and accountability, fostering a sense of reliability among consum-ers, employees, and the media. This trust is essential for rebuilding relationships and can significantly influence public perception during challenging times.

Second, ownership of the problem allows brands to control the narrative. By proactively addressing the crisis and accepting responsibil-ity, brands can shape the discussion surrounding the incident rather than allowing external voices to dictate the narrative. This proac-tive stance enables brands to communicate their perspective, outline corrective measures, and emphasize their commitment to resolving the issue.

Moreover, taking ownership can mitigate potential backlash. Brands that attempt to deflect blame or downplay their involvement risk escalating negative sentiments among stakeholders. Conversely, embracing accountability can reduce speculation, manage expectations, and ultimately lead to a more favorable response from the public.

Finally, ownership can create opportunities for improvement and growth. By acknowledging mistakes, brands can identify areas for enhancement and implement meaningful changes. This willingness to learn from a crisis not only strengthens the brand's operations but can also enhance its reputation in the long run, turning a potentially damaging situation into a catalyst for positive transformation.

Restoring Trust

When a brand acknowledges its role in a crisis, it signals to stakeholders that it values transparency and integrity. This act can be pivotal in restoring trust, which is often shattered during crises. By openly admitting to mistakes or oversights, brands demonstrate a commitment to accountability, showing stakeholders that they take the situation seriously and are willing to address the issue head-on. This candid approach helps dispel any doubts about the brand's intentions and capabilities, allowing for a more constructive dialogue with affected parties.

Moreover, taking ownership of the problem can facilitate a quicker recovery process. When a brand openly discusses the crisis, stakeholders are more likely to feel heard and understood, which can mitigate feelings of frustration or betrayal. This, in turn, fosters a sense of loyalty among consumers who appreciate the brand's honesty and commitment to making things right. In today's interconnected world, where information spreads rapidly, a swift acknowledgment can prevent rumors and speculation from gaining traction, allowing the brand to maintain greater control over the narrative.

Ultimately, embracing ownership not only aids in crisis management but also contributes to long-term brand equity. By reinforcing a culture of accountability, brands can build stronger relationships with their stakeholders, making them more resilient in the face of future challenges. As consumers increasingly gravitate toward brands that prioritize ethical practices and transparent communication, those that own their mistakes can cultivate a positive reputation that stands the test of time.

Demonstrating Accountability

Brands that take responsibility for their actions demonstrate accountability, which is essential in today's consumer landscape. As consumers become increasingly aware of corporate behavior and social responsibility, they expect brands to act ethically and transparently. When a crisis arises, stakeholders—including customers, employees, and investors—look to brands not only for effective solutions but also for a sense of integrity and moral responsibility. Brands that embrace accountability show that they prioritize their stakeholders' trust and well-being, which can help foster loyalty and long-term relationships.

Taking ownership of a crisis also signals to stakeholders that a brand is willing to learn from its mistakes and improve. This proactive approach can enhance the brand's reputation, as consumers appreciate transparency and honesty. In contrast, brands that evade responsibility risk alienating their audience and facing backlash, which can lead to significant long-term reputational damage. By recognizing the impact of their actions and committing to ethical standards, brands position themselves as leaders in their industries, capable of navigating challenges while maintaining consumer trust and loyalty.

Moreover, demonstrating accountability can create a competitive advantage in the marketplace. Consumers are more likely to support brands that align with their values, especially those that prioritize ethical behavior and social responsibility. Brands that effectively communicate their commitment to accountability not only manage crises more effectively but also pave the way for future success and resilience in a rapidly changing landscape.

Reducing Long-Term Damage

Brands that deflect blame or deny responsibility can face prolonged backlash and significant reputational damage. When a company refuses to take ownership of a crisis, it often fuels public anger and frustration, leading to negative media coverage and eroding trust among stakeholders. Consumers and the public expect accountability; failing to deliver can make it appear as though the brand is more concerned with protecting its image than with addressing the concerns of those affected. This deflection can result in a loss of customer loyalty, reduced sales, and a tarnished brand reputation that may take years to recover from.

In contrast, acknowledging the problem allows brands to begin the healing process more quickly. By taking ownership, brands demonstrate a commitment to resolving the issue and restoring trust. This approach not only reassures stakeholders that the brand is taking the situation seriously but also opens the door to constructive dialogue. When consumers see a brand actively addressing its mistakes, they are often more willing to forgive and support it in the long run. Additionally, this accountability can lead to more effective crisis management strategies, as the brand can gather valuable feedback from stakeholders to improve its practices and prevent future incidents.

Ultimately, ownership is not just about admitting fault; it's about showing a genuine commitment to rectifying the situation and learning from it. By embracing responsibility, brands can turn a crisis into an opportunity for growth and improvement, enhancing their reputation and reinforcing their connection with consumers.

How to Balance Owning the Problem With Managing Blame

While ownership is essential, brands must also navigate the delicate balance of taking responsibility without absorbing undue blame. It's important for brands to acknowledge their role in a crisis, but they should also clarify the context and contributing factors to avoid being solely blamed for the situation. This involves a nuanced approach where brands recognize their accountability while also addressing external influences or systemic issues that may have contributed to the crisis.

For instance, in cases where a crisis results from a complex interplay of factors—such as industry-wide challenges or regulatory shortcomings—brands should emphasize their commitment to addressing the issues at hand without allowing themselves to bear the brunt of blame for circumstances beyond their control. This helps to maintain a level of fairness in public perception while still demonstrating accountability.

Additionally, brands can focus on proactive measures taken to prevent future incidents, reinforcing their commitment to continuous improvement. By showcasing initiatives that go beyond the immediate crisis response, brands can effectively communicate their dedication to ethical practices and consumer safety. This forward-thinking perspective can help mitigate potential backlash and foster a more favorable view among stakeholders.

Ultimately, the key is to strike a balance between transparency and strategic communication. By owning the problem while also contextualizing it, brands can enhance their credibility and trustworthiness, paving the way for a more resilient reputation in the long run. This balanced approach not only facilitates effective crisis management but also contributes to building stronger, more sustainable relationships with stakeholders.

Focus on the Facts

When communicating about the crisis, it's crucial to stick to the facts. Providing a clear, honest account of what happened fosters transparency and helps build trust with stakeholders. Avoiding defensive language is essential; using terms that could be perceived as blaming others can exacerbate tensions and damage the brand's reputation further. Instead, focus on outlining the events as they occurred, acknowledging any mistakes made by the brand, and emphasizing the steps being taken to address the situation.

For instance, instead of saying, "We had to deal with unforeseen circumstances caused by external factors," it would be more effective to state, "We encountered unexpected challenges that affected our operations, and we take full responsibility for the impact on our customers." This kind of language not only shows accountability but also avoids alienating stakeholders who might feel that the brand is deflecting responsibility.

Moreover, sticking to the facts helps to minimize speculation and misinformation, which can spread rapidly during a crisis. By being forthright about the details and the brand's response, stakeholders are less likely to fill in the gaps with rumors or assumptions. This factual approach reassures stakeholders that the brand is in control of the situation and committed to resolving it.

Ultimately, a commitment to clear and factual communication lays the groundwork for restoring trust and credibility. By focusing on honesty and accountability, brands can better navigate the crisis and emerge stronger on the other side.

Highlight Systemic Issues

When addressing a crisis, it's beneficial to frame the situation within the context of larger systemic issues rather than solely emphasizing individual mistakes. This approach allows brands to maintain accountability while mitigating personal blame, which can often lead to defensiveness and prolonged reputational damage.

By highlighting systemic factors, brands can demonstrate a broader understanding of the challenges they face. For example, instead of only acknowledging a lapse in quality control that led to a product recall, a brand might address how industry-wide supply chain disruptions or regulatory changes contributed to the situation. This contextualization helps stakeholders see the crisis as part of a larger narrative rather than a simple failure on the part of the brand.

This strategy not only alleviates some personal blame but also positions the brand as part of a larger ecosystem that is actively working to improve practices and standards. It shows that the brand is aware of the challenges and complexities of its industry, which can foster a sense of empathy and understanding among stakeholders.

Moreover, framing the crisis in this way can also open the door for constructive dialogue about industry-wide improvements. It enables the brand to advocate for necessary changes while demonstrating that it is committed to being part of the solution, rather than simply reacting to problems as they arise. This proactive stance can help rebuild trust and enhance the brand's reputation in the long run.

Ultimately, by recognizing the systemic issues at play, brands can navigate the crisis more effectively, showing that they are not only taking responsibility but also understanding the broader implications of their actions and decisions. This approach reinforces their commitment to accountability and transparency, fostering stronger relationships with stakeholders.

Emphasize Solutions

Shifting the focus from blame to solutions is crucial when addressing a crisis. Instead of dwelling on what went wrong, brands should communicate the specific actions they are taking to rectify the situation and prevent future occurrences. This proactive approach not only demonstrates accountability but also reassures stakeholders that the brand is committed to improvement and responsible management.

When a crisis arises, stakeholders are often more concerned about how the brand will respond than about assigning blame. Therefore, brands should clearly outline their plans for remediation. This can include steps such as enhancing quality control measures, implementing new training programs for employees, or collaborating with industry experts to develop better practices. By focusing on these solutions, brands convey a message of determination and resilience, indicating that they are not merely reacting to the crisis but actively working to ensure it doesn't happen again.

Additionally, brands can engage stakeholders in their solution-oriented efforts. This might involve inviting customer feedback on proposed changes or establishing a forum for discussion around industry best practices. Such engagement fosters a sense of community and shows that the brand values its stakeholders' insights and concerns.

Moreover, transparent communication about these solutions builds trust. Stakeholders are more likely to feel confident in a brand that acknowledges its mistakes while also demonstrating a commitment to improvement. By sharing progress updates and celebrating milestones achieved in the remediation process, brands can reinforce their dedication to rectifying the issue.

By shifting the narrative from blame to solutions, brands can effectively manage crises while enhancing their reputation. This proactive stance not only mitigates potential fallout from the crisis but also positions the brand as a responsible and trustworthy entity that learns from its experiences.

Showing Empathy and Addressing Concerns of Affected Stakeholders

Empathy is a critical component of effective crisis management. When a crisis occurs, stakeholders, especially those directly affected, are often experiencing significant emotional distress. Addressing their concerns with genuine understanding can play a vital role in rebuilding relationships and restoring trust in the brand. This empathetic approach not only acknowledges the hardships faced by stakeholders but also demonstrates that the brand values their feelings and experiences.

During a crisis, it is crucial for brands to actively listen to the concerns of affected stakeholders. This involves engaging with them through various channels, such as social media, customer service, and community forums. By providing platforms for stakeholders to express their feelings, brands can gain insights into their perspectives and respond accordingly. Acknowledging their pain or frustration with sincere messages can help stakeholders feel heard and understood, which is the first step toward healing.

Moreover, empathy in communication can help humanize the brand. By showing compassion and understanding, a brand can create a connection with its audience, reinforcing the idea that it is not just a faceless corporation but a community member that cares about its stakeholders. This connection can be pivotal in mitigating reputational damage, as stakeholders are more likely to forgive a brand that acknowledges their suffering and shows a willingness to support them.

Additionally, demonstrating empathy goes beyond mere words. Brands should take tangible actions that reflect their commitment to addressing the needs of those affected. This could include offering support programs, financial compensation, or community initiatives aimed at helping those impacted by the crisis. By following through on empathetic communications with concrete actions, brands can further solidify their dedication to rebuilding relationships and trust.

Empathy is essential in crisis management as it fosters understanding and connection with stakeholders. By actively listening, communicating compassionately, and taking actionable steps to support affected individuals, brands can navigate crises more effectively and emerge with stronger relationships. Empathy not only aids in crisis recovery but can also enhance a brand's long-term reputation and loyalty among its stakeholders.

Active Listening

Engaging with stakeholders to understand their feelings and concerns is vital during a crisis. This engagement can take various forms, including direct communication, social media interactions, and the establishment of dedicated channels for feedback. By prioritizing open dialogue, brands can gain invaluable insights into the emotional state of their stakeholders and tailor their crisis response accordingly.

One of the most effective ways to engage with stakeholders is through direct communication. This can include sending personalized emails, hosting town hall meetings, or conducting phone interviews with affected individuals. Such initiatives allow stakeholders to voice their concerns and feel acknowledged, creating a space for genuine conversation. Listening attentively during these interactions not only fosters trust but also equips brands with critical information to inform their crisis management strategies.

Social media platforms serve as an immediate and accessible means for brands to connect with their audience during a crisis. By actively monitoring and responding to comments and messages, brands can demonstrate that they are listening and care about the opinions of their stakeholders. Engaging with users through polls, Q&A sessions, or live updates can also provide a platform for stakeholders to express their feelings while giving brands the opportunity to address their concerns in real time. This two-way communication fosters transparency and can help mitigate negative sentiment.

Additionally, establishing dedicated channels for feedback, such as hotlines, online surveys, or feedback forms, allows stakeholders to express their concerns in a structured manner. These channels can help brands collect quantitative and qualitative data regarding stakeholder sentiments, which can be invaluable for understanding the broader implications of the crisis. Brands can use this feedback to identify common themes, address specific issues, and inform their overall response strategy.

Acknowledge Impact

Publicly acknowledging the impact of a crisis on affected stakeholders is a crucial step in effective crisis management. By validating their feelings, a brand demonstrates that it genuinely cares about its audience and is committed to making amends. This acknowledgment serves as a foundation for rebuilding trust and can significantly influence how stakeholders perceive the brand during challenging times.

When a crisis occurs, affected stakeholders—whether customers, employees, or community members—often experience a range of emotions, including fear, anger, and confusion. By recognizing these feelings publicly, brands show empathy and understanding, which can help mitigate negative sentiment. For example, a brand might issue a statement that explicitly acknowledges the hardships faced by stakeholders due to the crisis, expressing sincere regret for any distress caused. This type of communication not only humanizes the brand but also creates a sense of connection with stakeholders who may feel overlooked or marginalized.

Moreover, acknowledging the impact of the crisis allows a brand to take ownership of the situation. It demonstrates accountability and reinforces the brand's commitment to rectifying the issue. This approach can be especially effective when combined with clear communication about the steps the brand is taking to address the problem. By showing that it understands the consequences of its actions and is actively working to make things right, a brand can foster goodwill and strengthen its relationship with stakeholders.

In essence, public acknowledgment of the crisis's impact on stakeholders is a vital component of a compassionate and effective crisis response. By validating stakeholders' feelings and demonstrating a commitment to addressing their concerns, brands can not only alleviate some of the immediate fallout but also lay the groundwork for a more resilient reputation in the long run. This proactive engagement can turn a challenging situation into an opportunity for growth and improvement, ultimately benefiting both the brand and its stakeholders.

Tailored Communication

Crafting messages that specifically address the concerns of different stakeholder groups is crucial during a crisis, as it ensures that each group feels heard and valued. The first step is to identify the key stakeholders impacted by the crisis, which may include customers, employees, investors, suppliers, community members, and the media. Each group has unique concerns and information needs, necessitating tailored messaging.

For customers, the focus should be on safety, product quality, and the steps being taken to resolve the issue. Reassuring them about their well-being and outlining actions to prevent future occurrences can help mitigate anxiety. Employees should receive messages that address their job security and the company's commitment to providing support during the crisis. It's essential to share information on the company's plans for moving forward and how employees will play a role in the recovery process. Investors will require insight into the potential impacts on business performance and the strategies being employed to mitigate risks, emphasizing transparency and reassurance about the long-term vision for recovery.

When communicating with suppliers, brands should discuss the situation's impact on supply chains and any changes to existing contracts, express appreciation for their partnership, and assure them of a commitment to maintaining strong relationships. Community members should be acknowledged regarding the crisis's effect on their local environment, with brands outlining how they plan to contribute to recovery efforts, such as donations or collaborations with local organizations. For the media, providing clear and accurate information is essential for helping them report on the situation. Proactively sharing updates and designating a point of contact for inquiries can facilitate effective communication.

Utilizing appropriate channels for each group is vital. Social media may be effective for quickly reaching customers, while email newsletters might be more suitable for internal communications with employees. Press releases can be used to engage with media and investors. Each message should reflect empathy and understanding of the stakeholders' feelings, acknowledging their concerns and frustrations while conveying a commitment to addressing the situation responsibly. Encouraging feedback from stakeholders can foster trust and demonstrate that the brand values their input. By ensuring that messages are tailored to the unique concerns of different stakeholder groups, brands can enhance their credibility, build trust, and promote a sense of community during a crisis, ultimately laying the foundation for stronger relationships in the future.

Apologies That Work: Crafting Sincere, Effective Responses

A well-crafted apology can be a powerful tool in crisis management, but it's essential to recognize that not all apologies are created equal. For an apology to be effective, it must be sincere and address several key components that resonate with stakeholders. First and foremost, a genuine apology should acknowledge the wrongdoing or harm caused, demonstrating an understanding of the issue at hand. This acknowledgment is crucial in validating the feelings and concerns of those affected, as it shows that the brand is taking the matter seriously. Table 8.1 presents the key elements of a sincere apology along with examples of effective versus ineffective apologies.

In addition to recognition, a sincere apology should express remorse. This means articulating genuine regret for the situation and its impact on stakeholders. It's not enough to simply say "I'm sorry"; the message

Table 8.1 This table presents key elements of a sincere apology, highlighting the differences between effective and ineffective apologies to guide organizations in crafting responses that promote accountability and trust

Apology component	Description	Effective example	Ineffective example
Acknowledgement	Recognizing the mistake or harm caused.	"We acknowledge that our product failed to meet safety standards."	"Some customers had issues, but we think it was overblown."
Explanation	Providing context or reasons without making excuses.	"The issue occurred due to a manufacturing error that we are addressing."	"We didn't think it was a big deal; errors happen."
Expression of regret	Clearly stating remorse for the harm caused.	"We are truly sorry for the distress this has caused our customers."	"We're sorry if you felt upset."
Commitment to change	Outlining steps to prevent future occurrences.	"We are implementing stricter quality controls and a thorough review process."	"We'll look into it if we have time."
Reparative action	Offering restitution or support to affected stakeholders.	"We are offering refunds and support to all affected customers."	"We can't do much about it now."

should convey empathy and understanding of how the crisis has affected others. This emotional connection can help rebuild trust and demonstrate that the brand values its relationship with its stakeholders.

Moreover, an effective apology must include a commitment to change. Stakeholders need assurance that the brand is not only acknowledging its mistakes but is also taking concrete steps to prevent similar issues from occurring in the future. This could involve outlining specific actions the brand plans to implement, such as revising policies, enhancing training programs, or increasing transparency in operations. By demonstrating accountability and a proactive approach, brands can reinforce their commitment to improvement.

Finally, it's vital that the apology is delivered in a timely manner. The longer a brand waits to address the issue, the more room there is for speculation, anger, and distrust to grow. A prompt and transparent response, accompanied by a heartfelt apology, can significantly mitigate reputational damage and demonstrate a brand's dedication to its stakeholders. An effective apology in crisis management requires sincere acknowledgment of the problem, expression of genuine remorse, a commitment to change, and timely delivery, all of which can help restore trust and credibility in the brand.

Be Specific

Clearly articulating what the brand is apologizing for is a crucial element of an effective apology. Specificity in the apology demonstrates that the brand not only understands the issue at hand but also acknowledges the impact it has had on stakeholders. By detailing the particular actions, decisions, or events that led to the crisis, the brand can convey a sense of accountability and ownership over its mistakes.

For example, instead of offering a vague apology for "any inconvenience caused," a brand should specify the nature of the problem, such as, "We apologize for the contamination of our product, which resulted in health risks for our customers." This level of detail shows that the brand is aware of the specific harm caused and is willing to confront the reality of the situation head-on.

Additionally, being specific about the issue can help to eliminate ambiguity and reduce speculation among stakeholders. When brands articulate exactly what went wrong, it allows for a more transparent dialogue and helps to rebuild trust. Stakeholders are more likely to feel reassured when they see that the brand is addressing the exact nature of the crisis rather than glossing over it with generalized statements.

A well-crafted apology should clearly state what the brand is apologizing for, demonstrating an understanding of the specific issues involved. This clarity not only fosters trust but also signals a commitment to accountability and resolution, ultimately aiding in the brand's recovery from the crisis.

Express Regret

Using language that conveys genuine regret is essential for crafting an effective apology during a crisis. Phrases such as "We are truly sorry for …" resonate more deeply with stakeholders than generic statements like "We apologize for the inconvenience." This type of language shows empathy and acknowledges the emotional and practical repercussions of the crisis on those affected.

When brands articulate their regret sincerely, they create a more personal connection with their audience. This genuine tone indicates that the brand recognizes the severity of the situation and the pain it has caused, whether it be financial loss, health risks, or emotional distress. For instance, saying, "We are truly sorry for the distress and uncertainty caused by our product recall" demonstrates that the brand is not only aware of the facts but also understands the feelings of those impacted.

Additionally, expressing regret in this manner can help mitigate feelings of anger or disappointment among stakeholders. When consumers see that a brand acknowledges the impact of its actions and communicates a heartfelt apology, it can significantly influence their perception of the brand's sincerity and commitment to making amends. This genuine expression of regret can play a crucial role in rebuilding trust and fostering goodwill in the aftermath of a crisis.

Ultimately, using empathetic and sincere language in an apology signals to stakeholders that the brand cares about its impact on their lives. It fosters a sense of understanding and can pave the way for more constructive dialogue, making it easier for the brand to navigate the recovery process and restore its reputation.

Commit to Change

An effective apology during a crisis must go beyond expressing regret; it should also include a clear commitment to change. This commitment reassures stakeholders that the brand is taking the situation seriously and is dedicated to preventing similar issues in the future. To craft this part of the apology effectively, brands should start by identifying the root cause of the crisis. This transparency helps stakeholders understand that the brand has conducted a thorough investigation and is addressing the underlying problems.

Next, brands should outline specific actions they will take to rectify the situation, such as enhancing quality control measures, improving employee training programs, or implementing new safety protocols. For instance, a food brand might announce a commitment to more rigorous testing of ingredients to prevent contamination. Establishing measurable objectives that the brand aims to achieve as part of its commitment to change can further enhance credibility. This could include setting a goal to reduce product recalls by a certain percentage within the next year or achieving specific safety certifications.

Providing a timeline for when stakeholders can expect to see these changes implemented helps build trust and shows that the brand is taking immediate action to resolve the issues at hand. Additionally, encouraging stakeholder involvement in the improvement process, such as soliciting feedback or creating advisory panels that include customers and employees, fosters a sense of community and shared responsibility. Finally, brands should commit to ongoing communication about the steps taken to prevent similar crises, providing regular updates to reassure stakeholders that the brand is following through on its promises. By incorporating these elements into the apology, brands can effectively communicate their commitment to change, restore trust with stakeholders, and position themselves as organizations that learn from their mistakes and strive for continuous improvement.

Case Studies

Several brands have successfully navigated crises by taking ownership of the problem, leading to positive outcomes.

Nestlé and the Water Crisis

Nestlé faced significant backlash for its water extraction practices during drought conditions, which raised serious ethical and environmental concerns. As communities struggled with water scarcity, the company's operations in areas experiencing severe drought drew criticism from activists and consumers alike. In response to the mounting pressure, Nestlé took ownership of the problem by publicly acknowledging the concerns surrounding its water extraction practices. This move signaled to stakeholders that the company recognized the impact of its operations on local communities and the environment.

Nestlé committed to implementing sustainable water practices, which included reassessing its water extraction methods and engaging with local communities to understand their needs better. By addressing the crisis transparently and outlining specific steps toward improvement, the company aimed to rebuild trust and demonstrate its commitment to corporate responsibility. Although the backlash was significant, Nestlé's proactive approach allowed it to mitigate some of the damage to its reputation. By fostering open dialogue and taking tangible actions toward sustainability, Nestlé positioned itself as a brand that is willing to learn from its mistakes and prioritize the well-being of the communities it serves. This incident serves as a testament to the importance of ownership in crisis management, illustrating that a sincere acknowledgment of issues can pave the way for recovery and positive change.

Toyota and the Acceleration Crisis

Another notable example of a brand that took ownership of a crisis is Toyota during the unintended acceleration crisis in 2009 to 2010. The automotive giant faced significant scrutiny and backlash after reports emerged of vehicles accelerating unexpectedly, leading to accidents and fatalities.

In response, Toyota quickly took ownership of the problem by publicly acknowledging the issue and halting sales of affected models. The company launched a massive recall, which involved millions of vehicles worldwide, demonstrating its commitment to addressing the safety concerns of its customers. Toyota's then-CEO, Akio Toyoda, delivered a heartfelt apology to the public, emphasizing the company's dedication to customer safety and satisfaction.

Additionally, Toyota implemented extensive measures to improve its quality control and safety protocols, including revising its engineering practices and investing in new technologies to enhance vehicle safety. This proactive response not only addressed the immediate crisis but also aimed to restore consumer confidence in the brand. By taking ownership of the problem and showing a genuine commitment to change, Toyota was able to mitigate reputational damage and ultimately rebuild its brand image over time. The incident serves as an important reminder of the significance of accountability in crisis management and the positive outcomes that can arise from taking responsibility.

Volkswagen and the Emissions Scandal

One notable example of a brand that did not take ownership of a problem is Volkswagen during the emissions scandal that came to light in 2015. The scandal revealed that Volkswagen had installed software in their diesel vehicles designed to cheat emissions tests, which misled regulators and customers about the true level of harmful emissions produced by their cars.

Initially, Volkswagen's response was defensive and evasive, with top executives denying knowledge of the wrongdoing and downplaying the severity of the issue. Instead of taking immediate responsibility, the company attempted to shift the blame to a few engineers. This lack of ownership not only resulted in a significant backlash from consumers and regulators but also led to long-lasting reputational damage.

The consequences for Volkswagen were severe, including billions in fines, a sharp decline in consumer trust, and a dramatic drop in sales. Additionally, the company faced numerous lawsuits and a loss of market share, especially in the United States. This failure to take ownership compounded the crisis, demonstrating that a lack of accountability can exacerbate the fallout from a brand crisis.

United Airlines and the Passenger Removal Incident

Another example of a brand that did not take ownership of a problem is United Airlines during the infamous incident in 2017 when a passenger, Dr. David Dao, was forcibly removed from an overbooked flight. The incident was captured on video and quickly went viral, sparking outrage and backlash against the airline (Figure 8.1).

Initially, United Airlines' response was inadequate and defensive. The CEO, Oscar Munoz, issued a statement describing the incident as "reaccommodating" the passenger, which many interpreted as dismissive of the seriousness of the situation. Instead of taking immediate responsibility and acknowledging the distress caused to Dr. Dao, the airline attempted to shift the narrative by emphasizing its policies on overbooking and its need to accommodate crew members.

This lack of ownership exacerbated public outrage and led to a significant decline in the airline's reputation. The incident resulted in widespread media coverage, a drop in stock prices, and a significant backlash from consumers who felt that United Airlines did not prioritize customer safety and dignity. It took several days and mounting pressure before Munoz issued a more sincere apology and acknowledged the company's role in the incident. However, the initial failure to take ownership contributed to the prolonged damage to United Airlines' brand reputation.

Conclusion

Taking ownership of the problem is a cornerstone of effective crisis management. It demonstrates accountability, empathy, and a

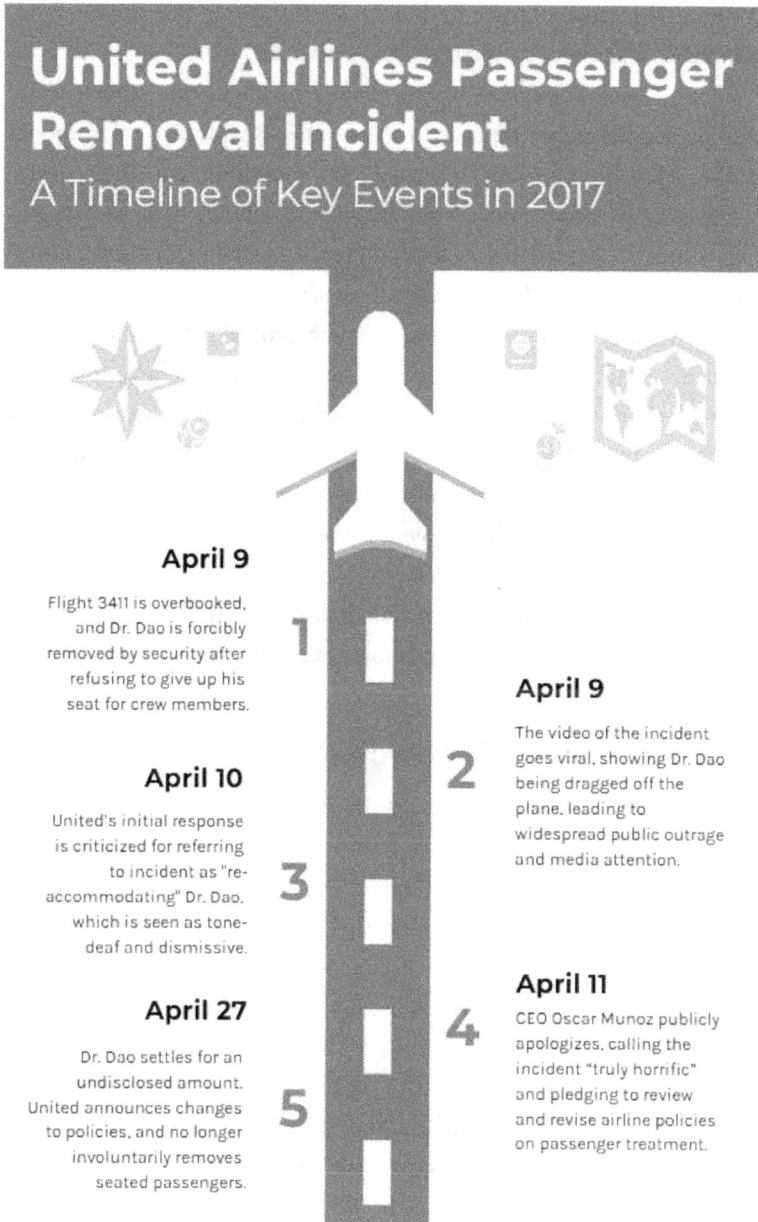

United Airlines Passenger Removal Incident
A Timeline of Key Events in 2017

April 9

Flight 3411 is overbooked, and Dr. Dao is forcibly removed by security after refusing to give up his seat for crew members.

April 10

United's initial response is criticized for referring to incident as "re-accommodating" Dr. Dao, which is seen as tone-deaf and dismissive.

April 27

Dr. Dao settles for an undisclosed amount. United announces changes to policies, and no longer involuntarily removes seated passengers.

April 9

The video of the incident goes viral, showing Dr. Dao being dragged off the plane, leading to widespread public outrage and media attention.

April 11

CEO Oscar Munoz publicly apologizes, calling the incident "truly horrific" and pledging to review and revise airline policies on passenger treatment.

Figure 8.1 United airlines passenger removal incident

commitment to addressing the issue, which are essential for maintaining trust and credibility. Acknowledging responsibility allows brands to connect with stakeholders on a human level, showing that the organization values transparency and is dedicated to doing what is right.

The examples discussed in this chapter highlight the importance of owning a crisis rather than deflecting blame. Brands that take responsibility and communicate their plans for resolution can often turn a challenging situation into an opportunity to rebuild trust and loyalty. Conversely, those that fail to own the problem risk deeper reputational damage and prolonged stakeholder dissatisfaction.

Ownership is a proactive and ongoing process. Organizations that foster a culture of accountability and implement structures for transparent reporting and feedback are better positioned to manage crises effectively. By taking swift and sincere actions, brands can not only mitigate immediate fallout but also lay the groundwork for recovery.

Ultimately, owning the problem is the first step toward demonstrating leadership in the face of adversity. It sets the stage for rebuilding trust, strengthening stakeholder relationships, and emerging from a crisis with a more resilient and credible brand identity.

Further Reading

Chan, E.Y., and M. Palmeira. 2021. "Political Ideology Moderates Consumer Response to Brand Crisis Apologies for Data Breaches." *Computers in Human Behavior* 121: 106801.

Lee, So Young., and L. Atkinson. 2019. "Never Easy to say 'Sorry': Exploring the Interplay of Crisis Involvement, Brand Image, and Message Appeal in Developing Effective Corporate Apologies." *Public Relations Review* 45 (1): 178–88.

Lee, SoYoung, and Taemin Kim. 2024. "Brand Recovery After Crisis: The Interplay of Relationship Norms and Types of Brand Apology in Consumer Responses to Recovery Efforts." *Journal of Marketing Communications* 30 (6): 637–59.

Wang, L., E.Y. Chan, and A. Gohary. 2023. "Consumers' Attributions in Performance-and Values-Related Brand Crises." *European Journal of Marketing* 57 (12): 3162–181.

Yuan, D., G. Cui, and L. Lai. 2016. "Sorry Seems to be the Hardest Word: Consumer Reactions to Self-Attributions by Firms Apologizing for a Brand Crisis." *Journal of Consumer Marketing* 33 (4): 281–91.

CHAPTER 9

R = Rebuilding Trust

Overview

- Outlines steps to regain customer trust and loyalty after a crisis.
- Discusses the balance between short-term actions and long-term reputation repair.
- Explores strategies like rebranding or repositioning to rebuild relationships.
- Includes examples of brands that effectively restored trust and strengthened stakeholder bonds.

Once the immediate crisis is resolved, the next vital step is rebuilding trust. A brand's reputation can take a significant hit during a crisis, but with intentional strategies and actions, it can recover and emerge stronger. Trust is the foundation of the relationship between a brand and its stakeholders, and it must be carefully nurtured after a crisis has occurred. This chapter discusses essential steps for recovering after a crisis, including acknowledging the impact of the crisis on stakeholders, demonstrating empathy, and taking concrete actions to prevent future issues. It also explores strategies for restoring customer trust, emphasizing the importance of transparent communication, accountability, and consistency in messaging. Furthermore, this chapter highlights successful case studies of brands that have navigated this critical phase effectively, showcasing how they rebuilt their reputations and regained stakeholder confidence. By examining these examples, brands can learn valuable lessons on the importance of trust and the steps necessary to cultivate and maintain it in the aftermath of a crisis.

Steps for Recovering After the Crisis Is Resolved

Recovery begins as soon as the crisis has subsided, and brands must be proactive in initiating the rebuilding process. The first step is to conduct a postcrisis evaluation, which involves analyzing the crisis's impact on the brand and identifying the lessons learned. This evaluation should focus on understanding what went wrong, assessing the effectiveness of the brand's response, and determining areas for improvement. By thoroughly examining the crisis, brands can gain valuable insights that will inform their future strategies.

Next, engaging with stakeholders is crucial. Brands should reach out to customers, employees, and other relevant parties to understand their feelings and concerns regarding the crisis. This engagement can take various forms, such as surveys, focus groups, or direct communication through social media platforms. By listening to stakeholders and acknowledging their perspectives, brands can demonstrate their commitment to rebuilding trust and ensuring that their voices are heard.

Finally, clear and transparent communication about the steps taken to address the issues that led to the crisis is essential. Brands should keep stakeholders informed about the progress made in implementing changes and improvements. Regular updates can reassure stakeholders that the brand is committed to learning from the experience and preventing similar issues in the future. By maintaining open lines of communication and demonstrating accountability, brands can gradually rebuild trust and restore their reputations.

Conduct a Postcrisis Evaluation

Assessing the effectiveness of a crisis management response is a critical step in the rebuilding process. Brands must carefully evaluate their actions during the crisis to identify what worked well and what fell short. This evaluation should involve analyzing key performance indicators such as stakeholder sentiment, media coverage, and customer feedback. By examining these metrics, brands can determine the impact of their crisis response on their reputation and stakeholder relationships.

One effective strategy during a crisis may have been timely and transparent communication, which can help to quell misinformation and foster trust. However, brands must also identify areas where their response may have lacked effectiveness, such as delays in communication or failure to address specific stakeholder concerns. Recognizing these shortcomings is essential for developing more effective strategies in future crises.

Gathering feedback from stakeholders is equally important in this assessment process. Brands should reach out to customers, employees, and other relevant parties to solicit their opinions on the crisis response. This can be achieved through surveys, interviews, or focus groups, allowing stakeholders to share their experiences and suggestions for improvement. By actively listening to stakeholders and incorporating their feedback into future strategies, brands can better align their crisis management efforts with stakeholder expectations, ultimately enhancing their preparedness for any future challenges.

Engage With Stakeholders

Continuing the conversation with stakeholders is essential for effectively rebuilding trust after a crisis. Brands must actively engage with customers, employees, and partners, showing that they value their input and concerns. This ongoing dialogue not only helps to reinforce transparency but also fosters a collaborative environment where stakeholders feel heard and appreciated.

For customers, this can involve regular updates about the steps the brand is taking to address the issues that led to the crisis. Brands can use various channels such as social media, newsletters, and community forums to keep customers informed and encourage feedback. By addressing customer concerns directly and promptly, brands can demonstrate that they are committed to improving their products or services and are willing to make necessary changes based on consumer input.

For employees, maintaining open lines of communication is crucial for rebuilding morale and trust within the organization. Brands should hold regular meetings, town halls, or feedback sessions to discuss the crisis's impact, share updates on recovery efforts, and provide a platform for employees to voice their opinions and suggestions. This approach fosters a sense of inclusion and encourages employees to feel more invested in the brand's recovery journey.

Engaging partners and other stakeholders in the recovery process is equally important. Brands can collaborate with partners to share insights, strategies, and best practices for crisis management. This cooperative approach not only enhances the brand's credibility but also demonstrates a commitment to collective improvement and accountability. By fostering a sense of partnership and collaboration, brands can strengthen their relationships with all stakeholders and pave the way for a more resilient and trusted future.

Communicate Progress

Regularly updating stakeholders on the steps taken to address the issues that led to the crisis is a crucial element of rebuilding trust. This transparency reassures stakeholders that the brand is not only aware of the problems but is actively working to implement positive changes. By providing consistent updates, brands can foster a sense of accountability and demonstrate their commitment to continuous improvement.

These updates can take various forms, including detailed reports, newsletters, or social media posts, tailored to the specific concerns of different stakeholder groups. For customers, sharing information about product improvements, safety measures, or service enhancements can help rebuild confidence in the brand. Similarly, for employees, updates on internal changes, training programs, and support initiatives can bolster morale and engagement.

Moreover, being open about challenges faced during the recovery process can further humanize the brand. Acknowledging setbacks, while communicating the lessons learned, shows stakeholders that the brand is committed to growth and integrity. This candid approach not only helps to mend relationships but also creates a foundation for long-term trust and loyalty. By maintaining regular communication and demonstrating genuine commitment to change, brands can effectively reassure stakeholders and pave the way for a stronger, more resilient future.

Strategies for Restoring Customer Trust and Brand Loyalty

Rebuilding trust is not a one-time effort; it requires sustained commitment and action. To effectively restore trust and loyalty, brands should implement several key strategies that focus on consistently delivering on promises, creating value-added experiences, and fostering two-way communication with stakeholders.

First and foremost, delivering on promises is essential for rebuilding trust. Brands must ensure that they follow through on commitments made during and after a crisis. This involves not only rectifying the specific issues that led to the crisis but also upholding the brand's overall values and standards. By consistently meeting or exceeding stakeholder expectations, brands demonstrate reliability and integrity, which are crucial for restoring trust.

Creating value-added experiences is another vital strategy. Brands should seek to enhance customer interactions by providing exceptional service, personalized experiences, and meaningful engagement. This could include offering exclusive benefits, rewards programs, or educational resources that resonate with stakeholders. By going above and beyond to add value, brands can foster a deeper emotional connection with their audience, helping to rebuild loyalty and trust.

Finally, fostering two-way communication is critical in the trust-building process. Brands must actively engage with stakeholders, encouraging feedback and open dialogue. This can be achieved through various channels, such as social media, customer surveys, and community events. By listening to stakeholders and responding to their concerns, brands can create a sense of partnership and collaboration. This transparency not only helps to address any lingering issues but also reassures stakeholders that their voices are valued and that the brand is committed to continuous improvement.

Rebuilding trust requires a multi-faceted approach that emphasizes delivering on promises, creating valuable experiences, and maintaining open communication. Through these strategies, brands can cultivate lasting loyalty and emerge from crises with a stronger, more resilient reputation. At the same time, there are different strategies for rebuilding trust in the short-term and in the long-term, as Table 9.1 depicts.

Deliver on Promises

Following through on commitments made during the crisis is a fundamental step in rebuilding trust. If a brand has promised changes or improvements in response to a crisis, it's crucial to deliver on those promises consistently. Failing to do so can lead to skepticism and disappointment among stakeholders, which may further damage the brand's reputation.

When brands demonstrate accountability by implementing the changes they promised, it shows stakeholders that they take their concerns seriously and are committed to making things right. For instance, if a company promised to enhance its safety protocols after a crisis, it should ensure that these measures are effectively put in place and regularly communicated to its audience. This not only reassures stakeholders but also reinforces the brand's credibility.

Moreover, consistent delivery on commitments can foster a sense of loyalty among customers and other stakeholders. When they see that a brand is dedicated to following through on its promises, it cultivates confidence in the brand's ability to manage challenges effectively in the future. This can transform a negative experience into an opportunity for the brand to demonstrate its resilience and commitment to improvement.

In essence, maintaining a consistent track record of fulfilling commitments made during a crisis is vital for restoring trust and rebuilding the brand's reputation. By prioritizing transparency and accountability, brands can create a positive narrative that helps to heal relationships and enhances long-term loyalty.

Create Value-Added Experiences

Re-engaging customers after a crisis is crucial for rebuilding trust and loyalty, and offering value beyond just products or services can play

Table 9.1 This table compares short-term and long-term strategies for restoring customer trust after a crisis, showcasing successful examples of brands that have effectively navigated trust recovery through transparency, engagement, quality improvement, community support, and rebranding efforts

Strategy type	Description	Short-term strategy	Long-term strategy	Example
Transparency	Being open about the crisis and the steps taken to resolve it.	Share immediate updates on crisis management.	Regularly publish transparency reports and updates.	Johnson & Johnson after the Tylenol crisis.
Customer engagement	Actively involving customers in the recovery process.	Host Q&A sessions to address customer concerns.	Create loyalty programs that reward customer feedback.	Starbucks' approach after the racial bias incident.
Quality improvement	Enhancing product or service quality postcrisis.	Quickly resolve product issues and offer refunds.	Invest in R&D for quality assurance and innovation.	Samsung's response after the Galaxy Note 7 recall.
Customer support	Demonstrating commitment to the community.	Participate in community outreach initiatives.	Establish partnerships with local organizations for ongoing support.	Patagonia's commitment to environmental causes.
Rebranding	Refreshing the brand image to signify change.	Launch a campaign focused on accountability.	Develop a long-term branding strategy emphasizing core values and ethics.	Dunkin' Donuts rebranding efforts after the food safety issues.

a significant role in this process. Brands can create meaningful connections with their customers by implementing initiatives that go beyond traditional offerings.

One effective approach is to develop loyalty programs that reward customers for their continued support. These programs can provide exclusive benefits, discounts, or points that can be redeemed for future purchases, encouraging customers to remain loyal to the brand. Such programs not only incentivize repeat business but also demonstrate that the brand values its customers and appreciates their commitment during challenging times.

Additionally, community engagement initiatives can foster a sense of belonging and connection. Brands can support local causes, participate in community events, or even launch initiatives that address relevant social issues. By actively participating in the community, brands show that they care about the well-being of their customers and the broader society, enhancing their reputation and reinforcing customer loyalty.

Educational content is another valuable way to engage customers. By providing resources, tutorials, or informative articles that resonate with customer interests, brands can position themselves as thought leaders in their industry. This not only adds value to the customer experience but also keeps the brand at the forefront of customers' minds, reinforcing their connection to the brand.

Re-engaging customers after a crisis involves offering value that extends beyond products or services. By implementing loyalty programs, engaging with the community, and providing educational content, brands can strengthen relationships with their customers and foster long-term loyalty, ultimately aiding in the recovery of their reputation.

Foster Two-Way Communication

Encouraging feedback and dialogue with customers is essential for rebuilding trust and ensuring that their voices are heard. Implementing mechanisms for ongoing communication can significantly enhance a brand's relationship with its customers, fostering a culture of openness and collaboration.

One effective way to facilitate this feedback loop is through surveys that solicit customer opinions on various aspects of the brand's products or services. By regularly conducting surveys, brands can gather valuable insights into customer preferences, satisfaction levels, and areas needing improvement. This not only shows customers that their opinions matter but also provides the brand with actionable data to refine its offerings and address any concerns that may arise.

In addition to surveys, creating feedback forums or dedicated platforms for customers to share their thoughts and experiences can further promote dialogue. These forums allow customers to engage with one another and with the brand, creating a community atmosphere where customers feel valued and involved. By responding to feedback and engaging in conversations within these forums, brands can demonstrate their commitment to listening and adapting based on customer input.

Moreover, transparency in addressing feedback is crucial. When customers see that their suggestions are being taken seriously—whether through product adjustments, service improvements, or policy changes —they are more likely to feel a deeper connection to the brand. This reciprocal relationship not only strengthens loyalty but also helps brands identify emerging issues before they escalate into larger problems.

Fostering feedback and dialogue with customers through surveys, feedback forums, and transparent communication channels is vital for rebuilding trust. By valuing customer input and actively engaging with their concerns, brands can create a loyal customer base that feels invested in the brand's success and future.

Long-Term Reputation Repair: Actions Versus Words

Words alone are insufficient for repairing a damaged reputation; brands must prioritize actions over rhetoric. While effective communication is essential during a crisis, it is the consistent follow-through on promises that ultimately restores stakeholder confidence. Consistency is key to demonstrating genuine commitment to change and accountability. When brands consistently deliver on their promises and adhere to their stated values, they begin to rebuild the trust that may have been lost during a crisis.

Emphasizing positive changes is also crucial in the rebuilding process. Brands should highlight the specific actions they are taking to rectify issues and improve their practices. By showcasing tangible improvements—whether in product quality, customer service, or community engagement—brands can reinforce their commitment to doing better. This not only helps to counter negative perceptions but also serves as a reminder that the brand is evolving and learning from past mistakes.

Moreover, building trust through engagement is an ongoing effort that requires sustained interaction with stakeholders. Brands should actively seek to involve customers, employees, and partners in the rebuilding process by encouraging feedback and facilitating open dialogue. This collaborative approach not only fosters a sense of community but also demonstrates that the brand values stakeholder input and is committed to making meaningful changes based on that feedback.

Repairing a damaged reputation demands a concerted effort that goes beyond mere words. By prioritizing consistent actions, emphasizing positive changes, and engaging with stakeholders, brands can rebuild trust and emerge stronger from a crisis. Actions truly speak louder than words, and it is through these deliberate efforts that brands can repair their reputations and restore stakeholder confidence.

Consistency Is Key

Ensuring that messaging aligns with actions is critical for rebuilding trust after a crisis. When a brand communicates intentions or promises but fails to follow through with corresponding actions, it creates a gap that can lead to skepticism among stakeholders. This discrepancy not only undermines the credibility of the brand but can also exacerbate the negative perceptions formed during the crisis. Stakeholders, including customers and employees, are more likely to feel betrayed if they perceive that a brand's words do not match its deeds.

To avoid this pitfall, brands must adopt a transparent approach, where their communications accurately reflect their operational realities. This alignment can be achieved by setting realistic goals and timelines for change, then transparently reporting progress against these commitments. For instance, if a brand promises to improve its sustainability practices, it should share updates and results on those initiatives, showcasing tangible improvements and demonstrating accountability. Such transparency helps mitigate skepticism and reinforces the brand's commitment to its stated values.

Moreover, consistent messaging reinforces the brand's narrative and helps rebuild stakeholder confidence. When stakeholders see that a brand is not only talking about change but also actively implementing it, they are more likely to trust the brand's intentions and engage positively. This approach fosters a sense of reliability and integrity, which is essential for long-term relationship building.

Aligning messaging with actions is vital for restoring trust and credibility after a crisis. By ensuring that promises are met with genuine efforts and transparent communication, brands can effectively mitigate skepticism and build stronger, more trusting relationships with their stakeholders.

Emphasize Positive Changes

Highlighting the positive changes made as a result of a crisis is essential for rebuilding trust and demonstrating a brand's commitment to improvement. By showcasing specific enhancements in product quality, customer service, or ethical practices, brands can effectively communicate their dedication to addressing the issues that led to the crisis.

For instance, if a brand faced criticism over product quality, it could detail the steps taken to enhance manufacturing processes, invest in higher-quality materials, or implement more rigorous quality control measures. Sharing testimonials or case studies from satisfied customers can further reinforce the positive impact of these changes, illustrating a tangible commitment to providing superior products.

In terms of customer service, brands can highlight the implementation of new training programs for employees that focus on improving customer interactions. This could include initiatives like enhanced response times, personalized service approaches, or the introduction of new support channels such as live chat or dedicated customer care teams. Publicizing these improvements through various communication channels—such as social media, press releases, and newsletters—can effectively reach a broad audience and signal to stakeholders that the brand is taking meaningful steps to enhance their experience.

Additionally, if the crisis brought to light ethical concerns—such as labor practices or environmental sustainability—brands should actively communicate their efforts to address these issues. This might involve sharing partnerships with reputable organizations to ensure ethical sourcing, adopting sustainable practices, or initiating community engagement programs that give back to affected communities. Highlighting these positive changes not only demonstrates accountability but also positions the brand as a responsible and socially aware entity.

By consistently showcasing these improvements, brands can foster a renewed sense of trust and loyalty among stakeholders, emphasizing their commitment to not just recovering from a crisis but emerging stronger and more resilient.

Built Trust Through Engagement

Consistently engaging with stakeholders through meaningful interactions is a crucial aspect of rebuilding trust and repairing a brand's reputation after a crisis. This ongoing dialogue allows brands to demonstrate authenticity and a genuine commitment to improvement, which can significantly help mend relationships over time.

To foster these meaningful interactions, brands should prioritize open lines of communication with their stakeholders, including customers, employees, and partners. This can be achieved through various channels, such as social media platforms, newsletters, and in-person events. Actively soliciting feedback and encouraging discussions around their products or services can show stakeholders that their opinions are valued and taken seriously. For instance, brands might conduct surveys, host Q&A sessions, or create forums where stakeholders can voice their thoughts and concerns.

Moreover, it's important for brands to respond to feedback in a timely and thoughtful manner. Acknowledging suggestions, addressing complaints, and making adjustments based on stakeholder input can demonstrate a brand's commitment to continuous improvement. This responsive approach helps create a sense of partnership, where stakeholders feel they have a stake in the brand's evolution.

Additionally, brands can share updates on their progress toward implementing the changes promised during the crisis. By regularly communicating these advancements—such as improvements in product quality or customer service initiatives—brands can keep stakeholders informed and engaged. Sharing success stories or milestones achieved as a result of stakeholder feedback reinforces the idea that the brand values their input and is committed to making positive changes.

The April 2017 United Airlines incident involving Dr. David Dao, who was forcibly removed from an overbooked flight, became a public relations crisis. United's initial response on social media—stating they were "looking into the matter" (Figure 9.1)—appeared to be swift, acknowledging the issue without delay. However, the company struggled to follow up with decisive, visible actions that addressed the widespread outrage over Dr. Dao's treatment. This lack of effective follow-through on their promise to address the incident publicly caused efforts to restore trust with passengers to falter, leading to ongoing criticism. Many perceived United's handling as insincere and reactionary, failing to bridge the gap between online acknowledgment and real, impactful action.

Overall, consistent engagement, authenticity, and responsiveness in these interactions can help rebuild trust and strengthen relationships with stakeholders, ultimately leading to a more resilient brand in the long term.

Rebranding and Repositioning After a Crisis (If Necessary)

In some cases, a brand may need to consider rebranding or repositioning to recover effectively from a crisis. This process involves several crucial

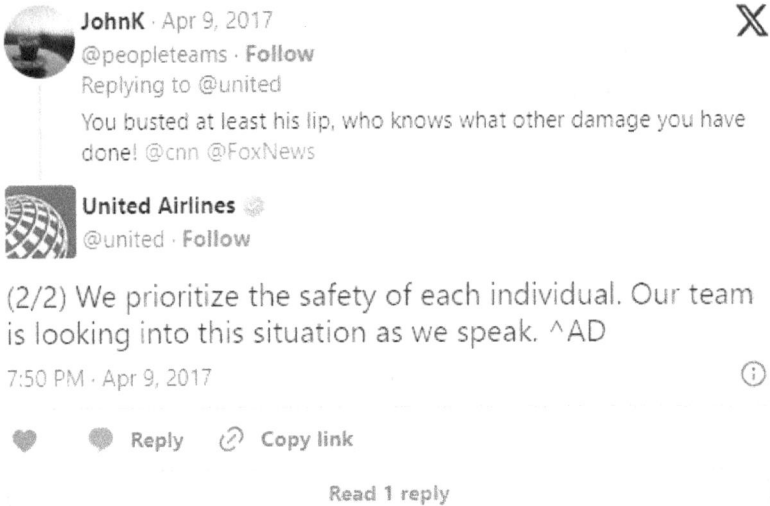

JohnK · Apr 9, 2017

@peopleteams · **Follow**

Replying to @united

You busted at least his lip, who knows what other damage you have
done! @cnn @FoxNews

United Airlines

@united · **Follow**

(2/2) We prioritize the safety of each individual. Our team
is looking into this situation as we speak. ^AD

7:50 PM · Apr 9, 2017

♥   🔁 Reply   Copy link

Read 1 reply

Figure 9.1 John K/United Airlines

steps, beginning with an evaluation of the current brand perception
among stakeholders. Understanding how the crisis has altered public
sentiment can provide valuable insights into what aspects of the brand
may need to be changed or emphasized. Conducting surveys, focus
groups, or social media analysis can help brands gauge the feelings of
their audience and identify specific areas for improvement.

Once the evaluation is complete, developing a new brand narrative becomes essential. This narrative should reflect the lessons learned
from the crisis and articulate the brand's commitment to change. A
compelling narrative can help reshape the brand's identity, emphasizing
its strengths and values while addressing any shortcomings revealed
during the crisis. This new story should resonate with both existing and
potential customers, creating a connection that fosters loyalty and trust.

Effective communication of these changes is vital for successful
rebranding. Brands must ensure that their messaging is clear, consistent, and aligned across all channels. This may include updating logos,
taglines, marketing materials, and even social media profiles to reflect
the new direction. Additionally, engaging stakeholders in the rebranding process can help create a sense of ownership and buy-in. Brands
might consider launching a campaign that invites customer feedback

on the rebranding efforts or sharing behind-the-scenes insights into the transformation journey.

Ultimately, rebranding or repositioning after a crisis is not merely about changing visual elements or messaging; it requires a deep understanding of the brand's values and a commitment to living up to them. By thoughtfully evaluating brand perception, crafting a new narrative, and effectively communicating changes, brands can emerge from a crisis with renewed strength and a more positive reputation.

Evaluate Brand Perception

Conducting market research is essential for understanding how a crisis has affected brand perception and identifying potential areas for rebranding. The process involves several key steps. First, brands should distribute surveys to gather quantitative data from a broad audience, focusing on questions that assess brand awareness, customer loyalty, and overall perception before and after the crisis. This approach helps identify shifts in sentiment and any lingering negative associations. Additionally, organizing focus groups with diverse stakeholders, including customers, employees, and industry experts, can provide qualitative insights into how the crisis has impacted perceptions and what specific aspects of the brand may need re-evaluation.

Another important step is to monitor social media platforms to analyze conversations surrounding the brand. Tools that track sentiment analysis can help gauge public opinion, identify trends, and highlight areas of concern. It's crucial to pay attention to recurring themes in comments, shares, and posts related to the crisis. Brands should also assess how competitors are positioned in the market postcrisis, as understanding their strategies can provide insights into potential gaps in the brand's approach and highlight areas where rebranding may be beneficial to distinguish the brand from negative associations.

Conducting a thorough audit of all brand materials, including logos, messaging, and marketing campaigns, is also necessary. This audit allows brands to evaluate whether these elements align with the desired brand image moving forward, identifying outdated or negatively associated components that may need rebranding. Implementing ongoing feedback mechanisms, such as customer service channels, online reviews, and feedback forms, can further gather insights into how stakeholders view the brand's current initiatives, informing necessary changes and improvements.

Once the research is complete, brands can analyze the findings to pinpoint specific areas where rebranding could effectively distance them from negative associations. This may involve updating the brand's visual identity, altering messaging to focus on positive changes, or repositioning the brand within the market to emphasize new values and commitments. By thoroughly understanding the crisis's impact on brand perception, companies can make informed decisions that facilitate successful rebranding efforts and help restore trust with stakeholders.

Develop a New Brand Narrative

If rebranding is deemed necessary, it is crucial to craft a new narrative that aligns with the brand's core values and vision for the future. This narrative should begin by acknowledging past mistakes, taking responsibility for the impact they had on stakeholders, and illustrating a sincere understanding of the issues at hand. By openly addressing these challenges, the brand demonstrates accountability and transparency, which are vital for rebuilding trust.

Following this acknowledgment, the narrative should shift focus to the brand's commitment to improvement. It should articulate clear, actionable steps the brand will take to rectify past mistakes and prevent similar issues in the future. This could include initiatives aimed at enhancing product quality, implementing ethical business practices, or fostering a more inclusive company culture. By detailing these commitments, the brand signals to its audience that it is not only aware of past shortcomings but is also dedicated to making meaningful changes.

Additionally, the new narrative should reflect the brand's aspirations and vision moving forward. It should paint a picture of the brand as a responsible and forward-thinking entity, one that prioritizes stakeholder well-being and sustainability. This vision can be reinforced through storytelling that highlights positive changes, community engagement efforts, and collaborations with stakeholders. By creating a narrative that authentically addresses past issues while celebrating future goals, the brand can effectively reposition itself in the market, fostering renewed loyalty and trust among its audience.

Communicate Changes Effectively

When launching a rebrand, it's essential to clearly communicate the reasons behind the change and the steps taken to create a more trustworthy brand. Transparency during this process is critical to gaining acceptance from stakeholders, as it helps to alleviate concerns and rebuild confidence. By articulating the motivations for the rebrand—whether stemming from lessons learned during a crisis, changes in market dynamics, or a shift in company values—brands can help their audience understand the rationale behind the transformation.

Providing detailed information about the specific steps taken to ensure a more trustworthy brand is equally important. This might include initiatives aimed at improving product quality, enhancing customer service, adopting more ethical business practices, or implementing rigorous quality control measures. By sharing these details, brands not only demonstrate accountability but also show that they are committed to meaningful change. Engaging storytelling can enhance this message, making the reasons for the rebrand relatable and emphasizing the brand's commitment to its stakeholders.

Additionally, brands should create multiple touchpoints for communication throughout the rebranding process. This can involve utilizing social media platforms, email newsletters, press releases, and community events to keep stakeholders informed and engaged. Encouraging feedback and dialogue allows brands to listen to their audience's concerns and suggestions, fostering a sense of collaboration. Ultimately, a transparent and well-communicated rebranding effort can significantly enhance trust, allowing brands to emerge from a crisis with renewed credibility and a stronger connection to their audience.

Case Studies

Several brands have demonstrated resilience and successfully rebuilt trust following crises, such as Oxfam that, eventually, was able to rebuild trust after the sexual misconduct scandal in 2018. Meanwhile, Johnson & Johnson's handling of the Tylenol cyanide crisis in 1982 showcased their commitment to consumer safety through swift action and transparent communication, allowing them to regain trust over time. Similarly, Pepsi's 1993 incident involving a false claim about a syringe in a can was managed effectively through transparency and a strong public relations campaign, ultimately reinforcing the brand's commitment to quality.

In contrast, Wells Fargo serves as a cautionary tale of a brand that did not successfully rebuild trust after its fake accounts scandal. Despite implementing changes and replacing leadership, the bank struggled to restore its reputation. The initial failure to take full ownership of the problem, coupled with ongoing scrutiny and public skepticism, hindered their recovery efforts. This example highlights the challenges brands face when they fail to adequately address crises and rebuild stakeholder confidence.

Oxfam and the Sexual Misconduct Scandal

The Oxfam scandal that erupted in early 2018 centered around allegations of sexual misconduct involving staff members in Haiti following the 2010 earthquake. Reports surfaced that some Oxfam employees had engaged in sexual exploitation and abuse while on a humanitarian mission. This scandal was particularly damaging for Oxfam, an organization dedicated to humanitarian aid and social justice, as it contradicted its core values and raised serious questions about its commitment to safeguarding vulnerable populations.

Initially, Oxfam's response to the scandal was met with criticism for its perceived lack of transparency. However, the organization quickly recognized the gravity of the situation and took decisive steps to address the crisis and rebuild trust. Oxfam publicly acknowledged the allegations, launched an internal investigation, and cooperated fully with external inquiries. This openness was crucial in signaling to stakeholders that the organization was taking the matter seriously.

In the aftermath of the scandal, Oxfam implemented a series of reforms aimed at strengthening its safeguarding policies and practices. The organization established a new global safeguarding team, enhanced training programs for staff on issues of harassment and misconduct, and introduced more rigorous vetting processes for employees and volunteers. These actions demonstrated a commitment to accountability and a willingness to learn from past mistakes.

Oxfam also engaged in transparent communication with the public and its supporters, regularly updating them on the progress of its reforms and initiatives to prevent future incidents. By being forthright about the challenges it faced and the steps it was taking to rectify them, Oxfam was able to gradually restore its reputation and rebuild trust among its stakeholders. The organization emphasized its dedication to ethical practices and safeguarding vulnerable populations, reminding supporters of its vital work in humanitarian efforts worldwide. As a result, Oxfam has been able to move forward from the scandal, although it continues to be vigilant in its commitment to maintaining the highest ethical standards in its operations.

Johnson & Johnson and the Tylenol Crisis

In 1982, Johnson & Johnson found itself in the midst of a significant crisis when several individuals tragically died after consuming cyanide-laced Tylenol capsules. This crisis not only posed a serious threat to public health but also jeopardized the company's reputation and consumer trust. However, Johnson & Johnson's response to the crisis demonstrated a commitment to transparency and consumer safety. The company promptly initiated a nationwide recall of all Tylenol products, removing approximately 31 million bottles from store shelves, which reflected their prioritization of consumer safety over profits.

Moreover, Johnson & Johnson effectively communicated with the public, providing timely updates about the situation and their ongoing efforts to address it. Their approach included press conferences, public statements, and collaboration with health authorities, which helped to reassure consumers that the company was taking the situation seriously. In addition to addressing the immediate concerns, Johnson & Johnson also committed to enhancing safety measures, including the introduction of tamper-proof packaging.

Through these actions, Johnson & Johnson not only managed to mitigate the immediate crisis but also laid the groundwork for regaining consumer trust. Over time, Tylenol was able to re-establish itself as a trusted brand in the pain relief market, demonstrating that effective crisis management, characterized by transparency and accountability, can lead to recovery and long-term success. The company's proactive measures and commitment to consumer safety served as a model for effective crisis management, showcasing the importance of taking ownership of the problem and prioritizing stakeholder welfare.

Pepsi and the Kendall Jenner Ad Controversy

Pepsi's 2017 advertising campaign featuring Kendall Jenner became a flashpoint for controversy, drawing significant backlash for its perceived insensitivity to social justice movements. The commercial depicted Jenner leaving a photoshoot to join a protest, where she handed a police officer a can of Pepsi, seemingly bridging the gap between law enforcement and protestors. Critics accused the ad of trivializing serious issues such as police brutality and racial inequality, leading to accusations of cultural appropriation and exploitation. The backlash was swift and fierce, with many consumers expressing their outrage on social media.

In response to the mounting criticism, Pepsi acted quickly by pulling the advertisement and issuing a public apology. The company's statement acknowledged that the ad did not resonate as intended and recognized the need to better understand the complexities surrounding social issues. This swift action demonstrated a willingness to accept accountability for the misstep and signaled to consumers that Pepsi was committed to addressing the concerns raised by the public.

Moreover, Pepsi's handling of the crisis involved engaging in dialogue with stakeholders to rebuild trust. The company sought to learn from the incident by conducting internal reviews and reassessing its marketing strategies to ensure they align with contemporary social issues and consumer expectations. By demonstrating a commitment to learning from its mistakes and showing sensitivity toward social justice, Pepsi aimed to restore its reputation and reassure consumers that it values ethical marketing practices. Although the incident was a significant misstep, Pepsi's proactive response illustrated the importance of ownership and accountability in crisis management, setting the stage for rebuilding trust with its audience.

Wells Fargo and the Fake Accounts Scandal

Another historical example of a brand that struggled to rebuild trust after a crisis is Wells Fargo following its fake accounts scandal in 2016. The scandal erupted when it was revealed that employees had opened millions of unauthorized accounts in customers' names without their consent, driven by aggressive sales targets and a toxic corporate culture. This unethical practice led to significant legal and financial repercussions for the bank, including hefty fines and settlements.

Wells Fargo's initial response to the crisis was criticized as insufficient. The bank's leadership, including then-CEO John Stumpf, was accused of failing to take full responsibility for the actions of employees and the systemic issues within the organization. Stumpf's testimony before Congress, where he repeatedly emphasized the actions of "a few bad apples," further fueled public outrage and skepticism about the bank's accountability.

Despite efforts to implement reforms and regain public trust, such as replacing the CEO, restructuring the bank's sales practices, and enhancing oversight, the damage to Wells Fargo's reputation persisted. Customers were wary of the bank's intentions, and public sentiment remained largely negative. The bank continued to face scrutiny from regulators and the media, and its efforts to rebrand and reposition itself were met with skepticism. Even years after the scandal, Wells Fargo still struggles with the lingering effects of the crisis, demonstrating the difficulties of regaining trust once it has been lost.

Conclusion

Rebuilding trust after a crisis is a long-term commitment that requires consistency, transparency, and meaningful actions. Trust, once damaged, can only be restored by demonstrating genuine accountability and a willingness to learn from mistakes. This process involves more than just words; it demands that organizations back their promises with concrete actions that align with their values and the expectations of their stakeholders.

Throughout this chapter, we explored the importance of taking deliberate steps to reconnect with stakeholders, from implementing strategies to restore customer loyalty to engaging in community outreach and transparency initiatives. Case studies of brands that successfully navigated the trust recovery process demonstrate that resilience is possible when organizations commit to rebuilding relationships thoughtfully and proactively. These examples also show that trust recovery can strengthen a brand's reputation, as stakeholders often value organizations that demonstrate growth and accountability in the face of adversity.

Rebuilding trust is not a one-size-fits-all approach. Each crisis presents unique challenges, and the strategies employed must reflect the specific needs and concerns of the affected stakeholders. By prioritizing long-term trust recovery as an integral part of crisis management, brands can emerge stronger, fostering deeper loyalty and credibility.

Ultimately, rebuilding trust is not just about overcoming a crisis; it is about seizing an opportunity to demonstrate the brand's core values and commitment to its stakeholders. In doing so, organizations not only recover from setbacks but also lay a foundation for future growth and a stronger, more enduring relationship with their audience.

Further Reading

Greyser, S.A. 2009. "Corporate Brand Reputation and Brand Crisis Management." *Management Decision* 47 (4): 590–602.

Hegner, S.M., A.D. Beldad, and S.K.O. 2014. Heghuis. "How Company Responses and Trusting Relationships Protect Brand

Equity in Times of Crises." *Journal of Brand Management* 21: 429–45.

Shin, H., R. Casidy, A. Yoon, and So-Hyang Yoon. 2016. "Brand Trust and Avoidance Following Brand Crisis: A Quasi-Experiment on the Effect of Franchisor Statements." *Journal of Brand Management* 23: 1–23.

Singh, J., B. Crisafulli, and M.T. Xue. 2020. "'To Trust or Not to Trust': The Impact of Social Media Influencers on the Reputation of Corporate Brands in Crisis." *Journal of Business Research* 119: 464–80.

Yannopoulou, N., E. Koronis, and R. Elliott. 2011. "Media Amplification of a Brand Crisis and Its Affect on Brand Trust." *Journal of Marketing Management* 27 (5–6): 530–46.

CHAPTER 10

M = Monitoring and Learning

Overview

- Guides brands on tracking key performance indicators like sentiment and sales postcrisis.
- Encourages conducting postmortem analyses to identify lessons learned.
- Provides strategies for refining crisis management plans based on past experiences.
- Features case studies of brands that successfully adapted through learning and monitoring.

The final component of the **STORM Framework**—monitoring and learning—focuses on the critical process of tracking brand health after a crisis and implementing the necessary changes to prevent future issues. Continuous monitoring allows brands to assess the effectiveness of their crisis response and identify areas for improvement. By analyzing stakeholder feedback, social media sentiment, and brand perception metrics, companies can gain valuable insights into how they are viewed postcrisis. This ongoing evaluation not only helps brands stay informed but also allows them to be proactive in addressing any lingering concerns.

Learning from past experiences is equally essential in this process. Brands that reflect on their crisis management strategies can identify what worked and what didn't, paving the way for more effective responses in the future. This adaptability can be crucial in rebuilding trust and ensuring that similar issues do not resurface. For instance, brands like Chipotle successfully revamped their food safety protocols and communication strategies after facing significant challenges in the past. By actively monitoring the impact of their changes and seeking continuous improvement, they were able to regain customer loyalty and confidence.

The monitoring and learning phase is vital for any brand looking to recover from a crisis. By committing to ongoing assessment and adaptation, companies can transform challenges into opportunities for growth and reinforce their reputation in the long run. The experiences of brands that have successfully made comebacks underscore the importance of this final component in the **STORM Framework**, showcasing that resilience is not just about recovery but also about evolution and improvement.

Tracking Brand Health After a Crisis: What to Look for

Once the crisis has subsided, brands must actively monitor their health and performance to understand the impact of their crisis management efforts. Key indicators to track include customer sentiment, brand loyalty metrics, and market position. By regularly analyzing customer sentiment, brands can gauge public perception and identify any lingering negative feelings associated with the crisis. This feedback can be gathered through surveys, social media listening tools, and direct customer engagement, allowing brands to adjust their strategies as needed.

In addition to customer sentiment, tracking brand loyalty metrics is essential for assessing the long-term effects of a crisis. Brands can analyze repeat purchase rates, customer retention, and engagement levels to determine whether they have successfully regained trust. Understanding shifts in market position relative to competitors is also crucial, as it highlights how well a brand is recovering compared to industry peers. This comprehensive monitoring approach enables brands to make data-driven decisions, ensuring they remain responsive to stakeholder concerns and can continue to strengthen their reputation over time.

Table 10.1 This table lists key performance indicators for measuring brand perception, customer sentiment, and overall health following a crisis, providing organizations with essential tools to evaluate their recovery efforts and monitor ongoing brand performance

Metric	Description	Purpose
Net promoter score	Measures customer loyalty and likelihood to recommend the brand.	Assess overall customer satisfaction and loyalty.
Customer satisfaction score	Evaluates customer satisfaction with specific interactions or products.	Identify areas for improvement in customer experience.
Brand sentiment analysis	Analyzes public sentiment through social media and online reviews.	Gauge public perception and emotional response to the brand.
Social media engagement rate	Measures likes, shares, comments, and overall engagement on social media platforms.	Understand how well the brand is resonating with its audience postcrisis.
Share of voice	Compares the brand's media coverage to competitors.	Evaluate brand visibility and presence in the market.
Website traffic and metrics	Tracks changes in website visits, page views, and bounce rates.	Assess interest in the brand and its recovery efforts.
Sales performance	Monitors sales figures pre- and postcrisis.	Determine the financial impact of the crisis on the brand.
Customer retention rate	Measures the percentage of customers retained over time.	Understand the effectiveness of trust recovery efforts.
Employee engagement score	Assesses employee morale and commitment to the brand postcrisis.	Evaluate internal brand health and culture.

Some metrics for tracking brand health postcrisis are also shown in Table 10.1.

Customer Sentiment

Regularly assessing how customers feel about the brand is essential for understanding the impact of crisis management efforts and for rebuilding trust. Utilizing surveys, focus groups, and feedback mechanisms can provide valuable insights into shifting perceptions. Surveys can be designed to measure customer sentiment and satisfaction, allowing brands to quantify how their image has evolved postcrisis. Additionally, focus groups offer a more in-depth exploration of customer attitudes and feelings, enabling brands to gain qualitative insights into specific issues and concerns.

Feedback mechanisms, such as social media engagement and customer reviews, also play a critical role in capturing real-time sentiment. By monitoring these channels, brands can identify emerging trends, respond to customer concerns promptly, and adjust their strategies accordingly. This continuous feedback loop helps brands stay attuned to their audience's needs and expectations, ultimately fostering a more responsive and customer-centric approach. By proactively seeking and acting on customer insights, brands can reinforce their commitment to improvement and further solidify their reputation over time.

Brand Loyalty Metrics

Measuring customer retention rates, repeat purchases, and loyalty program engagement is crucial for evaluating the effectiveness of a brand's recovery efforts following a crisis. Customer retention rates indicate how well a brand is succeeding in keeping its existing customers. A steady or increasing retention rate suggests that consumers are beginning to regain trust and feel confident in the brand's commitment to quality and improvement.

Repeat purchases provide insights into consumer behavior and indicate whether customers are willing to return after a negative experience. If repeat purchase rates rise, it signifies that customers are not only willing to give the brand a second chance but also finding value in its products or services. Similarly, analyzing loyalty program engagement helps gauge the effectiveness of strategies designed to incentivize customer loyalty. Higher participation rates in loyalty programs often reflect a stronger emotional connection between the brand and its customers.

By monitoring these metrics, brands can gain a clearer picture of how effectively they are restoring trust and loyalty. It allows them to identify areas needing further improvement and validate their crisis management strategies. Overall, tracking these indicators serves as a benchmark for measuring recovery progress and reinforcing a brand's dedication to its customers.

Market Position

Keeping an eye on market share, sales figures, and competitive positioning is essential for assessing a brand's recovery following a crisis. Market share indicates how well the brand is performing relative to its competitors and whether it is regaining the ground lost during the crisis. An increase in market share signals that consumers are returning to the brand and choosing its products or services over others, suggesting that trust is being restored.

Sales figures are a direct reflection of consumer demand and can provide insights into the effectiveness of the brand's recovery strategies. A rebound in sales can indicate successful efforts to reconnect with customers and meet their needs postcrisis. It also shows that the brand is effectively communicating its improvements and reinforcing its value proposition to the market.

Moreover, understanding competitive positioning allows a brand to assess its standing within the industry. By analyzing competitors' strategies and market responses, a brand can identify opportunities for differentiation and areas where it can leverage its strengths to reclaim market leadership. Overall, tracking these Key Performance Indicators is crucial for gauging a brand's recovery trajectory and informs future strategies to sustain growth and resilience in the face of challenges.

Monitoring Social Media Sentiment and Public Perception

Social media serves as a powerful tool for gauging public sentiment and can provide real-time insights into how a brand is perceived postcrisis. Brands can utilize social listening tools to monitor conversations and mentions across various platforms, allowing them to identify trends, concerns, and positive feedback related to their recovery efforts. By analyzing this data, brands can gain a comprehensive understanding of public perception and respond promptly to any emerging issues or criticisms.

Sentiment analysis further enhances this understanding by quantifying public sentiment toward the brand. By analyzing social media posts, comments, and reviews, brands can assess whether the overall sentiment is positive, negative, or neutral. This quantitative data can be invaluable in shaping communication strategies and ensuring that the brand addresses specific concerns that may arise.

The H&M controversy surrounding the "coolest monkey in the jungle" sweater (Figure 10.1) highlights the vital importance of brands actively monitoring public sentiment and social media discourse. When the advertisement featuring an African child model sparked outrage for its racially insensitive implications, H&M faced immediate backlash across various social media platforms. The brand swiftly responded by removing the sweater from sale and issuing a public apology, which demonstrates the need for brands to be attuned to their audience's reactions. Such incidents illustrate how timely and effective monitoring of public opinion can help brands navigate potential crises and preserve their reputations by allowing for immediate corrective actions. Ultimately, this situation underscores the necessity for brands to cultivate a proactive approach to crisis management, ensuring they remain aware of the broader societal context in which they operate.

Engagement metrics, such as likes, shares, and comments, provide additional context regarding how well the brand's messaging resonates with its audience. High engagement levels can indicate that stakeholders are responding positively to the brand's recovery efforts and are open to re-establishing a relationship. Conversely, low engagement may signal

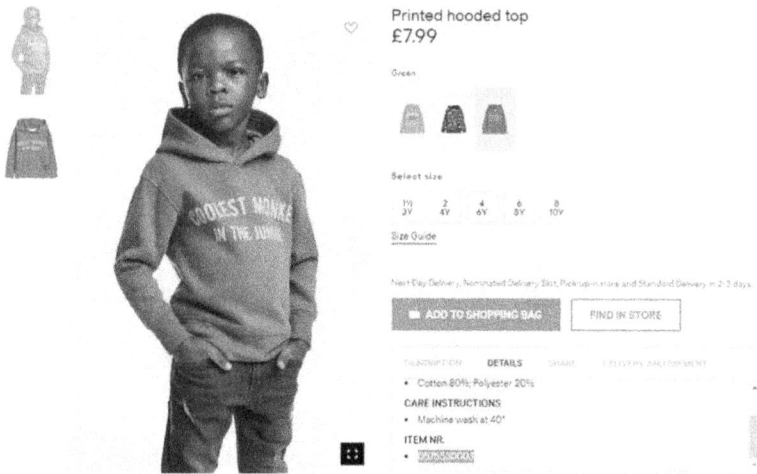

Figure 10.1 Printed hooded top

ongoing skepticism or dissatisfaction. By actively monitoring these social media metrics, brands can adapt their strategies, foster transparency, and engage meaningfully with their audience, ultimately aiding in the rebuilding of trust and reputation.

Social Listening Tools

Utilizing social media monitoring tools is essential for tracking mentions, comments, and hashtags related to the brand, especially in the aftermath of a crisis. These tools provide valuable insights into public conversations surrounding the brand, allowing companies to identify areas of concern or opportunity effectively. By closely monitoring social media platforms, brands can capture real-time feedback from customers, stakeholders, and the general public, helping them understand the immediate impact of their crisis management efforts.

For example, tracking specific hashtags related to a crisis or campaign can reveal how the brand is being discussed in various contexts, highlighting both negative sentiments and positive endorsements. Additionally, analyzing comments and mentions enables brands to gauge the effectiveness of their communication strategies and assess whether their messaging resonates with their audience. This proactive approach allows brands to respond swiftly to any emerging issues, engage with concerned customers, and address misinformation or negative narratives before they escalate.

Moreover, identifying trends in social media discussions can also unveil potential opportunities for the brand to enhance its image or reconnect with its audience. By recognizing themes that resonate positively, such as customer stories or advocacy, brands can leverage these insights to create targeted campaigns that reinforce their commitment to improvement and transparency. Ultimately, social media monitoring tools empower brands to stay attuned to their audience's sentiments, fostering a more responsive and adaptable approach to rebuilding trust and reputation.

Here are five top social media monitoring tools that brands can use to track discussions and sentiment during and after a crisis:

1. **Hootsuite** is a comprehensive social media management platform that allows brands to monitor multiple social media channels from a single dashboard. It offers features for tracking mentions, keywords, and hashtags in real-time, enabling brands to respond quickly to conversations about their crisis. Hootsuite also provides analytics to evaluate engagement and sentiment over time.

2. **Sprout Social** combines social media management with powerful listening and analytics capabilities. Brands can monitor keyword mentions, hashtags, and direct conversations, gaining insights into public sentiment surrounding their brand. The platform also facilitates engagement with followers, making it easier to address concerns and communicate updates during a crisis.

3. **Brandwatch** is a leading social media listening tool that offers advanced analytics and sentiment analysis. It allows brands to track discussions across various social media platforms and the web, providing deep insights into how the public perceives their crisis response. With its visual analytics features, brands can identify trends and adjust their strategies accordingly.

4. **Mention** is a real-time media monitoring tool that helps brands track their online presence. It alerts users to brand mentions across social media, blogs, and forums, enabling them to respond promptly to any discussions related to a crisis. With its user-friendly interface, Mention makes it easy for brands to stay informed and engaged with their audience.

5. **Talkwalker** is a powerful social media analytics and listening platform that provides comprehensive insights into brand sentiment and trends. It allows brands to monitor conversations across social media, blogs, and news sites, offering detailed analytics to understand public perception during a crisis. Talkwalker's visual analytics capabilities help brands identify emerging trends and assess the effectiveness of their messaging.

These tools are essential for brands looking to manage their reputation effectively during a crisis, allowing them to monitor conversations, respond to concerns, and maintain transparency with their stakeholders.

Sentiment Analysis

Implementing sentiment analysis is a critical step for brands aiming to understand public opinions and perceptions effectively, especially after a crisis. By categorizing sentiments as positive, negative, or neutral, companies can gain valuable insights into how their crisis management efforts are being received by customers and stakeholders. This analytical approach helps identify the prevailing mood surrounding the brand, enabling companies to assess whether their strategies are successful in rebuilding trust.

Sentiment analysis tools utilize algorithms to process vast amounts of social media data, customer feedback, and online reviews, providing a nuanced view of public sentiment. By analyzing the language used in these communications, brands can pinpoint specific concerns or positive sentiments that may arise in public discourse. For example, a surge in positive sentiment following a well-received apology or commitment to change can indicate that the brand is on the right track. Conversely, an increase in negative sentiment can signal that additional action is needed to address lingering issues.

Understanding these shifts in sentiment is crucial for adjusting communication strategies accordingly. If the analysis reveals that stakeholders remain skeptical despite positive changes, brands can tailor their messaging to further emphasize their commitment to improvement and accountability. By responding to public sentiment in a timely and thoughtful manner, brands can foster a sense of engagement and reassurance, ultimately facilitating a smoother recovery process and rebuilding trust over time.

Here are five effective tools that brands can use to implement sentiment analysis and understand public opinions and perceptions during and after a crisis:

1. **Lexalytics** offers advanced sentiment analysis and text analytics solutions. It can analyze social media posts, reviews, and other text data to determine sentiment, topics, and trends. Lexalytics provides customizable dashboards that allow brands to visualize sentiment over time, helping them understand how public perceptions evolve during a crisis.

2. **NetBase Quid** is a powerful social media analytics platform that specializes in sentiment analysis. It provides brands with insights into consumer opinions and emotions related to their brand and industry. The tool offers real-time monitoring of social media conversations, allowing brands to quickly identify changes in sentiment and respond appropriately.

3. **MonkeyLearn** is a no-code text analysis platform that allows brands to build custom sentiment analysis models. Users can analyze social media comments, reviews, and other textual data to extract insights about public sentiment. The platform also offers visualizations and integrations with other tools, making it easy to incorporate sentiment analysis into broader marketing strategies.

4. **Crimson Hexagon** (now part of Brandwatch) specializes in social media and consumer insights, providing brands with

detailed sentiment analysis and audience intelligence. The platform allows brands to track brand sentiment, identify key themes in discussions, and assess how different audience segments perceive the brand during a crisis.

5. **Sentiment Analyzer** is a straightforward tool that allows brands to analyze the sentiment of text data from various sources, including social media. It provides sentiment scores that help brands understand public opinion at a glance. While it may not have the advanced features of other tools, it's a useful option for quick sentiment assessments.

These tools are invaluable for brands seeking to gauge public sentiment, understand consumer perceptions, and adjust their crisis communication strategies accordingly. By analyzing sentiment data, brands can make informed decisions that enhance their reputation and foster trust among stakeholders.

Engagement Metrics

Tracking engagement metrics such as likes, shares, and comments on brand posts is essential for gauging public sentiment and measuring the effectiveness of crisis management efforts. High levels of engagement can signify that the audience is not only aware of the brand but is also interested in its content, reflecting a potential recovery in public perception.

When a brand experiences a crisis, monitoring these metrics allows it to assess the impact of its communication strategies in real time. For instance, an increase in likes and shares on posts addressing the crisis or outlining positive changes can indicate that stakeholders resonate with the brand's message. Comments can provide deeper insights into audience sentiment, revealing how consumers feel about the brand's actions and whether they believe the brand is genuinely committed to making amends.

Conversely, low engagement levels may suggest that the brand's efforts to rebuild trust are falling flat or that consumers remain skeptical. This information is critical for brands to pivot their strategies if necessary. By analyzing engagement metrics alongside sentiment analysis, brands can develop a comprehensive understanding of their recovery trajectory, enabling them to refine their approach and foster stronger connections with their audience. Ultimately, sustained engagement signals that consumers are willing to re-establish their relationship with the brand, paving the way for long-term recovery and growth.

Brands can use various tools to track social media engagement metrics, helping them measure their performance, understand audience interactions, and refine their strategies. Here are some notable tools:

1. **Hootsuite** is a comprehensive social media management platform that provides robust analytics and reporting features. Brands can track engagement metrics across multiple social media platforms, including likes, shares, comments, and follower growth. Hootsuite's customizable dashboards make it easy to visualize engagement data and identify trends over time.

2. **Sprout Social** offers in-depth social media analytics, allowing brands to track engagement metrics like post interactions, audience growth, and demographic insights. The platform provides detailed reports that help brands evaluate the effectiveness of their content and engagement strategies, enabling data-driven decision making.

3. **Buffer** is primarily a social media scheduling tool, but it also includes analytics features to track engagement metrics. Brands can monitor likes, comments, shares, and click-through rates for their posts across various platforms. Buffer's simple interface makes it easy to assess performance and optimize future content.

4. **Socialbakers** is an AI-powered social media marketing platform that offers detailed analytics and insights. Brands can track engagement metrics across different platforms and compare their performance to competitors. The tool provides benchmarks and recommendations to help brands enhance their engagement strategies.

5. **Agorapulse** is a social media management tool that provides comprehensive analytics for tracking engagement metrics.
   Brands can monitor comments, shares, and likes while also
   gaining insights into audience sentiment and behavior. The
   platform also allows brands to manage social interactions and
   respond to comments directly.

These tools help brands track engagement metrics effectively,
enabling them to understand how their audience interacts with their
content and refine their social media strategies to improve performance.

Learning From the Crisis: Conducting a Postmortem Analysis

Conducting a thorough postmortem analysis is essential for learning
from a crisis and ensuring that the brand is better prepared for future
challenges. This process begins by assembling a crisis review team,
which should include representatives from various departments such
as marketing, public relations (PR), legal, and customer service. This
diverse group can provide different perspectives on the crisis and the
brand's response, allowing for a comprehensive evaluation of what
occurred.

Next, the team should evaluate the effectiveness of the response
during the crisis. This involves analyzing the strategies implemented,
the communication methods used, and the overall execution of the
crisis management plan. Gathering feedback from stakeholders—such as
employees, customers, and partners—can provide valuable insights into
how the brand's actions were perceived and what could have been done
differently.

Finally, it's crucial to document the findings from this analysis.
This documentation should include a detailed account of the crisis,
the response strategies, outcomes, and lessons learned. By systematically
reviewing and recording these elements, the brand can create a reference
for future crisis management efforts. This postmortem analysis not
only helps the brand learn from its mistakes but also fosters a culture

of continuous improvement, enabling it to adapt and respond more effectively to future challenges.

Assemble a Crisis Review Team

Gathering a diverse team of stakeholders is a crucial step in conducting a thorough postmortem analysis of a crisis response. This team should comprise representatives from various functions within the organization, including crisis management, marketing, PR, and customer service. Each of these areas plays a vital role in managing a crisis and understanding its impact on the brand.

Crisis management experts can provide insights into the effectiveness of the initial response strategies and the decision-making processes during the crisis. Marketing representatives can offer perspectives on how the crisis affected brand perception and customer engagement, while PR specialists can evaluate the communication strategies used to convey the brand's message to stakeholders. Customer service representatives, on the other hand, can share feedback from consumers and clients, highlighting their concerns and how they felt the brand addressed (or failed to address) those issues.

By including a range of viewpoints, the review team can conduct a comprehensive evaluation of the crisis response. This collaborative approach ensures that all aspects of the crisis are examined, leading to a more informed analysis of what worked, what didn't, and how the organization can improve its crisis management strategies in the future. Ultimately, the insights gained from this diverse team will contribute to more effective preparedness and resilience in facing potential crises ahead.

When assembling a crisis review team, it's essential to consider team members with specific skills and traits to ensure effective crisis management and analysis. Here are some key qualities to look for:

1. **Strong communication skills:** Team members should be proficient in both verbal and written communication. They need to convey complex information clearly and effectively, ensuring

that all stakeholders understand the situation and the organization's response.

2. **Analytical thinking:** The ability to analyze data, identify patterns, and draw meaningful conclusions is crucial. Team members should be adept at evaluating the impact of the crisis and the effectiveness of the response strategies.

3. **Problem-solving abilities:** Crisis situations often require quick thinking and innovative solutions. Team members should be skilled in assessing problems and generating practical, actionable solutions under pressure.

4. **Emotional intelligence:** Understanding and managing emotions—both their own and those of others—is vital during a crisis. Team members with high emotional intelligence can navigate interpersonal dynamics and maintain a calm demeanor, which can help stabilize the team and reassure stakeholders.

5. **Adaptability:** Crises can evolve rapidly, requiring team members to adjust their approaches and strategies quickly. Flexibility and a willingness to pivot when new information arises are essential traits.

6. **Interpersonal skills:** Team members should be able to build rapport and trust with colleagues and stakeholders. Strong interpersonal skills facilitate collaboration and enhance the team's ability to work cohesively during a crisis.

7. **Experience in crisis management:** Prior experience in handling crises or working in high-pressure situations is invaluable. Team members with relevant backgrounds can draw from their experiences to guide the team's actions and decisions.

8. **Leadership qualities:** Individuals who demonstrate strong leadership capabilities can inspire confidence in the team and stakeholders. They should be able to make decisions, delegate tasks, and lead the team through challenging circumstances.

9. **Knowledge of the organization:** Team members should have a deep understanding of the organization's values, culture, and operations. This knowledge is crucial for aligning crisis responses with the organization's mission and maintaining brand integrity.

10. **Strategic thinking:** Members should possess the ability to think long-term and strategically about the implications of the crisis and the effectiveness of response efforts. This foresight can help in planning for recovery and future prevention.

By selecting team members with these skills and traits, organizations can enhance their crisis review team's effectiveness and ensure a comprehensive analysis of the crisis and its management.

Evaluate Response Effectiveness

Analyzing the effectiveness of crisis management strategies is essential for brands to learn from their experiences and enhance future responses. This evaluation involves identifying what worked well and what fell short during the crisis, along with extracting key lessons and pinpointing areas for improvement.

Brands that maintained open lines of communication with stakeholders often fared better. By providing regular updates and being upfront about the situation, these brands could build trust and demonstrate accountability. Additionally, quick, decisive action, such as recalling products or addressing issues, helped mitigate damage. Brands that acted promptly often prevented further escalation and regained consumer confidence.

Empathy and support played significant roles as well. Brands that expressed genuine empathy toward those affected by the crisis—such as customers or communities—were able to foster goodwill. By addressing emotional concerns and showing that they cared, these brands positioned themselves better to rebuild relationships. Furthermore, demonstrating a commitment to making necessary changes was crucial. Brands that outlined specific steps they would take to prevent similar crises in the future could reassure stakeholders of their dedication to improvement. Through these strategies, brands not only learned valuable lessons but also laid the groundwork for stronger relationships moving forward.

Document Findings

Conducting a thorough postmortem analysis is essential for learning from a crisis and ensuring that the brand is better prepared for future challenges. This analysis begins by assembling a diverse crisis review team comprising representatives from various departments, including crisis management, marketing, PR, customer service, and other relevant stakeholders. This diverse team is critical because each department brings unique perspectives and expertise that can help paint a comprehensive picture of the crisis response. A cross-functional team can effectively evaluate how different strategies impacted various aspects of the brand and its reputation.

Once the team is assembled, the next step is to analyze the effectiveness of the strategies implemented during the crisis. This includes assessing which actions were successful and which fell short, as well as exploring the reasons behind these outcomes. For example, effective communication might have helped build trust with customers and stakeholders, while delayed responses may have exacerbated the crisis. Identifying these patterns is crucial for drawing lessons that can inform future strategies. Furthermore, gathering feedback from stakeholders, including employees, customers, and partners, provides valuable insights into their perceptions of the crisis response. Their experiences and opinions can highlight areas that may not have been initially apparent, revealing gaps in the brand's approach or misconceptions that need to be addressed.

After evaluating the effectiveness of the response, it's important to document the findings in a comprehensive report. This report should include detailed analyses of both successful and unsuccessful strategies, along with recommendations for improvement. By systematically documenting the lessons learned, the brand creates a valuable resource that can guide future crisis management efforts. This documentation can serve as a reference point for training sessions and workshops aimed at preparing the organization for potential crises in the future. Additionally, sharing this report with the broader organization promotes a culture of transparency and continuous improvement, emphasizing that every crisis, no matter how challenging, is an opportunity to learn and grow.

A thorough postmortem analysis is vital for understanding the implications of a crisis and strengthening a brand's crisis management capabilities. By bringing together a diverse team, evaluating the response, gathering stakeholder feedback, and documenting findings, brands can create a roadmap for future preparedness and resilience. This commitment to learning not only enhances the brand's reputation but also fosters trust and loyalty among customers and stakeholders, ultimately positioning the brand for long-term success.

Implementing Changes to Prevent Future Crises

Learning from past crises is not enough; brands must also implement changes to prevent similar issues from arising in the future. One critical aspect of this proactive approach is revising policies and procedures. Organizations should carefully assess existing protocols to identify any weaknesses or gaps that contributed to the crisis. By updating these policies, brands can create a more robust framework that minimizes the risk of recurrence. For instance, if a crisis stemmed from inadequate communication channels, a brand might implement new protocols for internal and external communications, ensuring that all stakeholders are kept informed during a crisis.

In addition to policy revisions, training and development play a crucial role in equipping employees with the necessary skills and knowledge to handle future crises effectively. Organizations should invest in comprehensive training programs that cover crisis management, communication strategies, and specific departmental procedures. This training ensures that all employees understand their roles and responsibilities during a crisis, which can significantly improve response times and effectiveness. For example, conducting workshops and seminars can help staff recognize potential crisis indicators early on and equip them with the tools to respond appropriately.

Crisis simulation drills are another essential component of a proactive crisis management strategy. These drills provide a practical, hands-on experience that allows employees to practice their crisis response skills in a controlled environment. By simulating various crisis scenarios, brands can evaluate their preparedness, identify potential weaknesses, and refine their response strategies. Regular drills also foster a culture of readiness within the organization, reinforcing the importance of being prepared for unforeseen events. Moreover, these exercises can help build teamwork and communication among departments, ensuring a more coordinated response during an actual crisis.

Brands must take a multifaceted approach to prevent future crises by implementing changes in policies and procedures, investing in training and development, and conducting crisis simulation drills. These efforts not only enhance the organization's resilience but also demonstrate a commitment to continuous improvement and accountability. By learning from past experiences and taking concrete steps to address vulnerabilities, brands can foster greater trust and loyalty among stakeholders, ultimately positioning themselves for long-term success.

Policy and Procedure Revisions

Reviewing and updating existing policies and procedures based on lessons learned from past crises is crucial for enhancing a brand's resilience and effectiveness in future situations. One of the first steps in this process is to conduct a thorough evaluation of current policies to identify any weaknesses or inadequacies that contributed to the crisis. This assessment should involve cross-departmental collaboration to ensure a comprehensive understanding of the various factors at play. By fostering an inclusive approach, organizations can gain insights from diverse perspectives and experiences, ultimately leading to more effective revisions.

Enhancing quality control measures is often a vital aspect of this review process. If a crisis arose from product defects or safety concerns, it is essential to implement stricter quality assurance protocols. This could involve introducing more rigorous testing procedures, regular audits, and continuous monitoring of the supply chain. By prioritizing quality control, brands can reduce the likelihood of future crises and demonstrate a commitment to delivering safe and reliable products to their customers.

Improving customer service protocols is another critical area for revision. During a crisis, the effectiveness of customer communication can significantly impact a brand's reputation. Therefore, brands should assess how customer service representatives handled inquiries and complaints during the crisis and identify areas for improvement. This may include enhancing training programs to ensure that staff are well-equipped to manage difficult conversations, respond empathetically, and provide accurate information. Additionally, organizations could establish clear guidelines for crisis-related communication, ensuring that responses are consistent, transparent, and timely.

Revising crisis communication plans is also essential for effective crisis management. Brands should ensure that their communication strategies are up-to-date and tailored to address various stakeholder needs. This involves identifying key messaging, determining appropriate communication channels, and establishing a crisis response team with defined roles and responsibilities. By having a well-prepared communication plan, brands can respond swiftly and effectively in the event of a crisis, minimizing confusion and maintaining trust with stakeholders.

Reviewing and updating existing policies and procedures based on lessons learned is a proactive approach to crisis management. By enhancing quality control measures, improving customer service protocols, and revising crisis communication plans, brands can strengthen their overall resilience and readiness for future challenges. These changes not only contribute to preventing crises but also foster a culture of accountability and continuous improvement, ultimately benefiting the brand and its stakeholders in the long run.

Training and Development

Investing in training programs for employees that focus on crisis management, communication skills, and customer engagement is essential for enhancing a brand's resilience and response capabilities during a crisis. A well-prepared workforce can make a significant difference in how a brand navigates challenging situations, ultimately influencing stakeholder perception and maintaining trust.

Effective crisis management training should encompass various scenarios and equip employees with the skills to respond appropriately to potential crises. This includes understanding the organization's crisis communication protocols, knowing how to identify early warning signs of a crisis, and developing strategies for mitigating risks. By conducting scenario-based training sessions, employees can practice their responses in a controlled environment, enabling them to build confidence and familiarity with the necessary procedures. This proactive approach ensures that employees are not only aware of the protocols but also capable of implementing them effectively under pressure.

Communication skills are crucial during a crisis, as clear and transparent messaging can significantly impact stakeholder trust. Training programs should emphasize the importance of empathy, active listening, and conveying information succinctly. Employees must learn to communicate with clarity and confidence, especially when addressing customer inquiries or concerns during a crisis. Role-playing exercises can be particularly beneficial, allowing employees to practice their communication skills in realistic scenarios and receive constructive feedback. This training fosters a culture of openness and responsiveness, encouraging employees to engage with stakeholders authentically.

Customer engagement is another vital aspect of crisis management that training programs should address. Employees should be equipped with the tools and strategies necessary to engage customers effectively, even in challenging situations. This includes understanding customer needs and emotions, responding to feedback, and providing timely and accurate information. By investing in customer engagement training, brands can empower employees to handle difficult conversations with care and professionalism, turning potential crises into opportunities for relationship-building.

Moreover, preparedness at all levels of the organization is key to effective crisis management. This means ensuring that not only frontline employees are trained, but also management and leadership teams are equipped to make informed decisions quickly. Leadership training should focus on strategic thinking, decision making under pressure, and crisis leadership skills. By fostering a culture of preparedness throughout the organization, brands can create a unified response strategy that ensures everyone is aligned and ready to act when a crisis arises.

Investing in comprehensive training programs that focus on crisis management, communication skills, and customer engagement is crucial for building a resilient workforce. By preparing employees at all levels, brands can enhance their ability to navigate crises effectively, maintain stakeholder trust, and ultimately emerge stronger from challenging situations. This commitment to preparedness not only minimizes the impact of potential crises but also reinforces a brand's reputation as a reliable and responsible entity in the eyes of its customers and stakeholders.

Crisis Simulation Drills

Conducting regular crisis simulation exercises is a vital component of a brand's preparedness strategy, enabling teams to anticipate and effectively respond to potential crises. These drills mimic real-life scenarios and provide a controlled environment for practicing crisis management protocols. By engaging in these exercises, organizations can identify weaknesses in their response plans, enhance team coordination, and ensure that all employees are prepared to act swiftly and decisively in high-pressure situations.

One of the primary benefits of crisis simulation exercises is the opportunity to test and refine existing crisis response plans. During these simulations, teams can evaluate the effectiveness of their communication strategies, decision-making processes, and operational procedures. By analyzing the outcomes of these exercises, organizations can pinpoint areas that need improvement, whether it's in communication flows, resource allocation, or response time. This ongoing assessment allows brands to adapt their strategies to better align with best practices and evolving stakeholder expectations.

Moreover, crisis simulations foster a culture of preparedness within the organization. When employees actively participate in these drills, they gain firsthand experience in managing crises, which boosts their confidence and enhances their skill sets. This practical training reinforces the importance of collaboration and clear communication among team members. As employees learn to navigate the complexities of crisis management, they become more adept at anticipating challenges and devising effective solutions.

In addition to improving internal processes, regular crisis simulations also strengthen external relationships. These exercises often involve key stakeholders, such as PR teams, customer service representatives, and legal counsel. By collaborating during simulations, all parties can develop a unified approach to crisis response, ensuring that messaging is consistent and aligned across the organization. This alignment is critical for maintaining trust with stakeholders and ensuring that everyone is working toward the same goals during a real crisis.

Furthermore, the insights gained from crisis simulations can inform ongoing training and development initiatives. By analyzing the outcomes and feedback from these exercises, organizations can identify specific areas where additional training may be necessary. For example, if a simulation reveals gaps in crisis communication skills, targeted training sessions can be developed to address those weaknesses. This proactive approach ensures that employees are continuously developing their skills and staying prepared for future challenges.

Conducting regular crisis simulation exercises is essential for preparing teams for potential future crises. These drills not only help identify weaknesses in response plans but also cultivate a culture of preparedness and collaboration. By refining strategies, enhancing skills, and strengthening stakeholder relationships, brands can significantly improve their ability to respond to crises effectively and maintain trust in the face of adversity. Through consistent practice and evaluation, organizations can ensure that they are ready to act swiftly and effectively when faced with real-world challenges.

Case Studies

Several brands have successfully turned their crises into opportunities for growth by learning from their mistakes. For example, the Australian Broadcasting Corporation (ABC) received media attention for issues concerning sexual harassment and misconduct, but the corporation was able to establish guidelines and training programs to foster a safer and more inclusive workplace. Meanwhile, Nike faced backlash for featuring Colin Kaepernick in its "Just Do It" campaign. Instead of backing down, Nike embraced the controversy and reinforced its commitment to social justice, which strengthened brand loyalty and increased sales. Similarly, Kraft Heinz dealt with multiple product recalls by prioritizing quality control and transparent communication. By addressing safety concerns and engaging effectively with customers, they restored consumer confidence and improved their brand image. In contrast, Volkswagen failed to effectively monitor and learn from its emissions scandal in 2015. Initially, the company denied the extent of the issue, which damaged consumer trust further. Despite later attempts to address the scandal, their lack of transparency and accountability hindered recovery, illustrating the importance of timely and honest responses in crisis management.

Australian Broadcasting Corporation and Workplace Culture

The ABC controversy primarily refers to the events surrounding the handling of allegations against former presenter and journalist, the late Bruce Guthrie, and the broader scrutiny of the organization's workplace culture, particularly concerning issues of sexual harassment and misconduct.

In terms of monitoring and learning from the scandal, the ABC has taken several steps to address the concerns raised during this period. Following the controversy, the organization initiated an independent review of its workplace culture, which included examining policies related to harassment, discrimination, and employee safety. This review aimed to identify areas needing improvement and implement changes based on the findings.

The ABC has also established a new set of guidelines and training programs focused on creating a safer and more inclusive workplace. These initiatives included mandatory training on respectful workplace behavior for all staff, which helped raise awareness about sexual harassment and other related issues.

Moreover, the organization has committed to ongoing monitoring of its workplace culture and practices. By conducting regular surveys and reviews, the ABC can gauge employee sentiment and ensure that its policies effectively address concerns. The leadership has expressed a commitment to transparency and accountability, recognizing the need to learn from past mistakes and continuously improve the work environment.

While challenges remain, the steps taken by the ABC demonstrate an understanding of the importance of monitoring and learning from the controversy. By implementing changes and fostering a culture of openness, the organization aims to rebuild trust with its employees and the public. The ABC's efforts to address workplace issues reflect a broader recognition of the need for media organizations to prioritize ethical practices and create safe environments for their employees.

Nike and the Colin Kaepernick Controversy

Nike's decision to feature Colin Kaepernick in its "Just Do It" campaign in 2018 sparked significant backlash from various segments of the public. Kaepernick, a former NFL quarterback, became a polarizing figure after kneeling during the national anthem to protest racial injustice and police brutality. Despite the controversy surrounding his actions, Nike took a bold stance by aligning itself with Kaepernick, which was a clear indication of the brand's commitment to social justice issues.

Rather than shying away from the backlash, Nike leveraged the controversy to engage with its audience more deeply. The brand's messaging was clear: it stood firmly in support of those who fight for social change, resonating strongly with its core demographic, which includes younger consumers who value social responsibility and activism. Nike's willingness to embrace a figure like Kaepernick showcased its alignment with contemporary cultural movements, further solidifying its identity as a progressive brand.

This strategic decision ultimately paid off for Nike. The company reported an increase in sales following the campaign's launch, demonstrating that its core audience responded positively to its commitment to social issues. The brand's stock price also saw a notable rise, indicating investor confidence in Nike's ability to navigate the controversy successfully. By prioritizing authenticity and engaging in meaningful conversations about social justice, Nike not only strengthened brand loyalty among its supporters but also attracted new customers who appreciated its stance.

Nike's experience serves as a powerful example of how brands can turn potential crises into opportunities for engagement and growth. By embracing controversy and standing firm in its values, Nike effectively reinforced its brand identity, connected with its audience on a deeper level, and ultimately enhanced its market position. This case illustrates the importance of authenticity and conviction in branding, especially in an era where consumers increasingly seek out companies that align with their values and beliefs.

Kraft Heinz and Multiple Product Recalls

Kraft Heinz has encountered several challenges in recent years, particularly in the form of multiple product recalls that raised concerns about food safety and quality. These incidents, which included recalls of popular products like Kraft Singles and Heinz ketchup due to potential contamination and mislabeling, posed significant risks to the brand's reputation and consumer trust. In response to these challenges, Kraft Heinz took decisive actions to prioritize quality control and transparency, which have been crucial in restoring consumer confidence.

One of the key strategies employed by Kraft Heinz was a commitment to rigorous quality control measures. The company recognized that maintaining high standards for its products was essential not only for consumer safety but also for rebuilding its tarnished image. By enhancing its production processes and implementing more stringent checks, Kraft Heinz aimed to reassure customers that it was dedicated to providing safe and high-quality food products.

Additionally, transparent communication played a vital role in the company's crisis management approach. Kraft Heinz took the initiative to inform consumers promptly about the recalls, detailing the reasons behind the actions and the steps being taken to rectify the situation. This open dialogue helped to mitigate consumer fears and demonstrated the brand's accountability. By engaging effectively with customers through various channels, including social media and press releases, Kraft Heinz was able to maintain a line of communication that reassured the public of its commitment to safety and quality.

The efforts to prioritize quality control and transparent communication have yielded positive results for Kraft Heinz. As the brand worked to rectify past issues, it made significant strides in restoring consumer confidence. Customers began to recognize the company's dedication to ensuring safe products, leading to a gradual recovery in brand perception. By focusing on safe, high-quality offerings and effectively engaging with consumers, Kraft Heinz has shown that it can learn from its challenges and take meaningful steps toward regaining trust in the marketplace. This case highlights the importance of addressing crises head-on and making concerted efforts to foster transparency and accountability in rebuilding brand trust.

Volkswagen and the Emissions Scandal

A notable example of a brand that did not successfully monitor and learn from a crisis is Volkswagen in the emissions scandal that erupted in 2015. The crisis began when it was revealed that the company had installed software in its diesel vehicles to cheat on emissions tests, leading to significant environmental violations.

In the wake of the scandal, Volkswagen's initial response involved denial and a lack of transparency, which exacerbated the situation. The company underestimated the public and regulatory backlash, leading to a series of poor communication decisions. Instead of acknowledging the wrongdoing and engaging with stakeholders, Volkswagen's leadership tried to downplay the severity of the issue and initially failed to address the concerns of customers, regulators, and the media adequately.

As the scandal unfolded, Volkswagen was slow to implement necessary changes and did not monitor the public's sentiment effectively. The company faced multiple lawsuits, regulatory penalties, and a significant drop in consumer trust. The failure to learn from the crisis meant that Volkswagen struggled for years to restore its reputation, facing ongoing scrutiny and damage to its brand image.

While Volkswagen eventually took steps to improve its compliance and transparency, including significant changes to its corporate governance and management practices, the damage had already been done. The scandal highlighted the importance of proactive monitoring and learning in crisis management, as the initial failure to address the crisis transparently had long-lasting implications for the brand.

Conclusion

Monitoring and learning are the cornerstones of effective crisis management and long-term organizational resilience. The process of assessing brand health after a crisis, conducting postmortem analyses, and implementing lessons learned allows organizations to refine their strategies and be better prepared for future challenges. A robust commitment to monitoring ensures that organizations can detect emerging risks early, while a culture of learning fosters adaptability and continuous improvement.

This chapter has emphasized the importance of tracking key metrics, such as customer sentiment and engagement, as well as examining the outcomes of crisis response efforts. Tools and techniques, such as sentiment analysis and social media monitoring, provide valuable insights into public perception and help organizations tailor their ongoing communication and recovery strategies. Successful brands use these insights not only to correct missteps but also to strengthen their connections with stakeholders.

By embracing a proactive approach to monitoring and learning, organizations can transform crises into opportunities for growth. Developing systems that identify risks early and encourage accountability ensures that the organization is always evolving. Reflecting on what worked and what didn't creates a culture of resilience, empowering the brand to adapt swiftly in a rapidly changing environment. This iterative process of reflection and action is essential for navigating the complexities of modern business and maintaining stakeholder trust over the long term.

Further Reading

Becker, K., H. Nobre, and V. Kanabar. 2013. "Monitoring and Protecting Company and Brand Reputation on Social Networks: When Sites Are Not Enough." *Global Business and Economics Review* 15 (2–3): 293–308.

Hewett, K., and L.L. Lemon. 2019. "A Process View of the Role of Integrated Marketing Communications During Brand Crises." *Qualitative Market Research* 22 (3): 497–524.

Mirzaei, A, D. Gray, C. Baumann, L.W. Johnson, and H. Winzar. 2015. "A Behavioural Long-Term Based Measure to Monitor the Health of a Brand." *Journal of Brand Management* 22: 299–322.

Mohamed, K, and Ü.A. Bayraktar. 2022. "Analyzing the Role of Sentiment Analysis in Public Relations: Brand Monitoring and Crisis Management." *International Journal of Humanities and Social Science* 9 (3): 116–26.

Yang, C. 2022. "Strategies for Monitoring Brand Crisis Information Sharing by Weibo Users." In *Sharing Behavior of Brand Crisis Information on Social Media: A Case Study of Chinese Weibo*, 249–64. Singapore: Springer Nature Singapore.

CHAPTER 11

Preparing for Future Crises

Overview

- Revisits the STORM Framework with a focus on proactive measures.
- Details actions to establish crisis response mechanisms and communication plans.
- Stresses cultivating a culture of accountability and resilience.
- Encourages continuous improvement to adapt to evolving risks and stakeholder expectations.

In today's fast-paced and interconnected world, crises are inevitable for any organization, regardless of its size or industry. Whether caused by internal errors, external factors, or unpredictable circumstances, the potential for a crisis can have far-reaching effects on a brand's reputation, financial health, and customer trust. This makes proactive crisis management essential. Rather than waiting for a crisis to occur, organizations must anticipate potential risks, plan responses, and take steps to minimize the damage before an issue escalates. A well-prepared organization is more resilient, able to respond swiftly, and recover more effectively when challenges arise.

The **STORM Framework**—swift response, transparent communication, ownership of the problem, rebuilding trust, and monitoring and learning—provides a comprehensive structure for both responding to crises and preventing future ones. Each component serves a dual purpose: not only does it guide organizations through the immediate response needed during a crisis, but it also establishes processes that help reduce the likelihood of such events occurring in the first place. By approaching crisis management through this framework, businesses can build the resilience needed to navigate turbulent times while continually refining their ability to address emerging risks.

This chapter will delve into the elements of the **STORM Framework** in the context of crisis preparedness. It will explore how organizations can establish rapid-response mechanisms, develop transparent communication strategies, cultivate a culture of accountability, and ensure long-term trust rebuilding. Finally, we will discuss the importance of continuous monitoring and learning to adapt and strengthen crisis management strategies over time.

S = Swift Response: Establishing Crisis Response Mechanisms

In any crisis, time is of the essence, and a rapid, well-coordinated response can greatly minimize damage to a brand's reputation, operational stability, and stakeholder relationships. To achieve this, organizations must prioritize the establishment of a crisis response team, composed of key individuals from various departments, each with clearly defined roles and responsibilities. This team should include decision makers, communication specialists, legal advisors, and operational leaders, all of whom can mobilize quickly in the face of an unfolding crisis. By having a specialized team in place, organizations ensure that when a crisis occurs, everyone knows their responsibilities and can act efficiently without confusion or delay.

To maintain the crisis response team's readiness, regular training and simulation exercises are crucial. These exercises help the team rehearse their roles under realistic crisis conditions, enhancing their ability to make quick, informed decisions under pressure. Simulations allow team members to gain practical experience, identify gaps or weaknesses in the response plan, and refine their coordination. Regularly conducting these drills fosters a sense of preparedness and can instill the confidence needed to manage real crises effectively. Additionally, it helps create muscle memory within the team, enabling faster, more intuitive responses when faced with a genuine emergency.

A key component of swift crisis response is the implementation of preapproved response protocols. These are standardized procedures that guide the crisis response team through the initial stages of a crisis, providing a clear roadmap for immediate action. By establishing these protocols in advance, organizations eliminate the need for on-the-spot decision making, which can lead to delays and missteps. Instead, the team can follow an already agreed-upon plan that includes steps such as notifying key stakeholders, coordinating internal communications, and engaging with the media. These preapproved strategies help the team respond decisively and consistently, reducing the chances of further escalation.

Another essential element for ensuring a swift response is investing in early warning systems. These systems, such as social listening tools, media monitoring platforms, and comprehensive risk assessments, allow organizations to detect potential crises in their infancy. By continuously monitoring for signs of trouble—whether it's a brewing public relations issue, operational disruption, or external threat—companies can take preventative measures before the situation spirals out of control. Identifying warning signs early gives the crisis response team valuable lead time to prepare, ensuring they can act swiftly to either mitigate the damage or prevent the crisis entirely.

By establishing a dedicated crisis response team, engaging in regular training, implementing preapproved protocols, and using early warning systems, organizations can build the infrastructure necessary to respond swiftly to crises. These mechanisms ensure that the organization is not caught off guard and can act quickly to contain and manage any situation that arises.

T = Transparent Communication: Building Communication Plans

In a crisis, transparent communication is critical for preserving trust and controlling the narrative. Open and honest messaging reassures stakeholders that the organization is handling the situation responsibly, which helps to reduce confusion and the spread of misinformation. The first step in achieving this is to draft clear communication templates for various potential crisis scenarios. Having these preprepared templates enables organizations to respond swiftly with accurate, well-thought-out messages that align with the situation at hand. This foresight ensures that communication is not reactive but rather part of a planned response.

Equally important is regular communication training for spokes-people. Identifying and training specific individuals to serve as the organization's voice during a crisis ensures that all messaging is consistent, professional, and aligned with the organization's values. These spokespeople need to be adept at addressing difficult questions, managing public perception, and delivering the organization's stance with empathy and precision. Effective spokesperson training minimizes the risk of miscommunication and guarantees that the right tone is conveyed during high-pressure situations.

Another key component of transparent communication is under-standing the diverse audiences affected by a crisis. Organizations must identify communication channels appropriate for each audience—whether it be social media platforms for public updates, press relea-ses for media outreach, or internal communications for employees. Tailoring the message to the right channels helps ensure that the most relevant information is delivered to the right stakeholders promptly, helping maintain order and control throughout the crisis.

Furthermore, a robust media relations strategy is essential for managing interactions with the press during a crisis. By establishing strong relationships with journalists and media outlets beforehand, organizations can ensure more balanced and accurate coverage when challenges arise. Proactively engaging with the media in a transpar-ent and cooperative manner allows brands to shape their narrative, preventing damaging speculation or misrepresentation.

O = Ownership of the Problem: Cultivating Accountability Culture

Taking ownership of a crisis is crucial for building credibility and demonstrating accountability to stakeholders. When a brand openly acknowledges its responsibility during challenging times, it can better manage its reputation and foster trust among its customers and other stakeholders. To achieve this, organizations must embed a culture of responsibility throughout the company. This means ensuring that employees at all levels understand their specific roles and the significance of accountability in crisis situations. By cultivating this mindset, organizations can respond to crises with a united front, ready to take responsibility for their actions and decisions.

To reinforce this culture of ownership, it is important to establish a feedback loop that allows employees to escalate issues quickly. Creating a structured system for efficiently communicating concerns up the chain of command enables organizations to address problems before they escalate into full-blown crises. This proactive approach fosters an environment where potential risks are identified early, and solutions can be implemented in a timely manner, thus minimizing the impact of any adverse events.

Furthermore, developing policies for transparent reporting and crisis acknowledgment is essential. These policies should outline how the organization communicates its responsibility in the face of a crisis, ensuring that issues are openly acknowledged rather than deflected or downplayed. By adopting a transparent stance from the outset, brands can minimize reputational damage, facilitate the rebuilding of trust, and demonstrate their commitment to rectifying the situation. This level of accountability not only reassures stakeholders but also sets the foundation for stronger relationships moving forward.

R = Rebuilding Trust: Fostering Long-Term Relationships

Restoring trust after a crisis is not a one-time effort but rather a sustained, strategic process that requires ongoing commitment. A brand's reputation may suffer during a crisis, but with thoughtful actions and dedication, it can recover and even strengthen its relationships with stakeholders. To rebuild trust effectively, brands must invest in relationship-building initiatives that go beyond quick fixes. Postcrisis efforts should center on long-term strategies aimed at nurturing customer loyalty and reinforcing brand trust. These initiatives might include loyalty programs that reward continued patronage, personalized communication to enhance customer engagement, or community outreach activities that demonstrate the brand's commitment to its stakeholders.

Consistency is crucial in this rebuilding process. Brands must ensure that their messaging and actions reflect the organization's core values. This means maintaining transparency, being honest in all communications, and ensuring that the brand's recovery efforts align with its stated principles. Any misalignment between words and actions can further erode trust, so it is essential that messaging is consistently backed by genuine action.

Additionally, engaging in community and stakeholder outreach plays a pivotal role in rebuilding trust. Brands should take proactive steps to demonstrate transparency and accountability. This can involve hosting town hall meetings to listen to concerns, participating in community projects to give back, or offering public updates on progress made since the crisis. By showing a commitment to taking meaningful action, brands can gradually rebuild trust over time, fostering deeper connections with their audience and reaffirming their dedication to the community they serve. These long-term efforts not only restore credibility but also lay the groundwork for a more resilient brand, capable of navigating future challenges with integrity.

M = Monitoring and Learning: Continuous Improvement and Risk Mitigation

Preventing future crises hinges on a brand's ability to continuously monitor its environment and learn from past experiences. A proactive approach to real-time monitoring systems—which may include tracking customer sentiment through social media, analyzing sales patterns, and observing competitor actions—enables organizations to detect early warning signs of potential issues. By staying vigilant and aware of market dynamics, companies can address small problems before they escalate into significant crises, thus protecting their brand reputation and operational integrity.

Conducting postmortem reviews after a crisis is essential for extracting actionable insights that can guide future strategies. These reviews should analyze the crisis response in detail, evaluating what worked, what didn't, and why certain decisions were made. This reflective process allows organizations to refine their crisis management strategies by identifying both strengths and weaknesses. By learning from each event, brands can avoid repeating past mistakes, thereby strengthening their preparedness for any future challenges that may arise.

Regularly updating risk assessments and crisis management plans is crucial to ensuring that companies remain adaptable in an ever-evolving landscape. As new data emerges—from shifts in consumer behavior to changes in regulatory environments—plans should be revised to address current risks and vulnerabilities. This dynamic approach helps ensure that the organization is always equipped to handle future challenges, enabling swift and effective responses to potential crises.

Finally, fostering a culture of continuous learning within the organization is critical for enhancing crisis resilience. Encouraging feedback from employees at all levels and incorporating lessons learned into regular business practices promotes adaptability and innovation. This mindset of ongoing improvement not only strengthens the organization's resilience but also empowers employees to take an active role in crisis preparedness. By embedding a culture that values learning and adaptation, brands can enhance their readiness for future crises, positioning themselves to navigate uncertainties with confidence and agility.

Conclusion

The **STORM Framework** provides a comprehensive approach for organizations to prepare for future crises. By focusing on swift response, transparent communication, ownership of the problem, rebuilding trust,

Table 11.1 This checklist outlines essential actions brands should take to prepare for potential crises, including the establishment of communication plans, response mechanisms, and employee training, ensuring that organizations are equipped to handle unforeseen challenges effectively

Action item	Description	Status
Develop a crisis communication plan	Create a comprehensive plan detailing communication strategies for various crisis scenarios.	☐
Identify a crisis management team	Assemble a dedicated team responsible for crisis management and response.	☐
Conduct risk assessments	Evaluate potential risks and vulnerabilities that could lead to a crisis.	☐
Establish preapproved messaging templates	Develop templates for various crisis communications to ensure quick responses.	☐
Train employees on crisis protocols	Provide training sessions to prepare employees for their roles during a crisis.	☐
Set up monitoring systems	Implement tools to monitor social media and public sentiment regarding the brand.	☐
Create an escalation procedure	Outline a clear process for escalating issues that may lead to a crisis.	☐
Engage with stakeholders	Identify key stakeholders and establish communication channels for crisis updates.	☐
Regularly review and update the plan	Schedule periodic reviews of the crisis communication plan to ensure its effectiveness and relevance.	☐
Conduct crisis simulation exercises	Organize drills and simulations to test the effectiveness of the crisis response plan.	☐

and continuous monitoring and learning, brands can not only manage crises effectively but also prevent them from occurring.

A proactive approach to crisis management is essential. Regularly revisiting and updating crisis plans, coupled with ongoing training and simulations, ensures that organizations remain agile in the face of new challenges. This forward-thinking mindset helps build resilience and equips teams to respond confidently in times of uncertainty.

Ultimately, crisis preparedness should be embedded into the company culture. By fostering a sense of accountability, adaptability, and readiness across all levels of the organization, companies can ensure long-term resilience, safeguarding their reputation and maintaining trust with stakeholders.

Table 11.1 provides a comprehensive overview of the critical actions brands should undertake to effectively prepare for potential crises. The table outlines essential components such as developing a crisis communication plan, identifying a dedicated crisis management team, and conducting thorough risk assessments to evaluate vulnerabilities. It emphasizes the importance of preapproved messaging templates for quick responses, employee training on crisis protocols, and the establishment of monitoring systems to track public sentiment. Additionally, the checklist includes the need for a clear escalation procedure, engagement with stakeholders, regular reviews of the plan, and conducting simulation exercises to test response effectiveness. By addressing these key areas, organizations can enhance their readiness to navigate unforeseen challenges and mitigate the impact of crises on their brand.

Further Reading

Coombs, W.T., and J.S. Holladay. 2012. "The Paracrisis: The Challenges Created by Publicly Managing Crisis Prevention." *Public Relations Review* 38 (3): 408–15.

Coombs, W.T., and D. Laufer. 2018. "Global Crisis Management: Current Research and Future Directions." *Journal of International Management* 24 (3): 199–203.

Kash, T.J., and J.R. Darling. 1998. "Crisis Management: Prevention, Diagnosis and Intervention." *Leadership & Organization Development Journal* 19 (4): 179–86.

Rea, B., Y.J. Wang, and J. Stoner. 2014. "When a Brand Caught Fire: The Role of Brand Equity in Product-Harm Crisis." *Journal of Product & Brand Management* 23 (7): 532–42.

CHAPTER 12

Weathering the Storm and Emerging Stronger

As we conclude our exploration of effective brand crisis management, it's essential to reflect on the **STORM Framework**, which encompasses swift response, transparent communication, ownership of the problem, rebuilding trust, and monitoring and learning. These five components are crucial for navigating crises effectively and minimizing damage.

Brand crises are inevitable, stemming from operational failures, public relations missteps, or external threats. A swift response helps mitigate damage, while transparent communication fosters trust. Ownership of the problem is vital, as brands must acknowledge their role and communicate resolutions. Rebuilding trust is a long-term effort requiring accountability and commitment, and monitoring past experiences helps refine strategies for future challenges.

Cultivating a crisis-ready culture involves encouraging open communication, empowering employees, and prioritizing preparedness. By adopting the **STORM Framework** and fostering resilience, brands can not only survive crises but also emerge stronger and more committed to their stakeholders.

Recap of the STORM Framework

The **STORM Framework** provides a structured approach for brands to navigate crises effectively. Each component of the framework plays a vital role in crisis management.

S = Swift Response

Speed is of the essence in a crisis, as timely action can significantly influence the outcome and perception of the brand involved. When a crisis occurs, brands must be prepared to mobilize their crisis management teams swiftly, ensuring that a response plan is executed within the crucial first hours. The initial response is vital, as it sets the tone for how stakeholders perceive the brand's commitment to addressing the issue at hand.

A rapid response allows brands to demonstrate their dedication to transparency and accountability. By acknowledging the crisis quickly, brands can take control of the narrative before misinformation or speculation spreads. This prompt action not only helps mitigate damage but also shows stakeholders that the brand is proactive and serious about resolving the situation.

Moreover, having a well-defined crisis management plan in place allows brands to act decisively and effectively. This plan should outline specific roles and responsibilities for team members, communication protocols, and the steps necessary to address the crisis. By rehearsing these procedures through training and simulation exercises, brands can ensure that their teams are ready to spring into action when a crisis strikes.

In addition to internal preparedness, speed in communication with external stakeholders is crucial. Brands should be ready to disseminate accurate information to customers, employees, and the media quickly. This includes addressing the nature of the crisis, the actions being taken to resolve it, and any support available to affected stakeholders. By prioritizing speed in their response, brands can help maintain trust and confidence among their audience, ultimately contributing to a more effective crisis resolution process.

T = Transparent Communication

Honesty and transparency are paramount when communicating with stakeholders during a crisis. Clear and forthright messaging fosters trust, demonstrating that the brand is taking the situation seriously and values the concerns of its audience. When stakeholders perceive that a brand is open about its challenges and shortcomings, they are more likely to feel respected and valued, which can help mitigate negative perceptions.

Transparent communication involves providing accurate information about the nature of the crisis, the steps being taken to address it, and the expected timeline for resolution. Brands should avoid vague statements or downplaying the situation, as this can lead to skepticism and further erode trust. Instead, being candid about what went wrong and why it matters shows stakeholders that the brand is not only accountable but also committed to rectifying the situation.

Moreover, engaging in two-way communication is essential. Brands should encourage feedback and questions from stakeholders and be responsive to their concerns. This openness can help to alleviate anxieties and demonstrate that the brand is actively listening and prioritizing stakeholder interests. By addressing inquiries and acknowledging frustrations, brands can strengthen their relationships with customers and stakeholders, fostering a sense of partnership during challenging times.

Honesty and transparency in communication are critical components of effective crisis management. By providing clear, accurate information and engaging in open dialogue, brands can cultivate trust and demonstrate their commitment to addressing the crisis and prioritizing stakeholder well-being. This approach not only aids in crisis recovery but also lays a solid foundation for long-term loyalty and resilience.

O = Ownership of the Problem

Taking responsibility for the crisis and demonstrating empathy toward affected stakeholders is crucial for effective crisis management. When a brand acknowledges its role in the crisis, it sets the foundation for rebuilding trust. A sincere apology plays a pivotal role in this process; it conveys accountability and signals to stakeholders that the brand recognizes the impact of its actions. This acknowledgment can help to repair relationships and mitigate damage by showing that the brand values the concerns and feelings of those affected.

An effective apology should go beyond mere words. It should be genuine, acknowledging not only the specific actions that led to the crisis but also the emotions and hardships experienced by stakeholders. For instance, a brand that has faced a product recall should communicate not just the technical aspects of the situation but also express understanding of any inconvenience or disappointment caused to its customers. This approach fosters a sense of connection and can humanize the brand, making it more relatable to its audience.

Moreover, a sincere apology should be accompanied by a commitment to change. Stakeholders need to see that the brand is not only acknowledging its mistakes but also actively working to prevent similar issues from arising in the future. This could involve outlining specific measures taken to improve processes, enhance product safety, or implement better customer service practices. By following through on these commitments, brands can demonstrate their dedication to learning from the crisis and rebuilding trust over time.

Taking responsibility and showing empathy through a sincere apology are vital steps in crisis recovery. These actions help to repair damaged relationships and create a pathway for rebuilding trust with stakeholders, ultimately positioning the brand for a more resilient future.

R = Rebuilding Trust

Once the crisis is resolved, brands must prioritize rebuilding trust and loyalty among their customers, recognizing that this is a multifaceted process that demands both consistent actions and a long-term commitment. Trust is not easily regained; it requires brands to demonstrate reliability and authenticity in their communications and actions moving forward. This can be achieved through transparent practices, where brands openly acknowledge past missteps and clearly communicate their efforts to rectify those mistakes. By doing so, they signal to customers that they are taking their concerns seriously and are dedicated to improving their practices.

Moreover, brands should focus on delivering exceptional customer experiences as part of their recovery strategy. This includes actively listening to customer feedback, addressing grievances promptly, and showing genuine appreciation for customer loyalty. Engaging customers through loyalty programs, personalized communications, and targeted initiatives can help reinforce their sense of connection to the brand. By fostering a customer-centric culture, brands can create an environment where customers feel valued and understood, further enhancing their trust and loyalty.

In addition to consistent customer engagement, brands should also invest in social responsibility initiatives that align with their core values. By demonstrating a commitment to ethical practices and community involvement, brands can reinforce their dedication to making a positive impact beyond their products and services. Such initiatives not only resonate with customers but also help to rebuild a brand's image in the eyes of the public.

Ultimately, rebuilding trust and loyalty is an ongoing effort that requires brands to be vigilant, proactive, and responsive to customer needs. It is a journey that involves nurturing relationships over time and consistently living up to the promises made during the crisis resolution. By demonstrating a steadfast commitment to improvement and customer satisfaction, brands can successfully restore their reputation and solidify long-term loyalty among their customer base.

M = Monitoring and Learning

The process of crisis management does not conclude with the resolution of the immediate issue; rather, it is a continuous journey that requires ongoing vigilance and adaptability. Once a crisis is resolved, brands must engage in regular monitoring of their health and performance to ensure that they are effectively rebuilding trust and addressing any lingering concerns among stakeholders. This involves actively assessing customer sentiment through surveys, focus groups, and social media analysis. By gauging how customers perceive the brand postcrisis, organizations can identify potential areas for improvement and adjust their strategies accordingly.

Furthermore, tracking engagement metrics, such as likes, shares, and comments on social media platforms, is crucial for understanding public sentiment and gauging interest in the brand. High levels of engagement can indicate a positive recovery, while declining interactions may signal the need for further intervention. In addition to sentiment and engagement metrics, brands should closely monitor their market position by analyzing sales figures, customer retention rates, and loyalty program engagement. This data can reveal whether the brand is regaining lost ground in the market and can help organizations make informed decisions about their future strategies.

Learning from past experiences is equally essential. Conducting postmortem analyses of crises can help organizations understand what worked, what didn't, and why. This reflective process enables brands to refine their crisis management plans and enhance their overall resilience. By fostering a culture of continuous learning, organizations can prepare themselves to respond more effectively to future crises.

Ultimately, the commitment to continuous improvement not only strengthens the brand's reputation but also reinforces its relationship with stakeholders. By actively monitoring brand health and adapting strategies based on real-time feedback, organizations can lay a solid foundation for long-term success. This proactive approach ensures that brands are not just reactive to crises but are also equipped to thrive in an ever-evolving landscape, turning potential challenges into opportunities for growth and innovation.

Why Brand Crises Are Inevitable and Manageable

In today's fast-paced, interconnected world, brand crises are not just possible—they are inevitable. The rise of social media amplification, heightened consumer expectations, and the complexities of global supply chains can all contribute to potential crises that brands must navigate. As organizations operate in an environment where information travels instantly and public scrutiny is relentless, the stakes have never been higher. However, it's important to recognize that while crises may be unavoidable, they are also manageable with the right strategies in place.

A well-prepared brand can significantly mitigate the impact of a crisis and emerge stronger through effective crisis management.

Implementing proactive strategies allows organizations to respond with agility and confidence when issues arise. Understanding the nuances of the **STORM Framework** equips practitioners with the essential tools to face challenges head-on. This framework emphasizes the importance of swift response, transparent communication, ownership of the problem, rebuilding trust, and continuous monitoring and learning. By adhering to these principles, organizations can ensure that they are prepared to act quickly, communicate openly, and learn from their experiences.

In essence, while crises may pose significant threats, they also present opportunities for brands to demonstrate resilience and commitment to their stakeholders. By leveraging the **STORM Framework**, organizations can build a robust crisis management plan that not only safeguards their reputation but also fosters lasting relationships with customers and communities.

How to Build a Resilient, Crisis-Ready Brand Culture

Building a resilient brand culture requires more than just having a crisis management plan in place; it involves fostering an organizational mindset that prioritizes preparedness and adaptability. Organizations that actively cultivate such a culture can navigate crises more effectively and emerge stronger on the other side. Here are some key strategies to enhance resilience within a brand.

Embed Crisis Management in Training

To build a resilient culture, it is essential to make crisis management training an integral part of both employee onboarding and ongoing development programs. This ensures that every team member, regardless of their position or seniority, has a solid understanding of the organization's crisis response strategies and their specific role within that framework. By embedding this training from the outset, companies establish a proactive mindset across the workforce, ensuring that preparedness and accountability become part of the organizational DNA. Employees who are well-versed in their responsibilities during a crisis are more likely to act with clarity and confidence when unexpected challenges arise, preventing panic and confusion.

Training should encompass a comprehensive range of crisis management elements, including communication protocols, chain-of-command structures, and decision-making processes. Crisis simulations and scenario-based exercises can be particularly useful, providing employees with practical experience and helping them practice calm, effective responses in high-pressure situations. Regular updates and refresher courses should be scheduled to account for changes in personnel, new risks, and the evolving nature of crises in today's digital landscape. Moreover, this type of ongoing preparation empowers employees to not only react swiftly but also to anticipate potential risks, spot early warning signs, and take proactive measures to avert or mitigate crises before they escalate.

A well-trained workforce contributes to a unified, cohesive crisis response, enabling organizations to minimize disruptions, protect their reputation, and maintain stakeholder trust. Employees who understand the nuances of crisis management are better equipped to handle media inquiries, manage customer concerns, and collaborate across departments to restore normalcy. Ultimately, incorporating crisis management training into the core of the company's employee development programs not only prepares individuals to respond more effectively but also strengthens the overall organizational resilience, ensuring that the company can weather challenges and emerge stronger.

Encourage Open Communication

Creating an environment where employees feel comfortable raising concerns and discussing potential issues is vital for successful crisis management. Organizations that promote open communication are better equipped to identify and address problems early, preventing them from escalating into larger crises. Employees should feel empowered to speak up about potential risks or challenges without fearing retribution or negative consequences. This requires building a culture of trust where transparency is encouraged at all levels.

By fostering an open dialogue, companies not only mitigate risks but also create a more engaged workforce that feels a shared responsibility for the organization's well-being. Regular check-ins, open forums, and anonymous feedback channels can further enhance this communication, providing employees with multiple ways to voice concerns. These practices ensure that all perspectives are considered, from front-line staff to leadership, and create a proactive approach to identifying and managing potential crises.

In the long term, this openness contributes to a stronger, more resilient organizational culture, where employees are not just crisis responders but active participants in crisis prevention and preparedness. This inclusive approach strengthens the organization's overall readiness, making it more adaptable and capable of navigating future challenges with confidence.

Foster a Culture of Learning

A resilient brand culture thrives on continuous improvement and the commitment to adapt to changing circumstances. Organizations should place a strong emphasis on learning from both successes and failures, as this reflective practice is crucial for long-term growth. One effective way to do this is by conducting regular postmortem analyses after every crisis, regardless of the outcome. These thorough reviews allow teams to dissect each aspect of the crisis, pinpointing what strategies worked, which ones failed, and the underlying reasons behind those outcomes. This detailed understanding equips the organization with the knowledge to adjust and optimize their future crisis management protocols.

By engaging in this continuous feedback loop, organizations create a foundation for better decision-making and more effective responses in future crises. The insights gained from postmortems serve as valuable lessons that can be integrated into training programs, communication plans, and overall crisis preparedness efforts. Teams that embrace this approach are not only better equipped to handle future disruptions but also foster a culture that values resilience and adaptability. Leaders should encourage open, honest discussions during these analyses, ensuring that all perspectives are considered. This transparency and inclusiveness empower employees at all levels to contribute meaningfully to improving the organization's crisis readiness.

Moreover, promoting a culture of learning sends a powerful message throughout the company: that mistakes are opportunities for growth, not just failures. This mindset reduces fear of taking calculated risks and fosters innovation, as employees understand that continuous improvement is key to staying competitive and resilient. Over time, the organization becomes more adept at preventing crises before they escalate and more agile in responding to unforeseen challenges. By embedding this culture of learning, organizations can not only avoid repeating past mistakes but also elevate their overall preparedness, ensuring they are better positioned to navigate and thrive through future crises.

Engage With Stakeholders

Building strong relationships with stakeholders—such as customers, employees, and investors—is a vital strategy for fostering resilience, as these groups form the backbone of a brand's long-term success. Regular, meaningful engagement with stakeholders helps create a robust support network that becomes particularly valuable during a crisis. When an organization is proactive in nurturing these relationships, it can count on goodwill and loyalty from its stakeholders when facing difficulties. Engaging with stakeholders consistently, even when no crisis looms, fosters open communication and trust, creating a foundation of mutual respect that can help stabilize the organization during turbulent times.

By maintaining an ongoing dialogue with stakeholders, organizations can better understand their perspectives, expectations, and concerns, allowing them to align crisis management strategies with the needs of those they serve. This level of engagement ensures that when a crisis occurs, stakeholders feel heard and valued, which can significantly mitigate backlash or negative sentiment. It also enables organizations to respond in ways that are considerate of stakeholder priorities, making the crisis response more targeted and effective. The organization can gather feedback, anticipate potential issues, and adapt its messaging to address specific concerns, further reinforcing the trust and loyalty that stakeholders place in the brand.

This ongoing relationship-building does more than just prepare a brand for handling crises—it enhances trust and fosters a sense of security among stakeholders. Trust is a key currency in times of uncertainty, and organizations that have invested in their relationships will find it easier to retain stakeholder confidence when challenges arise. A well-established connection with stakeholders makes them more likely to stand by the organization through crises, offering their continued support as the brand works toward recovery. In this way, stakeholder engagement not only strengthens relationships but also provides a critical buffer that can help an organization weather crises with greater ease and resilience.

Conclusion

While crises are undoubtedly challenging, they also present unique opportunities for growth and transformation. Brands that effectively manage crises can emerge with enhanced reputations, deeper customer loyalty, and a stronger organizational culture. By leveraging the insights gained from a crisis, brands can innovate, refine their offerings, and improve their overall strategy, turning adversity into a catalyst for positive change.

Embracing a crisis as a chance for reflection can lead to meaningful improvements. Organizations can identify weaknesses in their operations, communication strategies, and customer engagement practices. This critical evaluation allows brands to adapt and evolve, ensuring that they are not only prepared for future challenges but also positioned to seize new opportunities that arise in the aftermath of a crisis. For instance, by recognizing shifting consumer preferences during a crisis, brands can pivot their strategies to align more closely with the evolving needs of their audience.

As we conclude this journey through the **STORM Framework**, it's essential to remember that crisis management is not solely about damage control; it's about cultivating resilience and adaptability within the organization. The lessons learned from crises can inform future practices, guiding brands toward more sustainable and effective operations. By fostering a proactive mindset and embracing change, brands can create a culture that is equipped to navigate uncertainty.

With the right approach, brands can weather the storm and emerge stronger than ever, transforming challenges into opportunities for lasting success. The **STORM Framework** equips organizations with the necessary tools to face crises head-on, ensuring that they are not just reactive but also proactive in their strategies. By adopting this framework, brands can build a resilient foundation that supports growth, enhances customer trust, and drives long-term success.

About the Author

Dr. Eugene Y. Chan is a professor of marketing at the Ted Rogers School of Management, Toronto Metropolitan University. He is a scholar in branding, brand crises, and corporate activism, with over 50 publications in leading journals on these topics. Dr. Chan teaches undergraduate and graduate courses and has received multiple awards. Recognized for his expertise, Dr. Chan's work informs both academic theory and practical strategies for navigating today's complex marketing landscape. He is also the author of *Consumer Behavior in Practice: Strategic Insights for the Modern Marketer.*

Index

www.ingramcontent.com/pod-product-compliance
Lightning Source LLC
Chambersburg PA
CBHW061151220326
41599CB00025B/4443